Local Lives

by Millen Brand

Local Lives

Millen Brand

"*Wherever men have lived there is a story to be told . . .*"
THOREAU'S Journal

Clarkson N. Potter, Inc./Publisher   NEW YORK
DISTRIBUTED BY CROWN PUBLISHERS, INC.

c.1

Inquiries should be addressed to Clarkson N. Potter,
Inc., 419 Park Avenue South, New York, N.Y. 10016.

Printed in the United States of America

Library of Congress Cataloging in Publication Data

Brand, Millen, 1906-
    Local Lives of the Pennsylvania Dutch.

    Poems.
    1. Germans in Pennsylvania—Poetry.   I. Title.
PS3503.R2576L6   1975   811'.5'2   74-28334
ISBN 0-517-51998-4

Published simultaneously in Canada
by General Publishing Company Limited.

First Edition

Designed by Ruth Smerechniak

Acknowledgments

Some poems first appeared in magazines and anthologies: a group of poems called *Local Lives* in *Cross Section 1945*, copyright 1945 by L. B. Fischer Publishing Corp.; "A Memory of Sweden" in the *American Swedish Historical Foundation Yearbook*, copyright © 1961 by the Foundation; "Legend for Now" in *Nexus*, copyright © 1972 by Wright State University; "Swinging off Swamp Creek" in *The Outsider*, copyright 1961 by Loujon Press; "Menno Simons," "Ernst Fuhrmann [Note]," "Ed Dry and His Farm," "The Honeymoon," "'Nervous,'" "Lisa," "Behold Beloved," "Pain," "The Weasel" in *Chelsea 28*, copyright © 1970; "Biafran Monody" in *Chelsea 29*, copyright © 1971; "Congo from the Pilgram Room" in *Chelsea 32*, copyright © 1973; "Behold Beloved" in *From the Belly of the Shark*, copyright © 1973 by Walter Lowenfels; "Local Light" and "Marvin Loes's Life" in *Chicago Choice*, copyright © 1961; "Local Light" in *Poets of Today*, copyright © 1964; "Local Light" in *The Writing on the Wall*, copyright © 1969 by Walter Lowenfels; "Bo-Cau" in *American Poetry Review*, copyright © 1975; "Dinner" and "Joe Heimbacher—The Run" in *Poetry*, copyright © 1947; "Blue Memory" in *New American Review #1*; "Chicago 1968" in *Agape*, May–June 1970; "Lost," "The Woman at the Spring Drip," "Death in the Trees," and "Brown" in *The New Yorker*; "Lost" in *The New Yorker Book of Poems*, copyright © 1969 by *The New Yorker*; "Our Friend, Papanahoal" in *Liberation*, copyright © 1959, and in *Seeds of Liberation*, copyright © 1964 by *Liberation*; "August 6, 1945" in *Liberation*, copyright © 1960, and in *1968 Peace Calendar*, copyright © 1967 by Denise Levertov Goodman; "The Table," "Streaking," "The Life of Isaac Stahl," "The Potter," "Censure," and "Story: The Extraordinary Account of Butter John" in *Poetry NOW*, copyright © 1974; "In Leo Reppert's Tavern" in *The Barataria Review*, copyright © 1974; "Great Age," "Ralph Berky," and "The Old Furnaces" in

This book, at her request, is for my mother, who was still flourishing in her ninety-fourth year as it was being finished.

Contents

Author's Note

In 1940, after a boyhood in New Jersey and many years in New York City, I began living on Crow Hill above Bally, Pennsylvania, with farmers as neighbors. Since I was descended on my mother's side from Pennsylvania Germans and had farmed with my father as a boy, I felt as if I was coming home on Crow Hill. I had a house, barn, and some acres of land, and for the first time in many years I had a sense of community.

A reaction to it was poetry. One part of my writing life had always been poetry, and it was natural that I should begin writing poems about the people around me there. I first wrote what the eighteenth century called "occasioned poems," a kind of journal of experience and accidental insight, but then I decided to be more deliberate, to go with notebook in hand and to say frankly that I wanted to write a poem about this one or that. I began to think of the poems as a book and I began to call the book *Local Lives*.

My family had left Pennsylvania with my great-grandfather Myers, so we had lost the *Deitsch*, the old Palatinate dialect that was still in use here. But my neighbors also spoke English, with a slight cadence of German. I picked up a little *Deitsch* myself and had to resist the temptation to drop too much of it into the book.

As it turned out, I was to write this *Local Lives* book for more than thirty years, with the unusual chance of following certain lives for this whole length of time. Most of the subjects of poems, at least of the full-scale ones, knew that I was writing about them and, without undue self-consciousness, talked as they would among friends. I used real names, only changing names and circumstances when I felt any chance of hurting anybody. To get certain freedoms, I made up characters, for example Delia Longacre and Elda Maria

Schwenk, and Joe Heimbacher as a type farmer. Fred Braun (pronounced in the German way, Brown) is partly myself.

I was impelled by a sense of valuable lives going unrecorded. I also believed that work was revelatory and had not been noticed enough compared with the singing and lute playing of life so much disliked by Menno Simons, founder of the Mennonite sect.

Some of the poems go back into history, and for them I preferably drew on original sources, as with the Chief Papanahoal poem written from two unpublished manuscripts.

The book includes skills, trades, ancedotes, ledger entries, letters, even two recipes. Why should poetry give all this up? Edward Field, who has liked to read the persimmon-pudding poem during readings of his own work, says, "My definition of poetry is 'the whole literary art.'"

Many of the poems have appeared in magazines and anthologies, acknowledged elsewhere, but I should mention that usually they were revised for this book, which has been in obsessive revision during most of its preparation. Writing it, rewriting it, using it to steadily widen my contacts with both the present and the past, and maybe even the future, has been so much a continuing gladness that it has been hard to agree to end it.

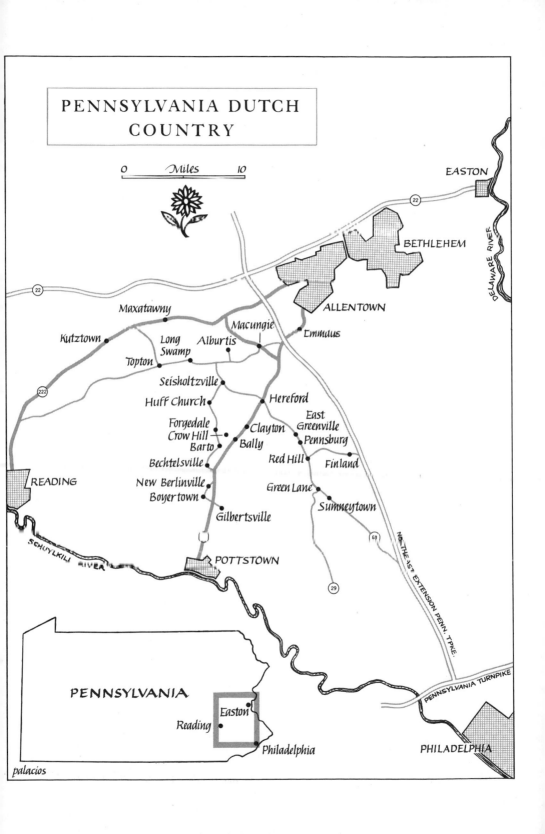

PENNSYLVANIA DUTCH COUNTRY

0   *Miles*   10

EASTON

22

BETHLEHEM

DELAWARE RIVER

22

ALLENTOWN

Maxatawny

Macungie

Emmaus

Kutztown

Long Swamp

Alburtis

Topton

Seisholtzville

Hereford

222

Huff Church

Forgedale
Crow Hill

Clayton

East Greenville

Barto

Bally

Pennsburg

Bechtelsville

Red Hill

Finland

READING

New Berlinville

Green Lane

Boyertown

Sumneytown

Gilbertsville

29

SCHUYLKILL RIVER

POTTSTOWN

NORTHEAST EXTENSION PENN. TPKE.

PENNSYLVANIA TURNPIKE

PENNSYLVANIA

Easton

Reading

Philadelphia

PHILADELPHIA

palacios

PART ONE

BREAD

Heat fat. Pour it into the flour.
Some salt for sweat and for the sea
Some sugar for the little ones' tongues.
Add milk. Stir in yeast,
which is air, which is a deceit of leaven
that, like life, grows in the dark
Knead and set and knead again
and let the warmth of wood come in.
Let all in the house eat with health.

THE START

Joe Heimbacher lifts up the plow handles
and points the blade down into the ground
damp with the unabsorbed melt of spring,
wet in the spring wind.

Toward him runs a shiver of weeds
stiffened with winter and death,
cold, but ahead of his horses
green plates of mustard shine.

The wind moves on from the woods
across the straps, across his raised shoulders,
and now his look is severe
as he thrusts the blade down.

THE LIFE OF JOSEPHUS GERHARD

Butter Valley has been the steady dwelling
of this man, Josephus Gerhard,
between the two hours, the hour
that scraped the first wail, and the last
rise and fall, rise and fall.

"I was ninety-five July sixteenth.
Yes, old." He sits straight in his chair
across whose arms his tan stick lies,
a carefully placed bar.
His voice is burred but clear.
"Old. My eyes see less each year,
and I hear less and get weaker.
Yes, the going is down, though slow."
His skin is the lace shedding of a locust,
but with no new locust under the web.
"I was born on a Friday, yes.
I have an almanac of that year,
eighteen fifty-three. Down below Millside,
on that farm where the barn is, or was,
so close to the railroad. Burned down now.
I went to school in Palm,
in Stump Hall—other places.
I didn't like school, I didn't like to study.
Some like to work with the head."
He touches his naked head. "Not me.
I left school in spring, then worked
on my father's farm for a time.

"When I was twenty-two, I married.
Yes, I married Elizabeth Schultz.
You know, down there"—his finger gives one flick—
"the Chester Schultz farm near the mill
that used to be her father Amos's,
there she was born and raised.
I never thought to have her for life
until I was grown. Then the idea grew.

Yes, at her place,
there was a strawberry patch. One day
we went to the end of that patch
and my wife gave me some strawberries."
His silence considers that gift. "Well,
so I wrote her a letter. Yes,
that's what I did.
I didn't say it. I wrote a letter.
So it happened. So it came.

"Two years later we took this farm "
He indicates up the hill the buildings
clotted white under pines.
"It was a farm left, ignored, abandoned
for over a hundred years.
A hundred seventeen acres
and ten acres of woodland yet.
It was washed, nothing growing but weeds.
Gullies. Washed off, it was terrible.
I said I was afraid we couldn't make a living.
'Well,' my father-in-law said, 'you try it.'
So we started.
The fields were all scattered with stones:
They had that much that we piled them in heaps
like you piled manure in the old days.
With them we filled the gullies
Some gullies you could drive a horse through.
There were so many tree stumps!
I pulled them and threw them in,
I don't know what I put in,
but I filled the gullies and made ground.
Horses helped. I always knew horses
Yes, they were part of it. Once I had
twenty at one time in my barn.
So then instead of stones, manure.
So we made crop, we improved.
Farming, always farming.
No grass mowers. We mowed all by hand,
by scythe, and grain by cradle.
As a man would mow,
a woman was needed to bind.

She'd make a band out of a straw,
grab a bunch of it, make a twist,"
his hands work quick in the air,
following the woman's hands,
"stick it under, and that kept the grain together.
Yes, rye, that was so long
you didn't have to make a double band,
but the wheat, that was shorter,
that had to have two skeins for it."
In these skeins of rye and wheat,
the handwork of history comes to an end—
all reaches him in the lines of the reapers
crossing the fields, and so stops.
"I always had good help to help me.
I had one man eight years,
another thirteen. Ralph Berky's father,
a painter by trade, a schoolteacher by knowledge,
loaded my hay and grain twenty-two years."
He turns his stick so that it points away
out of the web of his hand,
out to the acres of the hill,
out to the ground his son now farms in new ways,
but which his own life reclaimed.
"I was at the barber's
and they were talking about communities.
I said in ours we loved one another.
One said that could not be said
of any community anywhere.
I said, 'Well, ours is that way.' "
As he holds his strong stick out,
he repeats, "Yes, ours is that way."

THE DANGER

Love, ai, the threat of that,
so that perhaps acres of earth and its stones are needed
        and drawn-out work and monotony
to balance that danger:

repressed cries,
furies of closeness,
spasms of eyes seeing eyes,
the scream of self-loss and, afterward,
the slow coming back to oneself.

THE HONEYMOON

When Reuben Nair became a widower,
he had only one son to home, no daughter.

He was old, his son young—
David, a boy sixteen,

strong, eyes *gut genunk,* steady,
ready

to help as he was needed.
All he could do, he did.

Two years later Nair sickened
and when life slackened

and he knew he must leave the boy,
he said, "Your brothers have farms, so

you will take this one.
It's large for one alone,

but you should do all right now.
In the spring, plow."

"I can plow, but I need a wife."
His father said, "Wife,

that is not hard to get.
A little harder to get good yet,

but you will manage it."
After he died,

David asked a brother for advice.
He got none, rather:

"You have heard what Father said.
Do as he said you shall."

Some few miles away
toward Reading lived a family

with many daughters, all hardworking
and all churchgoing.

One of these David met
and liked—Marietta Schwenk—

and as she was one of seven,
they agreed and agreed when.

She had some things to bring,
a few boxes, linen and bedding,

so he drove to fetch them at the appointed noon.
They were married at sundown.

The next morning he plowed furrows,
and she dropped in the seed potatoes.

He, following, plowed each row in.
That was their honeymoon.

SEED
(Joe Heimbacher)

"When I've got seed, I want to get it in—
yes, get it in the ground, get it in the ground
as early as the ground can take it.
Or when I've got seed for later crops,

put that in, yes, put that in.
I would put it in the same day if I could.
Once it is in the ground,
you give it the care.
You work for it then."

ON PLOWING
(Joe Heimbacher)

"My father wanted no fields
with places for 'the pigs to eat'—
furrows like pig troughs,
any unevenness in plowing.
He set me in the straps and I was to go straight."

PAIN

Eli Spaar farms in an irregular hollow
thumbed out at the bottom to a duck pond
where, like a fence, a few sedge grow, the white ducks
floating toward them on their own reflections.
As summer ends, his joints commence to stiffen,
and he gets the frost's first warning
from the circle of shallow hills
where winter gazes at him with eyes
bright among the asters. Pain
climbs to his shoulders and neck.
He corners a duck in an open shed
and carries it, its white wings beating,
to the beheading block.
Day by day he dreams of summer,
dreams of a sun to thaw his pain.
Sometimes he stands completely still,
work stopped, as downhill

ice reaches out on the pond hardening
toward a hole where a spring
raises desperate nostrils
and breathes against the tightening ring.

SQUIRE FRANK BENFIELD
REMEMBERS THE OLD DAYS

"When I was five or so,
I and my brother, Seneca—
my brother was two years older—
we were water boys
for the Colebrookdale Railroad, being built.
In eighteen sixty-nine, my father
bought the farm and the old mill here,
so we lived here from then on."
His mind now goes back,
it is living into the old days:
"Take the lights that we had then.
In those days we had the *schmutzamschel,*
such a little oil lamp
that stayed always in one place.
Like a hand, the fat was in the palm
and the wick came out the end.
Even such a well-fastened lamp
we were afraid of, because of fire.
To make fire, we had no matches,
but rubbed stones or shot a fire *schloss.*
Schloss, such a lock that snapped. Or this happened:
When my mother, Lucinda, was a girl,
when the stove fire was out in the morning
(she told me this), she would be sent
across the meadow to a neighbor's
to fetch a little shovel of embers.
Listen now how they lived then.
She went barefoot, and when there was frost,
across the length of that long meadow
she walked back by the same track she had gone,

10

for there the frost was melted.
No,
we do not know how they lived in those days.
We have no idea of it."

ROUND

How small the warmth, how large the shadow
when Lucinda walked the meadow!

When her loan of coals cooled,
her heart had all the embers still.

When the embers faded there,
Frank heard their fire in the air.

When that fire itself was gone,
there was a burning in his bone.

When the hot coals of his bone
walked the small track back again,

how large the warmth, how small the shadow
in Lucinda's final meadow!

MAMIE KULP REMEMBERS
THE COLEBROOKDALE RAILROAD

"It's gone now,
but when I was a girl, Helen Bechtel and I
used to walk to Barto in the morning
and take the twenty-to-eight train
to Boyertown to school.
Farmers would be going in
to deliver milk for the creamery
and would give us a ride.

11

Helen was tall
and could climb up over the front wheel,
but I was little and had trouble."
She smiles. Still little. "The train then,
with all the stops, took twenty minutes.
Funny
how you don't forget."

STORY: THE EXTRAORDINARY
ACCOUNT OF BUTTER JOHN
(Squire Frank Benfield talking)

"Many years ago,
yes, in eighteen eighty-nine,
my first term as Justice of the Peace,
one morning, a Monday morning,
my wife wanted to wash the clothes, but
her iron kettle was gone.
She had seen it the day before,
and later that day, it seemed, a team had passed by
with a rattling wagon, the driver not known.
I said to watch out for the team—
if it should pass again, to let me know.
Some days later my wife told me
the team had passed again.
I put a string out the bedroom window
down to the ground and so to the road,
and I fastened it across the road.
At the end of the string, in the bedroom,
I put a bell, not loud, enough
that it would wake me. So,
my wife and I went to bed.
About two thirty the bell clinked.
A wagon was passing. My wife listened
and said it was not rattling so much,
but I said, 'Perhaps it is heavier now.'
So I jumped into my clothes

12

and I hurried down the road
and as the team pulled slow with its load,
I overtook it near the church.
I looked toward the morning and there
I could see the driver's head.
I thought that if his head turned,
I would walk past. If not,
I would find out, if I could, what he was hauling.
His head did not turn. I put in my hand.
As I felt, there was some butter in the wagon.
I took a handful of the butter
and tasted it. It was unfinished butter.
Butter was churned one day
and was finished the next.
I knew then what I must do.
I got some men together quickly
and we went after on horse,
and just at the top of the hill
before you go down to The Devil's Hole,
there we came up to the wagon.
The driver thought we would pass
and drew to the side, but we stopped.
'You're hauling butter,' I said.
'What's the reason you have unfinished butter?'
Well, he said, he had the butter
from the New Jerusalem creamery—
that's about seven miles toward Reading.
He said it had been wheeled by a wheelbarrow
over to a corner of a field.
There he found it. He was taking it
to see if he could find the owner.
I said, Wasn't it far to take it
to find the owner—in short,
I informed him, as he knew,
that it was stolen butter.
We marched him back to the hotel,
and one went to the constable
and got a warrant in shape
for this Butter John.
The next day we found out
the wagon he had he had hired,
but all the rest was stolen.

He had three hundred pounds of butter,
he had a stolen harness,
he had some gum boots of C. Y. Shultz,
one of the laborers at the creamery,
he had some sheets taken from a washline
he used to cover the butter,
yes, and he had even, to tie the load,
a strap of Painter Renninger's
from down at Sassamansville
that Renninger used to tie ladders.
So we came before the court,
and when the court had listened,
sentence was eighteen months.
While Butter John served this sentence,
it turned out he was wanted
in another county yet.
Yes, Northampton wanted him.
The iron kettle? No,
that I never got back.
I recovered for the others,
but I could not for my wife."

A LITTLE THING
(Squire Benfield talking)

" 'The Devil's Hole?' That's a stretch of road
from Huff's Church down toward Clayton.
In the days when that was a dirt road,
a farmer once drove with mules,
and his wagon got stuck in the mud.
The mules could hardly lift their legs.
'This's a devil of a hole,' he said.
Since then it's called The Devil's Hole.
That shows, doesn't it,
how long a little thing can be remembered?"

GOING BEHIND

Benson Diefenderfer
owns a few cows,
but he does not own a farm.
He works on shares for Sam Schoener.
"If he would buy good seed grain,
both of us would get the benefit,
but half his grain is bad.
I put my work into it too.
Is that fair to me?"
Diefenderfer's children help, but income
falls behind like a tagging dog.
"Fertilizer. I do what I can.
If he just put more into it,
both of us could take more out.
Look how the ground is getting."
He picks some up and throws it down
where it lies, a clod.
"I could hire myself out.
"I could take my cows and go.
I could find some farm to rent
and do better, so, than this."
He kicks the ground. Some fail
from misjudging their fields,
but he because "Sam Schoener
just wants to hold and wait,
just hold and wait, hold and wait,
until he can sell the place
for a big price. It'd serve him right
if I burned the whole thing down."

THE LIFE OF MAMA FRUH

A day of fall, a windless day
when from a summer cornice
dogwood hangs its fire of dying leaves
over signaling
buds.

It is Mama Fruh's birthday.
In the kitchen of the large farmhouse
she sits with her grown children,
her husband by her side,
he who has worked so hard
under dawn and under midday sun
so long. Always quiet.
A daughter, Lillian,
living at home with her husband
and children (this house covers many),
is sitting sidewise to the table
where her four brothers, finished eating,
talk and laugh. One is an engineer,
one an agronomist, one a teacher.
One farms nearby.
Those away talk with those at home
in the pause after the meal.
"Mama." "Yes." Lillian
speaks low through the noise.
"Yes, what is it?" Mama asks.
"You know that little coat I got Jackie
with the short sleeves. It made me think,
how you used to make us sweaters
in those days." Those days
of their childhood, so *schwer,* so hard,
when Mama used to knit them sweaters
with short, round sleeves, and the waists round
and not too long, like jackets.
The materials all she had,
unraveled thread strengthened with string,
knotted inside where the knots
would not show—so at least

16

they had something decent to wear
and were warm. "Mama." "Yes?"
"You still have somewhere, don't you,
one of those old sweaters you made?"
"Yes, in a drawer upstairs."
"Would you let me get it?
I'd like to see it again."
"I'll get it." And now the boys
listen, and become quiet
as Mama gets up and goes.
They hear the light step on the stairs.
They hear it again coming down,
and now not Mama comes in,
but someone shadowed and shy, timid,
a hider behind the garment held up.
The garment is surprisingly small—
and it has two colors, gray and a band
of red, a wine-red tone
as fine as the dogwood's leaves outside.
The stitches are small and even.
She pulls the sweater inside out,
and they see the remembered knots,
not showing. "Mama, it's pretty."
Now all at the table turn, shocked:
Behind them, Father is sobbing.
It is something he never does.
Quickly he controls himself.

A day of fall, a windless day
when foxglove lifts its green
curving stems of remembrance—
the same green of its spring,
unchanged, awaiting winter.

THE OLD FURNACES
(Percy Hertzog remembers his father)

"Slag I liked.
That was a sight when they dumped it,
it run down and lit everything up
so you could see it for miles."
His varnished chair
rocks in the nighttime kitchen.
His cigarette breathes gently. "Furnaces
used to be all around here,
Pottstown, Bechtelsville, yes, and Macungie,
Emmaus, Topton, and Alburtis.
All gone now except Bethlehem.
The one at Alburtis
I used to watch tapped many a night.
Four men with the big pick pick at it
and work till they get it open,
then the iron flowed out like water
into the sand, the molds.
I tell you the molds 'looked'—fresh made,
ready for the metal. They tapped it
at eight and twelve and four.
I stayed to see the second one at twelve.
I was nine or ten then and many nights
I would sneak out the house—yeah,
I guess my mother knew where I went,
but couldn't keep me, no, she couldn't."
He squeezes the end of his cigarette
and opens the slide door in the stove
and flicks the butt in. "My father
worked there fifteen years,
from about the time I was born
until the furnace closed. When I used to go,
he was on the bottom and top both in charging.
Yes, I would come
and my father would be on top
and the men would call, 'Percy's come!'
'Send him up!' my father would call back,
and they would put me between two buckets.

Once I tried walking up—
a stairway went zigzagging up—I near fainted.
After that I always went with the buckets.
So I would go to the top.
But I could not always go up.
Sometimes there was danger—gas.
If a top man was new, sometimes
he was overcome by the gas,
but the older men could tell it,
and kept some gauze, lighted it, and threw it in,
and so burned the gas.
There was two furnaces then,
Number Seven and Eight they called them.
Three men worked at the bottom
and one at the top, twelve-hour shifts.
When my father was top man,
he was quick; the men
could often get an hour to sleep.
Three buckets went up at a time,
and as soon as they were up,
he emptied them. Yes, he filled 'the bell,'
and when it got filled,
it went down slowly by itself, emptied,
then come up again. The charge
used coal, coke, limestone, and three kinds of mine:
red mine, a bluish kind, and salamander.
The salamander was heavy. No man
could lift a bucket of salamander.
Even a shovelful was hard.
Not that they shoveled the mine much.
The gondola cars was small, and they tipped them
and shoved them in, they had a handle for it,
and so scooped down the mine.
They dragged the cars back all by hand.
Yes, that was the method when my father
was top man.

"You would think
my father was big, but he wasn't.
No, he was small like me,
not much bigger than me.
One year he worked five days more

than there is days in the year.
Yes, that year he worked
three hundred and seventy days.
Man on one shift was sick
so after my father worked Thursday days,
he worked Thursday nights,
the twelve-hour shift, then again
his own shift Friday days.
That night when he went home
after working thirty-six hours,
come the foreman and said the man's still sick,
'Could you make shift again?' To coax my father,
he said, 'I'll give you a helper
and you won't have to do much,
just so somebody that knows is there.'
So Father went back to work!
Yes, my father he worked hard
and I never remember him tired.
He just kept working and if one said,
'Don't you want to rest now?' he said,
'I can rest when I'm dead.' "

THE WEASEL

From the stone wall
so close to Percy Hertzog's house that the stones' night shadow
reaches the pump and joins the pump handle,
a weasel glides. Its searching arch
red even in the moon
slips into the high grass
that looks like water. All is still now
where the grass bends toward the hen coop.

THE TEACHER
(Daniel Rohrbach)

"I was only eighteen
and I had children from six to fifteen.
That was young now to begin teaching,
but I was close to the children, I remembered
how it had been with me.
I came my own first day to school,
knowing not a word of English.
I remember it rained that day
and I sat on that rainy day
trying to learn by listening but could not.
One must fail by listening only, no?
The teacher got hot. Can one hear words
when the teacher shouts? I could not.
Beatings came later, yes, and fear
of that new language I could not learn.

"Well, on my first day as a teacher
come the shy ones, the little ones,
knowing no word at all
of this English now. As I hadn't.
I called the class to order, one by one
called roll, and the little ones,
so frighted by then, could hardly talk.
I said a few words in the dialect
and it was comforting to them.
Yes, they spoke better then,
I could understand their names.
So I made the start of teaching.
I set the older ones to copying
and called the little ones up front.
There was a row of them.
I told them they must learn English.
Had they some words of it yet?
Ja, they had, *ja ja ja.*
So they said even if they hadn't.
I told them they could surely learn.
'Look.' I took the chalk to the blackboard,

we had only a black-painted board then,
not the slate blackboards one has now,
and I drew a picture of an apple.
'Apple. *Now saag,* Apple.'
They said, 'Apple.'
'Un now saag, I have an apple.'
'I have an apple.'
Well, that first day come to an end,
and the little ones then knew
'I have an apple.' Yes,
each one could then go home,
knowing at least the few words.

"As I began, so I kept on,
and I would not say it was so hard,
no, not so hard at all,
as if I had used the cane."

A BRIEF STORY ABOUT
DANIEL ROHRBACH'S TEACHER

"I know Daniel Rohrbach's teacher.
There's a story about him.
He was one easy to get mad,
yes,
he had a short temper.

He was courting Daniel's sister
and one day sent Daniel home.
After school that day he came to the house
and didn't go
to the regular hitching spot, no,

he drove up by the porch ready
to drive away if Daniel's father spoke,
and that would end the courtship.
The father, knowing,
held his tongue and said nothing."

A CHILD BELOW DALE

Elda Maria Schwenk, bright-haired,
dips her long, bright legs
into the pool above Saylor's Mill,
casual, her life beginning.
Father Bally used to say,
"Alle anfang is schwer."
Every beginning is hard.
But it is not with her.

She passes an old tree. Small birds
skip along its drooping limbs.
She thinks: look so at the tree.
Each branch iss like a tree.
Ja, if it was stood up—so—
each branch could be a tree. Her thoughts
fall, unnoticed, between two languages.

THE DIALECT

There was no Germany when they emigrated.
Principalities, duchies, and kingdoms
loosed the feeding stream.
In seventeen sixty-six, Benjamin Franklin
standing to the British Parliament:
Q. "What number of white inhabitants
do you think there are in Pennsylvania?"
A. "I suppose there may be about
one hundred and sixty thousand."
Q. "What number of them are Quakers?"
A. "Perhaps a third."
Q. "What number of Germans?"
A. "Perhaps another third . . ." But that second third
about which he did not "speak with certainty"
was nearer a half. The seed brought from the slashed
bin in the center of Europe

23

took lasting root. Elda Maria Schwenk,
walking from Saylor's Mill to Forge Dale,
gives to the new world names
of *schtee, schtengel, veiolich*—
stone, stem, violet—names
that have come down almost unchanged
from the plats and fields of the Rhine.

THE EMIGRANTS

Whose minds are clear and whose hearts are stung
with contemporary unease
may think back to a different tongue

of Shultzes, Gerhards, Schwenks. They clung
to hope, embarking on the westward seas,
their minds clear and their hearts stung.

Redemptioners singing the song,
"Wir reisen nach Amerika"—who seek these
may think back to a different tongue,

the tongue of Menno, Pastorius among
the quietists, emigrants to peace,
their minds clear and their hearts stung.

Who watch today's computerized battles won,
the latest impersonal victories,
may think back to a different tongue,

hear a Pentecostal shuddering,
hear a voice speaking in the trees.
Whose minds are clear, whose hearts are stung
may think back to a different tongue.

OUR OWN, OR OTHER NATIONS

In 1681,
a pamphlet appeared in London, printed
by "Benjamin Clark Bookseller in George-Yard
and Lombard-street,"
whose title was: SOME ACCOUNT OF THE PROVINCE
OF PENNSILVANIA, BY WILLIAM PENN. Penn wrote:
"Since (by the good providence of God)
a Country in America is fallen to my lot,
I thought it not less my Duty
than my honest Interest to give
some publick notice of it to the World,
that those of our own, or other Nations,
that are inclin'd to Transport themselves
or Families beyond the Seas,
may find another Country added to their choice."
He said those who were "low" here
could there become "wealthy," one there
"being able to buy out twenty
of what he was when he went over"
after some period of "Industry and Success."
As to the place: "The Place
lies 600 miles nearer the Sun
than England . . . I shall say little in its praise,
to excite desires in any," but he still
could not help writing: "It may be
a good and fruitful Land"
with "Timber and other Wood"
and "Fowl, Fish, and Wild-Deer . . . plentiful."
As to land, he offered shares,
every one of which "shall contain
Five thousand Acres, free from any
Indian incumbrance, the price
a hundred pounds," pointing out
this was "land . . . for next to nothing."
Those who should go there were
"1st. Industrious Husbandmen and Day-Labourers,
that are hardly able (with extreme Labour)
to maintain their Families and portion their Children."

Also "Men of universal Spirits,
that have an eye to the Good of Posterity,"
those that "delight to promote
good Discipline and just Government
among a plain and well intending people."
But especially those "clogg'd
and oppress'd about a livelyhood"
who would find in the new "Country"
a new "Opportunity."
He then gave
the text of his Charter from the King,
withholding nothing, and ended:
"I desire all . . . who may be inclin'd
to go into those Parts, to consider
seriously the premises, as well
the present inconveniences,
as future ease and Plenty." And he asked
"Almighty God to direct us,
that his blessing may attend
our honest endeavour, and then the Consequence
of all our undertaking
will turn to the Glory of his great Name,
and the true happiness
of us and our Posterity. Amen."

The pamphlet appeared in Amsterdam as
*"Eine Nachricht wegen der Landschaft
Pennsilvania in Amerika,"*
and many in the Rhine countries
that William Penn had visited
read and reread it: Amen.

WORK

There is this story of the early days:
when a visitor from Philadelphia
arrived at a farm, the farmer said,
"I had to work hard to make hay,
now I must work hard to talk English."

26

B. FRANKLIN'S CHANGE OF HEART

In seventeen fifty-three, Benjamin Franklin,
attaché of the government
of the Pennsylvania proprietors
and, so, interested in the royal favor,
wrote a letter to Peter Collinson
about the Pennsylvania Germans:
"Few of their children in the country
know English. The signs in our streets
(Philadelphia)
have inscriptions in both languages,
and in some places only in German.
They . . . are allowed good in courts,
where the German business so increases,
that there is continued need of interpreters,
and I suppose in a few years,
they will also be necessary in the Assembly,
to tell one half of our legislators
what the other half says."
It was his feeling then
that with this German population,
"even our government will become precarious."
He went so far as to say,
"Those who come hither are generally
the most stupid of their own nation."

In seventeen sixty-six
he expressed himself differently
Nonresistant plain sects
to whom Penn had so much appealed
were now a minority of Germans, so Franklin,
speaking against the Stamp Act
before the British Parliament,
emphasized that the Germans
had had great experience as soldiers
in Europe and in the colonial wars,

and, said he, they were even more hostile
to the Stamp Act, wanting it abolished,
than the English colonists were.
It was true.

In seventeen seventy-four,
the Germans in Philadelphia
set up a "Correspondence Committee,"
telling other Germans in the colonies
about the events at Boston Harbor,
urging them to organize resistance.
They knew that the German immigrants
were all too familiar
with invasions of mercenary troops
and kingly wars. Their letters
were plain and sharp. When, two years later,
the Continental Congress
called for four volunteer companies
from Pennsylvania, five companies
enlisted just from among the Germans,
commanded by all German officers. By now,
the Northhampton County historian
William Beidelman wrote,
". . . there is no doubt that Franklin thought better
of his German fellow-citizens."

THE CLEANLINESS

Kroppa Berg. Crow Hill. On that slope
Percy Hertzog's wife, Mary,
likes the view, so her father
goes to neighbor Braun and says,
"Could I cut the saplings along the wall there
along your upper field, so Mary
can see out?" "Do so, yes,"
and Fred Braun gives the dependent father
two dollars for "cleaning brush."
The old man, bending his great back,
slowly cuts the saplings down,
and field and view are both clean.

CROW HILL

Kroppa Berg, Crow Hill,
is the high point
of Washington Township, the "township"
not a town but country
that stops at the town edge,
nervous, like a crow.

And *Post Yokel* is not a rustic fence post
but a hilltop rock where arriving mail
used to be announced by horn.
One can imagine the horn sounding yet
toward the watercress clouds spreading
in the springwater behind the pines.

Downhill from the Hertzogs', near the Yosts',
the trees
open wide on *Butter Dahl,* here
not a yellow valley really, but
streets, houses, and whining lathes—
the town the crow shies at, Bally.

FARMER YOST

July, and the ladle of the sky
pours the heat, but the Nevin Yosts
live sheltered. Noon shadow,
stealthily cool in the spruce
rising beside the Bally water system,
covers them,
and Crow Hill protects them with its shoulder
over their rooftop—Nevin, Ivy,
and three children, Hilda, Jerry, and Linda.
This noon Nevin is outside,
as he likes to be,
looking at a small flower sticking
out of a spiny clump: "I got Ivy

a portulaca this year at last.
They're a bright thing." At his touch,
the flute mouth shows its crimson groovings,
and all the flowers of summer shower him
with their reflections: zinnias,
lady-slippers opening
under their bushlike turret of green,
larkspurs, asters, cosmos,
marigolds, petunias.
"Once I bought some rare petunia seeds.
Such little things. I figured they cost
a hundred twenty dollars an ounce.
I got special earth and screened it
that there would not be the least lump.
I put it up on the roof there
to get the sun. Well,
not one seed of them all sprouted.
So I got common petunia seed
and threw it in the ground. They grew
and reseeded themselves from year to year.
Yes, there they are—
the shades may not be so fine,
but they are color at least."
His flower garden is by the long porch.
His vegetable garden on a wide hill terrace
is field size,
but he tills no other field.
He has a barn and shed.
All week he works, a cutter
at the "Bally Block," there makes a living,
but lives only
to get outside, to his phantom farm.
"I'll show you the cucumber patch."
Head up, he pushes through the beans,
stepping like a cultivating horse.
He searches under the cucumber leaves.
"That one I should have picked yesterday.
Ivy'll let me know about that one."
Lifting his feet again, coming out:
"You mustn't step on the vine ends.

They're touchy. If you step on the end,
the whole plant is likely to die.
Now, here we have strawberries,"
rows of them ripening,
and off to the west, wineberries or dewberries
shining their thin red drops against the woods.
" To the hill
there was raspberries when we came.
Then it got all grown over, there.
Now I've cleaned it out and they grow again,"
their thorny blades reddish in the shade.
"Twenty years ago when we came here,
the woods were to the garden wall.
Now I have them back. But it is work.
You must cut all over once a year
to keep it so." A wren skips beside him:
"Jenny Wren, she's a fast talker.
The birdhouse there, wrens nest in it." He goes
to the grape arbor now fully
raising its parasols to the sun:
"And here's a robin's nest. One day
Hildy shouted—I was in the garden—
'A black snake's eating the baby robins!'
I came running. All I could see
was a hanging loop. If I used the hoe,
I might drag down nest and all,
so I went in the house
and got the shotgun and shot him.
He came down in two pieces. Look.
Look here." The wood of the arbor
is nibbled with memorial shot holes.

He says, "Come. Let's have lunch."
At table, he bows to the blessing.
String beans and potato slices.
A pie is baking. Son Jerry asks,
"Will it be done to eat?" Ivy:
"It might be so if you eat slow."
Nevin: "For once he'll stretch it out."

Near Tamaqua,
some forty miles from Bally
up past Hawk Mountain in the spear of hills
that goes to the coal country there,
Nevin was born on a farm. There,
early like all farm boys, he began
to help his father—learned
how things come up from seed,
almost like something from nothing. Just earth
and work.
At ten, though, they moved into Reading.
Then when he came to Bally,
years later, grown,
he married Ivy Kemp. She was
sister of Mamie, wife of Ed Kulp,
manager of the Bally Block factory,
so Nevin worked in the "Butcher Block."
"I've worked in the 'Butcher Block'
twenty years now, cutting wood.
In one day we may cut
twenty-five hundred to three thousand feet.
That's a lot of trees now
to put in the drying kiln!"
Monotony—cut and cut.
Amusement: "If you see
a black and white dog there,
that's one we adopted.
He came in and lay down. Looked thirsty.
We hunted for a dish to give him water,
but couldn't find any. I cupped my hand
and gave him water from the cooler."

Pie eaten,
he goes outdoors again, goes
to the barn shed where a scythe
hangs by its long crook on a peg.
He takes it down and swings it.
"My father taught me how to scythe
and how to sharpen a scythe.
For grass you get a thin edge
that could cut a hair, but for weeds
it needs to be duller. If the blade edge

32

is too thin for that, it bends.
Yes, I learned all such things
at the old place."
Having mentioned "the old place," he says,
"Where I was born,
there was a house, a barn, yes,
there was quite a lot of buildings
that such a farm has. Many years
after I left, I went back there.
I drove up by a road I knew
and a mile and a half from the place
I started watching. I went carefully
and located it by the milldam,
but there was no buildings there.
I hunted over the ground
and found one patch of cement
that was left from the barn floor,
and that one patch of cement
was all there was of what had been.
I asked around. This's what happened:
It's coal country, and a colliery
had needed water and bought the place
and others near it to make a reservoir.
But then there was some legal action stopped them
so they tried to rent the place
but couldn't, and the mill
was out of use by that time,
so to save taxes, they tore all down."
He gazes around now at his own place,
the long porch of his low house.
"To tear such a place down," he says,
"the house, barn, everything.
Hard now to think of it,
that there where I was born,
not a thing now is left."

ECONOMY
(Nevin Yost)

"Here is my cider press," he says, amused
at the casklike object
that he bought to save money.
As to saving money, and why:
Not a few living on Crow Hill
have had thirty to a hundred dollars
total cash income some years
and paid the land tax yet.
"One summer
I saw some early apples on the ground
not bad enough to let rot,
not good enough to eat,
and not enough to take to the mill.
I looked for a hand cider press.
I had a hard time finding one.
Then I got this one
for seven dollars. It had a wooden cylinder
evenly studded with nail heads
to tear the apples apart
and grind them. After a year it broke.
Well, I figured,
I had seven dollars' worth of cider.
I didn't lose. So I put it by.
Then one from the block factory came
and said, 'You must fix that.'
I glued three pieces crossgrain
and so put nail heads in again.
At first I could grind the apples,
but the acid in the juice
worked on the glue and I found
one piece was turning, the others not.
I bolted them together, so,
and since then it's been all right."

CENSURE

Fred Braun
not long after he came to Crow Hill
broke through his two-foot house wall
to make an opening for a new window.
Behind the cemented surface of the wall
he found stones laid loose
in a mortar of straw and clay,
nest of immateriality
easy to pull out. Crumbling too.

When he built back
around the new window frame,
he cemented every stone,
even the inside ones.

He was let hear about that—
cement for the inside stones.
"Church work," neighbor Eline said.

ELLWOOD HUNSICKER

Ellwood Hunsicker had a field always troublesome,
something always eating at it, it seemed.
Crows—they especially angered him,
to see them walk like men
in a sheen of blue-black,
their legs springy and their wings adrag,
stabbing at the new-planted hills
and getting away so quick,
loping easily into the air
if he even appeared in sight.

One day he could stand it no more.
He took a double-barreled shotgun
and hid in some brush at the field edge
and when a few crows flew cautiously in,

he shot. Two fell. He shot again,
and another dropped to the ground. Good.
Let them lie there!
They could now nourish the field
they had so much stolen from.

MARVIN LOES'S LIFE

Elda Maria Schwenk watches beside her father
in the April morning sun. The scene is new to her.
In front of them under a lean-to roof
are wooden crates piled in a smother
one over another. And in these, packed too tight,
wings held down and heads unnaturally up
like all who are crowded too close together,
cockerels wait, within easy reach
of Marvin Loes, the caponizer, and his wife. "Another."
One grown cock yells across the farm
what could be exultation or alarm.

The caponizing takes place
on a tablelike board resting on a barrel.
Mrs. Loes puts a cockerel on the board,
stretching him out on his side. She attaches threads
to his feet and to one wing, and the threads
have lead weights on them, to hold him entrapped.
For a moment he flaps
his hooked-back wing across his bared side,
then cries at the brief sting
the knife gives as Loes under the wing
makes his incision and inserts his searching wire pliers.

Mrs. Loes tosses the bird into an empty crate where it peers
downward, blinking its hurt and discouragement.
"It'll be uncomfortable for a couple weeks,"
Schwenk says as Loes wipes some bloody streaks,
"but then it'll patch up. Grow twice the size,"
he says for his daughter's benefit.
And now she notices that the bloodied Mr. Loes

36

has one arm shorter than the other. His hand does not close
although he uses the fingers. His fast wrist
directs the knife cut and the plier twist
expertly. "None but him can do so many,"
his wife says, and again the wrist twists.
He frowns. He could be angry or indifferent.
Elda Maria thinks, though,
he likes it when the cut cockerel blinks.

ELDA MARIA SMILING

Elda Maria visits her grandmother
in the evening, and there is evening
over the aging eyes. Her grandmother thinks,
How I loved her father when he was small!
And everything about this child
is my son again—see him
there as he first stood up.
There is that cleft chin, that smile.
There he is with his smile!
"Child, *kum.* Come to me."
Again just for a moment
let me hold him to my breast.

BUYING EGGS

Wesley Kaesemeyer and his wife, Hilda, and a last grown son
      to home, Leslie, and Wesley's bachelor brother Hinton
      live together in a house typical of the old "large houses"
      of Washington Township,
houses that wombed outsize families, spreading room after
      room, each like a subhouse, some of the upper bedrooms,
      lacking heater vents from the downstairs stove, nerve-
      cold in winter,
so that the kids skipped shivering to the kitchen in predawn
      dark, carrying their clothes.

"Be quiet."
"Ach, ach, cooooooold!" *Kolt.* But warm now
this September morning
as Fred Braun comes in to buy eggs.

He greets Hilda. Hilda says, "Strange without Pop."
"Yeah, hard to get used to it."
The orderer, the order-giver. Her father-in-law
used to sit out on the porch that had two clotheslines
      on which his long underwear might be drying,
and he'd watch restlessly. He insisted on "everything in its
      place." He kept the farm under
a bleak eye of incessant reproof,
all listening to his will.

Now
Hilda sets a thick-crusted pie on the ledge of the kitchen
      coal stove.
"A cherry pie?" Braun says, spying through its slits.
"No, grape. Concord grape. Two hundred nine grapes."
"How do you know?"
"Well, I like to count. I have that way, I count as I work.
      Two hundred nine. Wesley brought in enough for two and
      I only used half." Grapes
from the drapery of two-rooted vine off the porch.
"I like cooking," she says. "But cleaning, no. I just can't
      clean the whole house no longer. I used to clean all
      through in one day. Not now. It takes me three days now—"
"The windows look as if you just washed them."
"I did, but I'll let them go a month now. No, I'm closing
      part of the house."

She changes the water in a mason jar holding two gladioli
      stalks. "Don't you think of Pop with the flowers?
      Wesley brings them in and keeps saying it's the last,
      like Pop. Then he brings two more."
Wesley comes in, carrying a cane. Braun says, "Nice flowers,
      those gladiolas of yours."
"Yes, but that's the end. I see we have pie."
"Fred come for eggs," Hilda says. "Will you get them?"
"Yes." Wesley holds up the cane, a tapering bare stick with
      a big curved handle that has a crinkle in it.

"Pop's cane. I cut it growing like this beside the creek and
        gave it to Pop. I think of him when I use it.
I use it to bring the cows in—tap them with it. But,
        before, I had to borrow it from Pop every time,
        and every time he'd say, 'You may take it, but you
        must bring it back.' Well, that's Pop.
Come see the pigs."

Five pigs snort and squint from their sty.
"Don't keep a sow no more," Wesley says. "Sometimes they don't
        throw and then it's a loss. No, I buy shoats now. These
        have raised good—not all for us, of course. One's for
        my sister, one for the boys, and one for the Reverend
        Johnson."
"Will you smoke hams this year?" Braun asks.
"Always smoke hams. But it's work. You must go a dozen times
        a day, more, so it don't flame. But anything that's good
        is work.
I'll use hickory again. Pop always used that. Some use apple,
        that's a good taste, some cherry, some sassafras even,
        but I do what Pop did. Not that I do everything like he'd want.
He never kept anything in the smokehouse, always kept it ready.
        But I have stuff in it now, so I'll have to clean it out.
        Pop'd raise hell if he knew."
Brother Hinton emerges from the barn, enthroned on the manure
        spreader. Wesley says:
"Pop liked to work. He'd work till he dropped, and sitting by
        was hard for him, you know? But Leslie now, I'm not so
        sure. I've seen him leave a field-end, quit early. Off
        to the girl friend's house."
The sun crosses the red barn and makes embossed rays of the
        neat rake marks in the barnyard. As Hinton disappears
        down the lane toward the fields, his spreader faintly
        rattling,
"But here I talk," Wesley says. "And you want eggs."

MENNONITE BEGINNINGS

Menno Simons, plain son
of Dutch peasants, born in Friesland,
read Luther, *On the Freedom
of a Christian Man,* and thought.
Thought against
Catholic dogma, state rule,
and tightened his weak flesh
toward the people's "hunger and need."
Strong only in "Him," he led
the brethren in the long search
for the church within the self,
danger always at his side.
Tjard Reynders sheltered him
"out of compassion and love"—
found out later, Tjard was broken
on a rack. Menno himself
fled and wrote, wrote and fled
until at last his years cracked.
When he died in Wustenfelde,
he was buried secretly
and war soon erased his grave.

Menno Simons:
"Our weapons are not weapons
with which cities and countries may be destroyed,
walls and gates broken down,
and human blood shed in torrents like water . . .
Iron and metal spears and swords
we leave to those who, alas,
regard human blood and swine's blood
about alike . . . Tell me,
how can a Christian defend Scripturally
retaliation, rebellion, war,
striking, slaying, torturing, stealing,
robbing and plundering and burning cities,
and conquering countries?
Our weapons are not swords and spears,
but patience, silence, and hope,
and the word of God."

40

T. J. van Braght wrote July twenty-third,
sixteen fifty-nine:
"Thou knowest, O my Savior and Redeemer,
the steadfast faith, the unquenchable love,
and faithfulness unto death,
of those of whom I have written."
He wrote of 4,011
burned at the stake . . . "bodies torn on the rack,
torn tongues, ears, hands, feet;
gouged eyes, people buried alive,
crucifixions, beheadings, stonings—"
An example among so many others
was Michael Sattler, tried
in fifteen twenty-seven
in the town of Ensisheim
for resisting infant baptism,
for not believing
Christ's blood and body were literally
present in the sacrament.
"You arch-heretic, you have seduced the pious,"
the Town Clerk said. Michael:
"God knows what is good."
"You desperate villain, I tell you
if there were no hangman here,
I would hang you myself
and believe that I had done God service."
The Ensisheim judges' sentence: "Michael Sattler
shall be delivered to the executioner
who shall lead him to the place of execution,
and cut out his tongue; then throw him upon a wagon,
and there tear his body twice with red hot tongs—"
In another trial, the witness said,
answering a question,
"We may have read the Gospel together."
Ques. "Where did you read it together?"
Ans. "At the dyke." Ques. "With whom did you read it?"
The inquisitors searched for names,
but none of the questioned gave names. Braght
reported that a steward said,
"They embraced a faith
which the lords and princes could not understand."
In one questioning:
Lords: "Will you not yet confess?"

Elizabeth: "No, my lords."
"Your mother is almost dead with grief."
"Though the door should stand open
and you should say, 'Go, only say: "I am sorry:" '
I should not go." Some were asked:
"Have you any books of Menno Simons?"
"I have a little book on the faith."
So they said, so questioners pursued,
and as they answered and as, from the hearing hall,
friends called out to comfort them,
fearless of their own arrest,
the number taken, tried, and condemned
began to overwhelm the judges.
It was a frenzy of testimony
to the power of belief. A defendant,
John Claess, leaving the court, said,
"You citizens bear witness that we die
for no other reason
than for the true word of God."
There were revolts. The citizens themselves
stormed the courts and tore up the stakes.
Even prosecutors suffered nausea.
At last the murderousness died down.

When the worst of it was over,
in the more "comfortable" time
beginning in the sixteen fifties,
van Braght wrote from memories, histories, and records
The Bloody Theater or Martyrs Mirror,
a detailed account
of the martyrs through the centuries,
a book of some twelve hundred pages,
two thirds of which tell of the torture and death
of the Anabaptist faithful
following the year fifteen hundred.
It lies today on many plain-sect tables.
In spite of its endless horrors,
it has love in it,
the arrested singing together in prison
from separate cells, the letters
of the condemned to their relatives,
sending consolation and what help they could
to those "keeping the faith."

Van Braght himself, a survivor,
in a commentary said,
"It is now better, quieter, and more comfortable,"
but "there is more danger now."
Many forget "what pertains to the soul
and on which everything depends . . .
If you are overcome by the world,
it will soon put an end
to your Christian and virtuous life,
without which latter the best of faith
is of no avail. Care, therefore, my dear friends,
equally well for both,
for the one is as important as the other.
Faith without the corresponding life,
or life without the faith,
can, will, and may not avail . . .
Knowing then, that we must care for both,
there remains nothing for us but to do it."

"THEY BRAKE BREAD"

A sixteenth-century writer
said of the Anabaptists:
"They brake bread with one another
as a sign of oneness and love,
helped one another truly
with precept, lending, borrowing, giving,
taught that all things should be common,
and called each other 'Brother.' "
At an Anabaptist baptismal service
in Strassburg in fifteen fifty-seven,
those being baptized were asked
"whether they, if necessity required it,
would devote all their possessions
to the service of the brotherhood,
and would not fail any member that is in need,
if they were able to render aid."
All were children of God, and the church
one family.

THE LAST FAMILIES IN THE CABINS

At a bend in the Bally-Dale road,
in a low growth of woods
an unused log cabin still stands,
its adze-squared timbers weathered
into black bars between the mortar,
and some of the bottom logs thrust out.
"There are few cabins left in these hills,
none lived in at the present time,"
the Reverend Elmer Johnson says. "In my young days,
when I began the flour route
for my uncle, Joseph Schultz, the miller,
in the late eighteen eighties,
there were still four families
lived in cabins. Only the poorest
by that time would live so.
My uncle gave me orders
my first day with the wagon,
when I would come to such and such a cabin,
a woman would come out,
and would have with her a receptacle.
She would say how much flour she needed.
I should give her what she asked.
As I was told, so it happened.
I came to a cabin, the woman came out.
She reckoned, so many loaves of bread,
and the children should have a small cake,
so she explained how much she needed.
I tried to give her more, but she refused.
'Only so much,' she said.
Then she said, 'I don't have money.'
'It's no matter,' I said as I was ordered,
and closed the wagon up and drove away.
Because people could not pay
was no reason why they should not eat."

IN THE PATH OF THE SETTLERS

"600 miles nearer the sun"—
what undershadows play
beneath the hackberry crown,
not just the shadows of leaves
 but moving caravels
 of skin, of smoke.
A flight of turkeys. "Peag."
 A cry to Europe's ardor—food, fields—"Wampum
in shells bored lengthwise." Plenty.
 Labadists warned Penn
that "scholars now coming among you will be apt
to mix school learning
amongst your simpler and purer language, and thereby
obscure the brightness of the testimony."
 But the ardor of scholars and "Day-Labourers" alike
smelling the west, irresistible
 "Fowl, fish, and Wild-Deer."
 Timber and other wood.
"Land . . . for next to nothing."

BEHIND GERMANTOWN

"And I must tell you that there is a breathing, hungering,
 seeking people, solitarily scattered up and down the
 great land of Germany, where the Lord hath sent me."
So Penn wrote after his trips to the Dutch and German
 countries, to Mulheim-on-the-Ruhr, to Frankfurt, and
 even as far as Kreigsheim near Worms on the upper Rhine.
Once George Fox went with him. Deep in his inner consciousness,
Fox honored Mennonite teaching,
insistent nonresistance, the will
to read what Christ taught, with the courage to do it.
As to the "hungering" Germans Penn spoke of,
they had reason to hunger.
Wars, wars, and wars—

wars of Emperor, lords, princes, prelates, knights, and burghers—
the Peasants' War waving its angry "shoe," and religious war
      waving its angry Cross.
So terrible were these wars that "people tried to
      satisfy hunger with roots, grass, and leaves; even
      cannibalism became more or less frequent.
The gallows and graveyards had to be guarded;
the bodies of children were not safe from their mothers."
(Oscar Kuhns)
In Württemberg alone, three hundred thousand people died, three
      quarters of the population.

Two years after the "Peace of Westphalia," which ended the
      Thirty Years War,
Francis Daniel Pastorius was born in Sommerhausen,
September 26, 1651.
Educated in five universities, he was fluent in Latin,
      Greek, French, Dutch, English, Italian, and Spanish,
and wrote them "macaronically" in his "commonplace-book."
In a memoir, he said:
"Upon my return to Frankfurt in 1682,
I was glad to enjoy the company
of my former acquaintances and Christian friends,
Dr. Schutz, Eleonora von Merlau, and others,
who sometimes made mention
of William Penn of Pennsylvania,
and showed me letters from Benjamin Furley,
also a printed relation concerning said province;
finally the whole secret could not be withholden from me
that they had purchased twenty-five thousand acres of land
in this remote part of the world.
Some of them entirely resolved
to transport themselves, families and all.
This began such a desire in my soul
to continue in the society,
and with them to lead a quiet,
godly, and honest life in a howling wilderness,
that by several letters
I requested of my father his consent."
His father gave his consent and some money.
Pastorius wrote this account of his reasons also:

"After I had sufficiently seen the European provinces and
        countries and the threatening movements of war,
and had taken to heart the dire changes and disturbances of
        the Fatherland,
I was impelled, through a special guidance from the Almighty,
        to go to Pennsylvania."
He went. Sailing ahead of the others,
he arrived in Philadelphia in August 1683
and was "heartily welcomed by Penn."
The others followed on the *Concord,* the German *Mayflower,*
        and all went by a narrow bridle path
to a "new colony," Germantown, where Pastorius helped them
        dig cellars and build huts
and get ready for the cold. There was "much hardship" the
        first winter,
but by the following fall
William Streypers could write home to his brother:
"I have been busy and made a brave dwelling-house, and under
        it a cellar fit to live in; and I have so much grain,
        such as Indian corn and buckwheat, that this winter I
        shall be better off than I was last year."
Cornelius Bom wrote: "I have no rent or tax or excise to pay.
        I have a cow which gives plenty of milk, a horse to ride
        around; my pigs increase rapidly so that in the summer
        I had seventeen, where at first I had only two."
These letters were brave.
Other accounts were darker.
All was not quite so prosperous there,
and Germantown was a preferred place,
with close access
to Philadelphia and the sea.

WILDERNESS

The wilderness,
later called the "New Elysium,"
was not quite that paradise to start.
Firstcomers died
in unused Indian caves

along the lower Delaware.
Log cabins were put up hastily.
Shoes were worn out and abandoned.
Roads followed Indian tracks
into a loneliness of fear and ague.
As the roads dwindled,
wagon wheels became the butt ends
of large trees; harnesses,
strips of untanned hide. But
there was no lessening of individual will.
In a stillness,
seed they carried—
potatoes, beans, flax, wheat—grew.
No gear whined in the wheat,
no hammer beat to make it.
It came up without sound.
It was there. The crop was harvested.
It was a start, it was food.
A man took a kernel of corn
and in its dried-up sides—
two troughs like sunken cheeks—
put his fingers. Hard,
silent, yellow, gaunt good hope.

DINNER

A kitchen table
that has held suet drippings,
the flower of the oil lamp
sinking.
Walls unpainted
graying to the far, the dark, of space,
as if trees still in their bark,
a woods edge,
had moved to the circle of lamplight.
The glow of red coals
printed on all their cheeks,
they sit and eat.

48

WHAT HE TOOK

Jeremiah Schultz rests against the headboard of his bed
in his second-floor farmhouse bedroom
that looks toward the well-pointed wall
of the old Schwenkfelder Cemetery.
He rubs at his bushy right eyebrow; his eyes,
all of him, tired from too long living;
past eighty and useless from the hips down
all his life. "I think now if a person
had this much of his thumb cut off, he'd know
how much he'd miss it." As a young man
he made himself "a little wagon"—a two-wheeled part wagon,
part drag—
the rail padded with rubber and open in back.
He lay down with his chest against the rail
and propelled himself by his strong hands.
He wore gloves and went faster than a man could walk.
He would go sometimes as far as ten miles,
and could get up a hard hill.
But that is all past now, his days of traveling are past.
Though kept,
the chariot of those years weathers now on the porch.
He sits with twilight behind his head,
and as he talks,
his voice is muffled by his untended beard.

"Ai ai ai, I taught school six terms.
The fourth term I took a school not far from here.
The farm near the school could not board me,
and I said I would go then to the hotel—
they would board me there. They said the woman there
had the worst temper in the county. So they said.
I said I wasn't afraid of her. So I went,
and that woman had no temper. No, sometimes
I thought she kept the steam too long.
That's the way it is, yes. I told them in winter

there would be times in the heavy snow or ice
when I couldn't make it to the schoolhouse in my wagon.
I asked how much it would be to get me there.
They said, 'We've got good strong children.
When you need help, they will help you and no charge.'
So I boarded there. Some months later,
this woman of the temper had a baby.
When it was two days old,
she called me from the second floor to come up
and I came up. I could manage stairs in those days.
She held the baby up for me to see.
From the middle of the floor where I sat, I said,
'When it's older, yes, if you will,
I want you should let me hold it.'
When the baby was ten days old,
the woman called, and said, 'Here she is.'
She had trust. I sat on a chair,
and she gave me the baby wrapped in its blankets.
I held it. 'Now,' she said, 'are you all right?'
'I'm all right,' I said; 'you can go now
and do whatever you want to do.' She left.
A little later she called up the stairs,
'Is the baby all right?' I said it was.
For an hour I sat holding the baby.
It moved so in my arms.

"Once she said,
'I'm going down the road to my niece's place.
The hired girl could take care of the baby,
but I'd feel better if you watched it.'
She was gone an hour and a half.
I never took my eyes from it once.

"When I was away over the Christmas holidays,
the baby died suddenly. Yes, it died.
When I came back, the woman told me and said,
'Since you did so much for the baby,
go to the bureau where her clothes are kept
and take whatever of hers you want.'
I found a sock the baby had worn.
It had a hole that was mended. I took it.

50

The woman said, 'You took a mended sock.
Why didn't you take something good?'
I said I wanted what the baby had had use of.
Yes, that's what I wanted. Something
the baby wore. So I kept it.
Yes, that's the way it is, that's the way it is."

THE CORRESPONDENCES

As Heimbacher guides his plow blade,
stones behind him on the ground
follow like birds, while steady overhead
a hawk cuts furrows straight as his.

THE SCHWENKFELDERS

A Silesian knight,
Casper Schwenckfeld von Ossig,
in the first half of the sixteenth century,
reacting against formalism,
literate, sane, free-spirited,
as a "protestant" insisted
on a minimum of theological dogma,
on purity of life rather than ritual
as a means of salvation.
His followers, called Schwenkfelders,
were many, like him, remarkably literate
(at twelve, Abraham Wagner
inscribed his Greek grammar
with three lines of his own Latin),
and they increased in two centuries
to about two thousand souls
in the eastern end of Germany.
By an all-too-human irony,
Lutherans and Catholics both opposed them.
The principality of Liegnitz

in seventeen nineteen
undertook to "convert" them back to Catholicism.
Now began several years of "persuasion"
of these Schwenkfelders and, that failing,
in Upper Harpersdorf, four women, one a young girl,
were put in stocks, forced to kneel
in front of the Catholic church,
in mid-December cold,
four days and nights. No Lutherans intervened.
The government threatened the Schwenkfelders
with fines and imprisonment.
They were forbidden to emigrate.
To enforce that, to try to keep them there,
no one was allowed to buy their farms.
If they left, they lost their land and buildings.

Melchior Schultz in seventeen twenty-six
called his three sons together
and said what many were saying:
"If you turn Catholic, you may keep your house . . .
For your sake we would much rather
enter on a road of misery."
He said that if they trusted "in God
and in the glory of His name,"
He would find "a way and place
where we may found a home again."
So, he and his sons and others
carrying a few parcels and possessions
too dear to leave behind—books, for example—
set out by night, and by stealth crossed
the Silesian border into Saxony.

THE VOYAGE

Count von Zinzendorf's Herrnhut,
that little babel of the sects,
took them in for some years tolerantly
but uneasily, then turned them out:

"Separatists will get out of Herrnhut."
Sunday, April 19th,
seventeen hundred and thirty-three,
thirteen souls, among them
David Shultze and his father and mother,
still carrying their small possessions,
a wreath of Latin and farm tools
and what they could store in memory,
left at noon for the Elbe,
their destination Pennsylvania.
Two days later, at Pirna,
they engaged for their river passage,
so down the river in two boats
past the ropes of the vines with their early
tendrils like horns of snails, singing
loss, loss, and rapture:
Deo gratia.
Delays on sandbars, always sand,
always shallows as if the grudging *fluss*
had not enough water, merely that,
to free them. Sometimes on the sandbanks,
they got off to lighten the boat,
sometimes stayed on in hope and haste.
So the curving land went past.
Pillentz, Dresden fortified,
and always forts and castles
rising along the occasional cliffs,
each prolonging a cliff face
with terror. To Torgau,
and on Sunday ("Jubilate")
to Wittenberg, fifteen miles
The next Sunday ("Cantate") in the afternoon
they passed Schnackenburg, four years before
rinsed with flame, fallen flat
in the waste of its own heat.
And now May lifted its heat
and spread it out sensuously
on the water. Quiet. Then wind.
Either no wind
or too much wind. The sails hummed,
and in the narrow river limits
the steersman could not keep the course.

One mile above Hamburg
they caught again on a sandbar
and had to wait for high tide.
They waited past that for morning.
Now four boatmen coming from Altona
out of the morning mist
and the diffused city. The Van der Smissens,
"incomparably nobleminded people,"
gave them kindness, food: of bread
"16 loaves, 2 Holland casks,
2 pots of butter, 2 roasts."
From Hamburg they took a vessel
going to Amsterdam, so they met
the first coasts of the sea.
David Shultze wrote in his diary:
"May 14th . . . we sailed toward the sea
and reached it in the afternoon."
They sailed on through the entire night.
Now the first seasickness,
the prelude to the deeper sicknesses
that were to come from slowness, the cobalt gloom,
the contagion of close air
rising from the wood, from the clothes,
from the presence of so many
in the dark crossing chamber.
Late on the night of the 16th, Amsterdam,
and with "joy" the following morning,
in a nodding sky-net of masts,
they disembarked, loading the baggage
on a *treckshuyt* or canalboat
that went behind a slow-gaited horse
to Haarlem, to their friends there.
Six Schwenkfelders joined them there.
At Haarlem, Cornelius Van Putten,
who had a pleasure garden, entertained them
with wine and tea, a round face
against hedges, against red house bricks—
a second benefactor
among the good Dutch "mercantiles."
June 16th they left Haarlem,
sailing all night on the Haarlem sea,
and as the early morning raised

54

thin lights behind the shore,
they passed by Leyden and The Hague,
and came in the afternoon to Rotterdam.
They who all their lives had been in one place
tacked now from city to city,
with reefing, unreefing, calling
doubt along the reefing ropes.
At Rotterdam they boarded a final ship,
the *Pennsylvania Merchant,* its captain
loading on, implored to load on,
one hundred fifty-five tons cargo
and over three hundred passengers.
The great sides worn and heavy,
the great hollow took them in.
The Gravendeel pilots, boarding,
were not pleased at the overcrowding,
which weighted the ship so
that it stuck on a sandbank
like the riverboats, setting out.
July 5th, they "reached the ocean"
and everybody began to vomit.
Now sea wind, again the North-Sea wind,
now the dependence on that element
that emerges from the variable sky—
angry, sudden, occasional, steady,
sweetly stealing, often abominable
and able to offer death.
The water ran hard with its white crests.
They entered the Straits of Dover.
When, July 9th, the wind blew harder,
they went further backward than forward
The next day still hard wind,
abating a little, but not much.
And the next day the first child died
even before England, a frail nine-year-old.
The small body was fitted in a sack,
and in the sack they put some sand,
that pursuing fringe of the sea,
and with the singing of a hymn
the sack slid down and out of sight.
"Nun lasset uns den Leib begraben."
At Plymouth they had to stop,

an English ship to pay the English toll.
While they waited in port there,
there was a good following wind,
but when they wanted to leave,
the wind was contrary. So they pitched,
so they tacked into a N.W. wind.
When the wind was favorable,
they hoisted twelve or thirteen sails
and swept rapidly along.
On August 3rd, young Johannes Naas
got up an hour before day
"in order to see how it was going."
David wrote, "He fell off of the ladder,"
the one going up from the hold.
What happened was this:
Wanting to watch the compass
that he kept track of each day,
he had tried to climb the ladder.
One of the passengers, still asleep,
had a cover lying entangled in the ladder,
and furthermore there had been a little rain
and it was slippery under the trap-hole.
When Johannes reached the top
and was about to climb on deck,
the one sleeping stretched himself
and, pulling on the coverlet,
knocked the ladder from under Johannes' feet.
He fell down from the top
and with his left side struck on the rungs,
and lay a long time half-conscious
before he could get up. He could not walk
for two weeks, but stayed in the hold
on his back in the swaying dark.
So for this Johannes Naas
time lengthened and the sea became
broken reflections
through opened portholes and windows.
And wind: at night "it lulled again."
Ships were seen in the distance.
If one came near, the captain
spoke through a megaphone,
making call and inquiry,

and sometimes one ship rounded another
in close circles again and again
with a violence of friendship
where to be friend means not an enemy.
August 4th, "our sailors" caught a fish,
large, resembling a hog in body,
entrails, and flesh, and even in the snout,
not a true dolphin. Calm.
A tack-wind, but not too strong.
Some women walked heavy with child,
exercising across the deck.
Several babies had already died.
At night lullabies sounded
of creaking cordage and running keel,
and life, cradled and rocked, slept.
Long tacks pushed toward the west
morning to night and night to morning
through the blue ocean shelves.
The 26th, in late afternoon,
they passed by a mast standing fast,
the point a half yard above the water
with rope still attached to it.
They went by, luckily at a rod's distance.
The captain had been drinking tea.
All saw the impossibility,
the fixed pole immovable
in the middle of the curling waves.
Over that one small upraised finger
the dark came as if walking on the water,
and the stars flashed out and, in their frost,
lifted before and sank behind,
calling the snows and foam of distance.
More strangeness: the following night
the ship rolled as if in a great gale
although it was calm. Wide flats
and phosphorescent pinpoints of light
spread like the night meadows of home
off in the dark. Increasing wind.
"We saw great flocks of birds."
September 7th. Toward evening,
the captain caught with a great iron hook
"a fish that is called a shark."

September 10th. The captain and the boatswain
had a boxing match. The captain won,
knocking the boatswain on the deck.
There were other fights, of anger.
Strong N.W. wind. At dinner
the cook poured seawater on the fire
to put it out, and the fumes
"went all over the ship."
The people thought it was on fire.
Such a great "furor" arose
that the captain and all the men
were frightened. A blaze of spilled fat,
any blaze in a bandbox of sails streaming up
stops the breath.
A land bird. A portent after long weeks
of edging to the north and south.
Now, from ahead, a large vessel.
Both ships slowed
and the captain lowered a boat,
rowing on the pews of the waves
toward the newcomer. The word:
Only four days from land!
The word was reason for rejoicing,
but there was more—half a bag of apples.
The captain brought the apples up the side
and the sight of that freshness, that red,
that blessed new world to be eaten
maddened all. He threw one.
They fell in heaps. They fought to get it.
He threw another and they rushed and fought,
they screamed for the beautiful apples.
The departing ship signaled farewell
and sailed on, eastering.
The next day "Winter's wife" died
and in the darkening evening
was let down into the sea.
She was not the first one, no,
and always it was women and children.
Storm clouds. Rain and thunder,
and after thunder, heavy waves rose.
All sails were furled, and the rudder fastened.
A burst of sea broke some shutter bolts

58

and shouted in, wetting beds,
loud in the dark. Stopped and again
loudened outside. They lay in dark,
captain, crew, and passengers,
wet in the wet bedclothes.
In the morning, David Shultze looked out
and to him it seemed the waves
were "as though they sailed among high mountains
covered with snow." On deck only one sailor
tied fast to watch by the rudder.
And roar and roar and shudder.
A day later the storm went down,
and in the following calm
the captain ordered a kettle of rice,
so the smell of its hot steam
comforted the people. They ate it.
Now a good breeze, stiff and steady,
carried them straight to the west.
At midnight, September 22nd,
the first soundings for land were made,
One hundred fifty rods and no bottom. It seemed
all right to go forward. The next morning,
soundings measured
fifty-five rods, then twenty,
but still no land in sight.
At four in the afternoon,
afraid of the coming dark,
afraid of the "stream called Delaware"
with sandbars in its mouth,
as night came on,
the captain reefed and lay by,
waiting for morning to go in.
The great sails, sea-rent and mended,
lapped on the spars. Few slept.
Many even sang in the dark,
sending their voices toward the land,
voices carrying
lassitudes and hungers, and prayer.
Auf Seel, auf, auf, was zauderst du.
This was the half-understood home,
strange land, uncertain hope,
this was where God had had them come.

Now at their feet river water
flowed by, tinged with earth.
In the morning, fog spilled toward them
smelling of the continent beyond,
and they advanced in the fog
under the slow push of the wind
and at noon saw land.
The pilots came out to them.
Yet before the entry of the river
they were held by a last storm
sudden in coming and sudden in going,
louder than any before,
so that it seemed an augury of terror
before a land dreamed of as peace.
The sound of it was "awful."
Yet the water no longer had
its former power of the deep,
no longer were they threatened;
they had reached salvation.
The 25th, they sailed gently in.
They had ended their journey
across "the very big sea."
Yes, it was "The Eÿnde with God."
So they sang. So they wept.

HOW MANY

How many through the centuries,
reading *The Martyrs Mirror* or living it,
must have had the thought: If only the world
was just my house or my yard or my farm
and the sky over it, if only
the past could die at dawn,
at birth, at some point
that stopped it.
But a stranger crosses the fields,
and memory and fear
break through the windbreak,
and the yard wall is down.

60

AUGUST 6, 1945

Fred Braun has just leaned out on a low windowsill
that needs painting. There are cracks in it,
but so far they have let no rain through.
They can wait a little longer.
This moment is his to enjoy,
looking at his apple orchard and two small plum trees
and under them a red napkin of bee balm.
It is beautiful and peaceful. His wife
is troweling a flower bed
along the house wall. He hears
the thud of an apple falling, part
of the nice lethargy of the day. And today
across the world
behind a plane, the *Enola Gay,*
there floats in the air, slowly descending,
a hardly visible thin tube
with a small fuse at one end
that will fire one of two parts
into the larger part at the other end
and explode this almost unnoticeable filament
with a light brighter than the sun. Below,
in the wooden city Hiroshima
can it not be that a man
has just rolled back one of his living-room shutters
and is looking out on his garden, thinking,
The morning glories on their bamboo sticks,
the blue sky,
how beautiful everything is! Let me enjoy it
I should be painting the shutters,
but they can wait.
The rain does not yet come through.

CLAUSA GERMANIS GALLIA

Five years after Pastorius had written about "the threatening
        movements of war"
and had taken his ship to America,
a certain person
        lifted heavy robes proudly
        up over his left arm to display
an aging but handsome thigh. *Le Roi Soleil.*
That drooping regal lip and eye initiated
        many
        less than necessary acts.

In September, sixteen eighty-eight, after secret conferences
        at Versailles,
Louis XIV authorized—for certain "limited French aims"—
an invasion of the Rhineland.
He meant it as a quick war (and a cheap one),
but nothing ever goes quite as planned.
The Dauphin rapidly captured
Heidelberg, Mayence, Philippsburg, Mannheim, Frankenthal,
        Speyer, some twenty cities
in a muddy, cold campaign,
but this easy success
depended on "the enemy," a Grand Alliance of northern troops,
being away fighting Turks in the east.
When the Turks were unexpectedly defeated
and that great sickle of Grand Alliance troops turned west,
Louvois, the general, consulted with Louis on strategy,
asking him
to let him "devastate" the Palatinate, to put a barrier
        between the enemy and France.
All food, all fodder, all houses, all towns, cities, all
        that could keep up troops—all was ordered
burned and destroyed.
It was an expensive operation
which Voltaire described later:
Directions were given (it was midwinter)

"to the citizens of all those flourishing and well-ordered
    towns, to the inhabitants of the villages"
that they leave.
Men, women, old people and children filled the roads and
    fields. Few were killed,
but all were made homeless.
The destruction was methodical. Mannheim was torn stone
    from stone, and then Louvois suggested
shipping the stones away,
that nothing be left with which to rebuild. Louis:
    "I do not doubt you will execute this
with all diligence." He saved some chapels,
but no houses anywhere. All went down in the laborious flood
    of fire and demolition.
Voltaire said,
if Louis personally had seen the suffering,
he would "himself have extinguished the flames," but "in
    the midst of pleasures,
he signed the destruction of an entire country."
To celebrate it,
he had a medal struck that said
CLAUSA GERMANIS GALLIA, Gaul is closed to Germany.
This was the logic, and of course what is logical must be
    done.
Europe was "horror-struck." The Germans called the French
    "Huns." Napoleon said of it, later:
"Only Wellington and I
are up to these things."

As the burning went on, some officers had difficulty
being ruthless enough.
Tesse let the people of Heidelberg
put out fires he had started. D'Uxelles "failed" to demolish
    castles and went slow with the torch.
Louis was angry. Louvois wrote, "The King
will remember those who don't obey . . . Everything must be
    burned."
The details of how farm women wept,
reddened with flame, and their men waited
and killed the French in their hearts
go unrecorded. Palatinate children afterward

grew up malnourished and stunted and, grown,
grasped at any hope. Some explored Boehme,
some the cabala, the Rosy Cross,
some looked for a "new Christianity,"
and some read the letters now coming back from "Amerika."

THE BAKER

Conrad Beissel, founder of the Ephrata Cloister
not far from Lancaster, Pennsylvania,
was born in sixteen ninety in Eberbach
in the Palatinate,
two years after the devastation. Brought up
"after the manner of the country,"
he was so frail and small, so undernourished,
he would say to his brothers,
"If you were so small as I,
you would have to be born again."
He apprenticed himself
to the (to him) ravishing trade
of baking bread. He supplied bread
in rebuilt Mannheim and Heidelberg.
He even baked kosher bread,
using oil instead of fat, so that Jews
"ran after him." He became a master baker.
He became the best baker of his time.
He also inclined to Pietism
and mystic arts, so that
the City Council of Heidelberg,
sadly noting his unorthodoxy,
put him in jail. They made him an offer:
If he would "go through" church (an established church)
only once a year, he could stay, it would be
a technical compliance.
He would not, so they exiled him.
After some wandering in the German kingdoms,
he came to America. At Germantown
when he tried to be a baker,
women refused to buy his bread, proud

of their own. He learned weaving
and began wandering again.
He studied doctrines, made friends with Mennonites,
taking their plain clothing,
and became "a Solitary"
with powers of trance allowing him to be
possessed by God: "Thus speaks the Lord."
He introduced antiphonal singing
"unequaled by any party in the Christian Church
from the days of Ignatius on." It was
"the choral singing of the angels."
He moved to the Cocalico
and lived in a "hermit hut,"
but others came, to live and sing,
and so began *Ephrata, Camp of the Solitary.*
"To feed the Solitary . . .
they erected a common bakehouse with brick ovens
and a room with mixing troughs."

BEYOND THE WALL:
THE LIFE OF THE REVEREND ELMER
ELLSWORTH SCHULTZ JOHNSON

"I was born on Wednesday,
June twenty-sixth, eighteen seventy-two,
in the small brick house, called the bakehouse,
next to the larger brick house
of our family farm in New Berlinville.
My grandmother, Elizabeth, did some spinning,
and would let me turn the reel for her.
When I was four, she died.
I sat outside the large house as she died,
and I recall my father coming down
with a basin. . . . So the spinning stopped.
That same summer my mother bought me
my first pair of boots, which had
bright leather tops. I wore them
to my other grandparents' home,

that of Amos and Elizabeth Schultz.
My aunt Elizabeth had recently married
Josephus Gerhard, who was then working
for my grandfather. Before dinner
Josephus sat down with me
on a step of the rear staircase
and, understanding my child's pride,
he gently touched the new shoe tops
and said, *'Ei was schoene Stiwel.'*
He has been my well-beloved uncle
for more than seventy years.

"My grandfather Isaac
told us about our name, how Johnson
was the English of Jansen,
and that Johnsons had been in Pennsylvania
since sixteen eighty-four.
My great-great-grandfather, Isaac's grandfather,
saw Washington at Germantown.

"Schooling has been much of my life,
and the first experience was early.
It came about through another person.
Before I was born, my grandfather Isaac
took into his home a boy to raise,
Ferdinand Hoffman, son of a minister
at Falconer Swamp. We grew close.
One day before I was five,
Ferdinand took me for a day to school,
or maybe it was a half day.
There I sat between two boys,
Ferdinand and another boy,
yes, I heard them spell,
so that world opened. At five,
by permission I went to school,
carrying my own green-covered primer,
my ABCs.
My mother, Susanna, helped me much;
much of my life as it is I owe to her.
Our family have long, in the struggle to live,
rested upon a firm belief
in the preeminence of Christ,

66

the Christ of the Sermon on the Mount.
We believe in that and we believe
in taking the utmost scruple
to preserve individual liberty.
My mother told me the stories of our faith,
the story of Schwenckfeld and the church
From her I had my first church history.
When I was eleven, my mother died,
she who had always said
she would see I got an education.
I lost hope then, yes, before long
I left school and worked on my father's farm.
Then I helped three years
at my uncle Joseph Schultz's mill.
It was there I drove the flour route.
One day after the many hours of work
and after sweeping up the mill,
I happened to open two books on the floor.
I sensed somebody was looking at me.
I looked up—another uncle was there,
one from an adjacent farm.

I tried to hide the books under some bags,
but he insisted on seeing them,
and, so, they were school books,
a geometry and a Latin.
He said, 'Elmer, do you want to study?'
I said I did.
He said, 'I'm afraid we've neglected you.
Your mother prayed you might go to school,
and you are going to go.'
He called my uncle Joseph. Together
they went to my grandfather Amos. Next day
my grandfather called me at one o'clock.
He mentioned my work at the mill,
he said the years of work were not wasted.
I knew what life was,
and I would study so much the better.
'Here behind the wall of the hills
we are still provincial.
We need now one to go out,
and bring the world back to us.'

He said I should have the ten years' education,
and as he would not live to see it through,
he put the money in my hand.
He told me where I was to go:
Perkiomen Seminary, Princeton
(it had good men to study under),
and last, New England
with its different religious ideas.
'You go there, you'll be safe.
Go to the Hartford Theological Seminary.'
So he laid out the work.
Three years later he died.
I faithfully carried the work through."

Ten years of study, ten years more in Europe,
where he did Schwenkfelder research,
then home. At home
he took as his pastorate Bally
and he built a house in Hereford
not far from Owen and Josephus Gerhard's.
There he has lived and there he lives today.
He went beyond the wall and returned.

CODA
(The Reverend Johnson talking)

"Yes, when I came back from Europe,
the day I came, they said Uncle Josephus
was up the hill with Owen, his son,
and I should go up. His granddaughter,
Frances—she was a little pudding,
yes, quite a lump—she wanted to go too,
so I let her. Halfway up the hill,
she tired. She wanted to be carried.
I carried her. But this is my point.
I found Uncle and Owen arguing,
Owen wanting something done one way,

Uncle another. I took Uncle's arm
and said, 'Now come down the hill.
You've bossed it long enough.' With that
he smiled at me, as he could smile."

JOSEPHUS GERHARD DRIVES THE SAFE
(The Reverend Johnson talking)

"When Uncle Josephus was twenty,
yes, before he was married,
the Pennsburg bank bought a safe,
six tons two hundred and forty pounds.
It arrived at the railroad station,
and the bank then offered a large sum,
ten dollars, to get it up the hill.
Uncle asked his father could he 'borrow'
two teams. His father outguessed him
and said, 'The ten dollars comes to me!
But I am glad you are confident
you can drive the safe up.'
Uncle hitched the two teams to the wagon,
and when the safe was on it,
went around, for a few minutes,
adjusting collars, lifting and leaving down,
talking to the horses, so they felt him.
Then he gave them the word to go.
None thought they would go,
nearly two tons to the horse,
for the wagon weighed too,
but the horses pulled and went.
Halfway up the hill waited a man
with a stone in his hand.
He got a quarter for his work.
When the wagon reached him, it stopped,
and he put the stone behind a wheel.
There, panting, the horses rested.
They fully got their breath,
and Uncle untwisted the chains

and again talked to them.
None now believed that on the hill,
the horses would start the wagon again,
but Uncle gave the word to go,
he just gave the single word
to the horses who knew him,
and again the horses pulled.

"Uncle delivered the safe, and duly
the ten dollars was paid to him,
and by him was paid to his father."

STORY: THE HORSE THAT LEANED DOWN ITS HEAD
(Henry Havighurst talking)

"Yes, I have reason to remember
how they did it—organized companies,
put a good surface on the roads,
and then you had to pay to go on them.
They had such a toll road to Hereford,
one to Green Lane, yes, a lot of them,
and they were good in wet weather.
It paid then not to drag through the mud.
Yes, but sometimes it got tiresome—
always a penny here, a penny there,
even two cents at places.

"I had a girl lived down near Sellersville,
a long drive and many tolls.
I used to drive it in the sulky,
light for the horse and, going light,
I could cut around across the fields
and get by some of the tollhouses.
Coming home late at night,
I wouldn't want to wake none—
the tolls were closed at ten o'clock—
no, I wouldn't want to wake them up
so at the bar in the road

70

I'd get out of the little sulky
and let down the horse's checkreins,
then him and me would lean down our heads
and go under the bar together.

"I went to see that girl near Sellersville
about a year. Yes, about a year.
Then a new family moved near us
that had a daughter. I got acquainted with her.
Then I had a quarrel with the other. One night
I drove to see the other and the next night
I was married to this one nearby.

"No, I was not happy from it.
You understand.
I keep remembering the tollhouses,
all the times me and my horse
bowed down under the bar.
At times I even think
I could have paid a few pennies more."

FROM A POINT BESIDE THE ROAD

"Yes, here the tavern stands
one day's oxcart journey from Kutztown
toward Philadelphia. The ox is gone,
but the tavern stays."
And if one sees a house close to the road,
it is likely a toll-road house,
where once the collector reached out
handily to the wagon seat.
The original meaning gone—
the oxen and the later trotters
and all the hurly-burly swinging by.
Words—songs—have held back
that clatter into nothingness.
Is it so with the stir that passes now?

THE OLD WINTERS

The Reverend Johnson
takes a visitor to see a landmark,
the great oak above Wolf's place, a tree
that was large before history.
Morning frost whitens its long limbs
that pale off into his recollection
of the old winters. "Those winters
are now almost forgotten," he says.
"We do not have now
that awful cold that made so many die
so that the old people would say
after one of those hard winters,
'We have reached another spring.' "
That was the cold his collateral forebear,
David Shultze, in his diary called
"frigidissime." "Snowed a great snow."
"Terribly cold; intensely cold."
In seventeen fifty-seven:
"Christmas night, December 25.
Fritz Reymer of Falconer Swamp
froze to death in the snow."
All winter long they sledged wood home
from the woodbin of the trees.
Flour mills shut for weeks,
streams being so frozen over
that the water was stolen from the wheel.
And snow. "Much snow."
"The potter died. . . . Then fell a deep snow."
In the snow, roads lost boundaries
and fences faded. Roofs as at Ephrata
pitched steeply down three stories
to drop the glittering drifts to the ground.
Wolf's oak has the record in its rings,
and past its arms the fields seem to echo
short steams of spring and late thaws,
lonely woods roads vaporous

with fogs of melting ice. Elmer Johnson
mentions to the visitor his pleasure
that those bitter winters are gone.
"Yes, it is easier now to be old."

A MEMORY
(Henry Benfield speaking)

"Funny what one remembers.
I remember one real bad winter a tramp come,
and he was old, not much strength   I got more now than he had.
He asked if we had cows, to keep warm,
a tramp'll never stay where there ain't cows,
and he wanted to stay the night. I let him. That night
        it snowed.
It stormed till next day you couldn't get through at all.
When we cleared the path to the barn,
the tramp come up to the house and asked to eat,
and since he needed, we gave. He stayed two weeks,
two weeks he stayed and each day ate.
Then come a sunny day.
He asked, so soft, could he stay yet another day.
'No,' I said, 'no,
now you must go.'
Then in his old, thin voice,
like this, he said, 'Well, if I gotta, I gotta.'
I never forget how he said that:
'Well, if I gotta, I gotta.'
So he went off down the road."

AMOS SCHULTZ'S LIFE

George Schultz, cousin of the diarist David,
in seventeen thirty-four,
a year after David made his voyage,
came with two brothers to Pennsylvania, part
of the Schwenkfelder group of that year.
On a knoll by a long meadow
near Fruitville in the New Goshenhoppen region,
the brothers put up a two-story log house,
and here George's son Isaac was born
and here, on May eleventh, eighteen nine,
Isaac's son Amos was born.
It was this Amos
who was to send his grandson Elmer Johnson
to school, preparing him to do research
on the *Corpus Schwenckfeldianorum,*
that garland of the sect's scholarship.
Johnson's mother, Susanna,
Amos's daughter, was named for her grandmother,
so upward and downward the vine spread
with the leaves and repetitional blossoms
of those "plain people" who, without dogma,
so much loved spiritual liberty.

Isaac, for all that he was a farmer
and lived in a log cabin,
wrote a Latin letter that "could shame
many later Latinists." He had Greek,
and of course both English and High German.
"He put Amos early to books,"
the Reverend Johnson says. "At six
Amos was a pupil in a little school
just over the top of a hill
by his father's house," and later
he was one of the few of his time
who went to a private school,
James Patterson's school
at Chestnut Hill near Philadelphia.
There is an extant bill:

74

"April 1, 1824
Mr. Isaac Schultz to James Patterson
For the tuition of Amos Schultz
3 mos.
$4.50. Fuel 50¢."
Amos in his homespun suit started school
with only two words of English,
"Yes" and "No." He studied hard,
he did not need the rod,
"Solomon's medicine," but grasped learning.
He wrote some poetry: ". . . *die Sonne klar,*
Die schönste Zeit auf Erden."
There is this story about him.
Once at term end,
he had to walk home forty miles.
They told him that if he sat down
on every milestone along the way,
he would run "the last few miles."
He did not find that he could.

At sixteen, schooling finished,
he helped on his father's farm
that raised wheat, rye, corn, barley.
Fields of straight blue flax. Hay.
Summers he worked in the fields,
winters he made straw hats
or shelled corn by hand.
His father had much to manage
and accepted his son's interest in accounts. Amos
kept a record of what the farm did,
so much yield "from each field and patch."
He kept a ledger of costs,
accurate "to the quarter of a cent."
A Schwenkfelder trait, that recording,
as if to the observing eye of God
all mattered, even the smallest thing.
An example—this was remembered
and eventually written down:
In eighteen twenty-nine
when Amos was twenty, he built a corncrib
for Father Isaac in a new "plantation"
Isaac bought at that time. Amos

framed the timbers together at home
and hauled them to the new place,
and one day, after such a trip,
he did not notice the early dusk come on.
He mounted his horse and started home.
All went well till he reached a wood
where a dense fog covered the path.
First he gave the horse the rein,
hoping it would find the way,
but the horse could not.
Then he "hollered," that the neighbor's dogs
might answer and he could "regain his bearings."
None answered. He "pondered his course,"
still slowly walking the horse.
He dismounted and began "to feel around"
for something to guide him. In the dark
he reached the stump of a tree
newly cut down. He felt it carefully
and "found that he recognized it."
From there he knew his way back to the path,
and so continued home, "rejoicing."
This story was loved
by his many children, in later time—
the father who could lose his way
and who could find it again.

Now came a great opportunity.
He had an uncle, Joseph,
who had a farm near Niantic.
This uncle, being without any children,
"cast about" to find his successor.
At first he considered Jonas Schultz,
a cousin of Amos,
but Jonas had extravagantly bought
three pair of calf leather boots
in a single year. That was sufficient
for him to rule Jonas out.
It was conveyed to him then
that Amos was "prudent and hardworking"
and had helped his father six years
in clearly exemplary ways.
He and Amos therefore

76

drew up a contract
that Amos was to work for him for a year
at from eight to ten dollars a month.
The day Amos left to go to Joseph
he still wore homespun clothes from head to foot
and all that he took he carried
under his arm tied in a handkerchief.
Before the year was out, Joseph died.
On his deathbed, he wrote a will
that his nephew Amos should take "the plantation"
with a fourth of its title granted him
as a dower in sign of affection.
The balance to be paid to the estate
in ten equal yearly installments.
Such an arrangement was not unusual
and was approved by the legatees.
The farm was run down, it was not well equipped,
but at least it would give Amos a start.
He had recently become engaged
to Elizabeth Kriebel, a distant cousin
on his father's side—a strong girl,
straight-lipped with an arrowy straight nose
and deep and faithful soft eyes.
She lived by the Zachariah Run,
motherless since she was six,
brought up by her older sisters.
They decided to marry at once,
the wedding to be the sixteenth of April,
eighteen thirty-three. After the marriage,
they drove all the next day
with Amos's brother Isaac (his father's namesake)
to the new farm near Niantic.
The farm had no carpets. No curtains. For light,
lamps that held a half pint of lard.
They used also tallow dips.
Stoveless, they cooked at the fireplace.
That first year
Elizabeth came down with typhoid.
Amos had scarlet fever during haying.
All in all,
it was not a good year "by his standards,"
but it was a beginning.

There was a maxim in those days:
"Man muss das geld nützen
und die Gebaude stütsen."
("One must save money
and patch up the place.")
Amos patched up his house.
He tore out the brick floors of the kitchen,
and throughout the downstairs story
changed the partitions, plastering
inside and out, and ceiled over.
Elizabeth was pleased.
Back of the barn he started
a new corncrib. Father Isaac,
when he saw how big it was to be,
"remonstrated" and said such a crib
his son would never fill.
Still Amos put it up.
Already in the year
though not a good year,
the debt on the farm was being paid.
There was much reason to hope.
As if in sign and seal,
a first child was conceived.

Now Amos agreed to take on
an unusual duty,
which came to him in this way.
There was no convenient church. In summer,
the Reverend Frederick Waage used to preach
under a big chestnut tree
at the Niantic crossroads. In rain,
the covering over them would leak
and so the worshipers decided
to make a meeting house safer than leaves.
For that, there must be money
and one to control the money. Amos
was more learned than the usual farmer—
"Wann mer eppes g'schrive wolle have"
("When one would have something written"),
one must go to him. So this Amos
who so carefully tallied the yields of crops
kept now the accounts of building contracts,

wood, plaster, window frames. Remembering
his own childhood when he had sat
three-hour sermons through on backless seats,
he made sure that the seats had backs.
He made the ridgepole tight.

The first child was Sarah. Seven more—
four girls and three boys—
were born in the years that followed,
ending with baby Elizabeth.
These eight Schwenkfelder Schultz children
benefited from a loving custom, that
of starting religion at home.
The child at home
lifted his eyes to God the Father
through Father and felt God near.
Amos's children
worshiped with his voice as he read
Weichenhan's Sermons or led
in his deep bass the singing of hymns
in *Weber's Note Buch.* They remembered
all their lives that in thunderstorms,
when they were frighted,
Father lit a lamp in the house
and gathered them around him to sing
songs they all knew and loved
and so they were comforted.

His children Amos raised without the rod
as he himself had been raised.
Joseph, the first son, remembers
that his father once found him in a misdeed
and stood without speaking. His silence
hurt more "than a severe whipping"
and it "made me stop and think."
Mother Schultz was still gentler.
"How we do grieve God," she said,
"should we be disobedient!"
but she and Amos taught more:
positive love.
It was son and grandson of theirs
who gave flour to such as needed

on the flour route, along the back roads, heaping
receptacles with such kindness
the bread tasted of it. But this kindness
went hand in hand with the work
asked by a provident God.

Before ten years were up,
Amos and Elizabeth, working together
and managing well, had paid for the farm.
A friend, coming by, found the yard
alive with little pigs and said,
"Hier vermehrt sich ja alles."
("Here all multiplies.") Sheds and barns
overflowed with manure.
One year Amos had twenty-four
"four-horse" loads of it
from the hogpens alone. He dug a cistern,
drained manure to it,
and to absorb the liquid
put in weeds, straw, and young brush
and lime with it. His corn so leaped,
neighbors wanted it for seed corn,
and he now easily filled the big corncrib.
He was always dreaming up "inventions."
Some laughed,
but the *aus dem Kipp* ("one out of his mind")
proved he had the laugh on them.
A field he trenched with stones "made crop."
They said his head ran to uncanny things
though within the limits God had set,
or some attributed it to "learning."

In eighteen forty, he was elected
Justice of the Peace for five years.
To help him now
he "brought with him" his brother Isaac,
Isaac who had never married
and who became his "farm manager."
Amos was a perfect justice,
made by temperament and presence
to be one. He was big.
He had wide shoulders and a large chest.

His eyes were heavily lidded.
His lip ends were always flexible,
but the right end of his lips
sagged a little as life advanced.
Under his white shirt collar
he wore a short necktie
with a knot hastily made.
Dispensing justice, he looked out
over his desk and imposed himself,
though quiet. One remarked
how exact his handwriting was.
He had this "minor" case:
Three young men "bent upon mischief"
placed Charles Binder's wagon on his fence.
Binder, catching them at this "mischief,"
asked three dollars damages.
Amos examined the wagon and fence,
and finding no harm done,
when the men pleaded guilty,
he awarded no damages
but a twenty-five-cent fine.
A woman coming in from the hills
told him about a misbehaving husband.
He wrote the husband a letter
for the woman to take back with her.
It was said the letter was persuasive.
Near and far
people came to him for advice,
satisfying with him a need
for concern, for authority.
He was reelected
for a second five-year term,
but at the end of that,
he refused to go on. Also
he refused all higher office.
He had something else in mind.

In the preceding years
he had bought three pieces of land:
one from Henry Huber,
one from John Himmelwright,
and one from Henry Landis.

Adding this new land to his own,
he made two equal-sized farms
that would later help his children.
In eighteen fifty-five, first
he planned for a house and barn
the other side of West Branch Creek
that ran through his property—
with a wink he talked
of his new home "in the West."
"The West" was just a step away,
but somehow the children felt
it was a strange place, not theirs,
and while the barn was going up,
they helped as needed,
but also scurried back home.

After harvest that same year,
he began to make bricks
for his new house, and the pit
where the brick gang dug clay
was to be—
for all was carefully thought through—
the pond for a later mill.
Three men and a boy were his brick gang.
One man at the "loam hole"
tempered the clay to the consistency
of bread dough without lumps or stones.
Another carried it to the molder
who worked at an open-air table,
like a baker putting dough
into bread pans. A boy
carried the boxes or molds
to a "hearth" where the clay could dry
ready for the firing. A kiln was built
like a small windowless house
"at the lower end of the willows"
and for weeks carts creaked back and forth,
carrying some eighty thousand bricks.
To make the work easier, as usual
Amos made an invention, a shaft
that saved the unhitching of the horse.

In eighteen fifty-seven, they moved.
Ah, the sadness of moving—
any move from "one's own home."
The children, especially the girls,
could hardly bear it. They cried. Yet
the new house was handsome and large,
and all was clean and fresh, smelling
of lime, paint, and paperhanger's paste.
Soon they found they began to like it.
The float of morning air from the creek
crossed the County Line Road—pleasant—
and they had room to spread out.

Now Amos was set to build the mill.
The small fall of the stream
had long worked on his mind
as he walked down the reed-tangled branch.
He had decided on the millsite, to be
near the County Line Road. The pond
had been dug there already,
and now his drafting pen on paper
raised up the mill's coming walls,
three stories and a half high,
the base fluttering like a skirt
to the penstock and the wheels.
He drew it all in precise lines. Hammers rang,
and all went up, frame and rafters shaping
in wood the nearly forty-foot building
housing gears and grinding stones,
bins and large high-ceilinged rooms:
He called it the County Line Mill
and it was a handsome one.

His son Joseph was the first miller,
and for him on the side road
a new house was built,
a square brick home.
For son Edwin on the second farm,
a similar solid home.
A final outbreak of the building passion:
Amos had bought a run-down farm

near Clayton in the center of *Butter Dahl,*
and when his youngest daughter,
his beloved baby Elizabeth,
married Josephus Gerhard,
he suggested Josephus try this farm.
He sensed in this young man
one who could take such an unpromising place
and do with it. To encourage him,
he built additions to the house and barn
and even made another "invention":
a canal, a "small water power"
that would pump the creek water
up to a reservoir at the barn.
So he helped his "son," as he called him.

It was time now to rest.
The Reverend Johnson said of Amos,
he did not like to be "conspicuous."
He and his wife retired in their "new house,"
in its hedged seclusion.
The children were nearby, and children
and grandchildren hunted them there
and asked to hear favorite family stories.
One: "Mama" in the early days
used to bring the men from the fields
"by blowing the big horn,"
but it seemed to give her toothaches,
so Amos "had made" a large brass bell
that weighed twenty-five pounds.
John Kehs, the local blacksmith,
fixed up a holder for it,
and the bell was put on the porch.
It was said it could be heard three miles.
A neighbor, admiring it,
asked would Amos "have one made for him
just the same as what he had."
Amos did, and when it was put up—
as it happened, on a Saturday evening—
he was there and of course
tried it out, ringing it.
Hardly had he done so
when a young man came to call

84

on one of the daughters of this neighbor.
Another daughter "minus a caller"
urged Amos to ring the bell again—
perhaps it would do as well for her.

Amos never put himself forward,
yet all respected him.
He was plain.
His son Joseph, describing him, said,
"When he went in the room to dress,
he came out in less than five minutes."
He could be firm at need,
but the Reverend Johnson says he ruled
"by admonitions of irresistible kindness."
Like Elizabeth he asked only
that none sadden the Lord.

The twenty-ninth of March,
eighteen ninety-one,
when she was seventy-eight, Elizabeth
"passed away to the dear Savior."

Her husband lived four years longer.
A day short of his birthday,
on May tenth, eighteen ninety-five,
in his eighty-sixth year
he "fell asleep." Through the clear spring weather
friends and family carried his coffin
down the County Line Road
to the Schwenkfelder Cemetery
and placed him there beside his wife.
On the double stone now on their two graves,
under "Father, Amos Schultz," it says only,
"We will meet again," and under
"Mother, Elizabeth Schultz,"
likewise, "We will meet again."

THE MOVING

Elizabeth Gerhard sometimes told Josephus
about her childhood. So all do,
and it draws man and wife together.
She told him about the great moving:
"Ah, it was such a thing
when the new house was built.
We did move then to a different county
even if it was but a step.
All through March,
Mother, sister Susanna, and Sarah
did prepare to move.
They were cleaning the new house,
but only four bedrooms were ready.
But so, they washed and cleaned bedding
and furniture—it was a great work—
and carried all across the creek.
On the twenty-first of March,
we were busy moving all day.
In the evening we did eat
the first time in the new home.
We had fried eggs for supper.
We sat at the big family table—
Father, Mother, Uncle Isaac, Sarah,
Susanna, Joseph, Anna, Edwin,
Owen, Lucina, and myself
and two workingmen.
The next day, Sunday, we had
no meeting—we had meeting
only every other week—
so after the morning's work was done,
we did dress ourselves cleanly
and Sarah, Susanna, and Anna
went into the south front room.
There were the washtubs and washbaskets
filled up still, not yet unpacked,
and all three did begin to cry.
Then came Lucina too—
she had taken a book—

86

and seeing her sisters there crying,
she sat with them on the floor
and did the same. So I found them
and joined them. All of us cried
and all of us sat so on the floor.
Mother came in and she kept brave.
She cheered us. She told us soon
there would be chairs to sit on, soon
we could straighten this room up
and lift the bookcase from the floor.
We went to the kitchen
and sat there reading awhile.
Grandfather Isaac Schultz
came walking in the yard,
and came in and did shake hands.
When he came to me, he asked,
'Hast du auch ein recht gutes Buch zu lesen?'
('Have you also a good book to read?')
He looked in my book and smiled. I had
Das Erste Lesebuch für Junge Kinder
(The First Reader for Young Children).
I did love to read that book
that had the English on the one side
and the German on the other.
Grandfather had come walking
all the way from his home
to our old home. As we were gone,
he did follow us to the new house.
So that first day we had company.
Still we did not feel at home,
and at noon when the boys
left the cows out to water,
the cows were lowing and crying too.
They too did not feel at home.
They made an awful noise that Sunday,
for animals notice things.
Yes, they too have feelings."
She smiled at herself as a child
weeping there with the cows.
"But later we loved our new home
and we knew that Father was right."

UNCLE ISAAC'S LIFE

Jacob in Genesis in the Bible
took his brother's patrimony.
Isaac Schultz helped build his brother's farm.
He was tireless at his brother's business.
He worked a hundred fifty-five acres.
He had no machinery
except one poor-running thresher.
He walked two pair of horses
back and forth the whole day
to shell four loads of corn.
He drove surplus grain to market.
He was on the road thousands of miles
with two-, four-, and six-horse teams.
To drive, he got up at two o'clock
when none other would be up
but Elizabeth to get his breakfast.
His brother's family was his family.
He would play his Jew's-harp
for little Joseph, or he would carry
Susanna on his back.
He sat at the table with them
and was glad just to be there.
So he worked thirty-three years.
He always did well with horses,
but one December day
he tried to gentle two new horses.
He hitched them up to the body wagon
and started from the yard. The sky
looked like snow over the Niantic hill.
As he rounded the corner,
the young horses bolted, getting control of him.
As he struggled,
the wagon overturned.
The reins, wapped around his wrists, dragged him,
and that threshing of him on the cold ground
shook out his life.

EDWIN FOX, BEEKEEPER

Bees and ants
are the glance
time took into future mind.
They are the mind of life
before the life of mind.

"You'd think they could think.
They can't."
But they can sting and go honeying—the bees
in Fox's two
flowering American elm trees.

A dozen go to each bud
and the undistractible hum sucks
both flower and gum, airlifting
propolis
and nectar back to the metropolis,

the tawny pseudocity of the hive.
Some slight defect of structure
keeps the insects small, the brainpan
minimal,
and so they do not change at all.

Bees found in Baltic amber,
preserved in that resinous chamber
sixty million years, might be
today
flying the shore of that same sea.

Man is deceived
that bees understand
how they must go to the elms
and through the wind
ascend from and descend

back to their boxed home.
Yet as the boxed swarm
in winter makes itself warm
by its own motion,
a central commotion

exactly fitted to the enclosing cold
(a fire of wings
flown standing still),
the beholder falters.
It must be some mind in those *keschta.*

"Look how they work the elms,"
Fox says toward the brassy zigzags
where the spring breaks into running particles,
the sun dividing
into many suns.

"For two or three days
they'll work them hard,
then go to something else. They're friendly with you.
No need to be afraid.
They won't sting you unless you're afraid."

The near-pathetic fallacy
of Braun's noticeable shrinking
amuses Fox whose high-pitched voice
sings
with a bee's zing:

"My father had bees, so as a boy
I practiced with his smoker and veil
and, later, had my own.
But it was chance
that I started myself." He squints

up through the buzzing boughs and says,
"It was a spring early like this,
and there was an old cornfield
and one stalk
still stood up. They talk

90

about 'solitaries'—that means a swarm
that gets on a bush or tree alone—
and here one had fastened on that stalk
and stayed there
while the scouts went about. It seemed

a good, heavy swarm. I decided
to beat the scouts out, and hive it. I did,
and I got two 'supers' of honey from it.
I did well.
I guess that was my downfall."

He got more bees, splitting hives
or buying some—"three-banded Italians"
and gray and black "Caucasians"—others.
Occasionally
a neighbor would report a stray,

a swarm perhaps a yard long
threatening
to head for the eaves. To stall that off,
call Fox
and he would hurry over with his box.

Like most beekeepers,
honey cultivators, honey reapers,
he did not live
only from the bee,
that uncertainty,

but had another life. "I was born
September twenty-seventh, eighteen ninety-three,
on a farm in Maxatawney Township.
When I was about nine,
we moved to Huff's Church, down

from Squire Benfield there. I went to grade school there."
Then to high school and Kutztown Normal School,
helping farm but wanting to teach.
In nineteen sixteen, young,
though not as young

as Daniel Rohrbach when he began,
he took his first one-room schoolhouse
in Harlem, in Hereford Township. School—swarm—
not the same word
but the brood frame of a brain stirred

by awareness.
Small as the little ones were,
that first awareness
burned in their eyes
and left a lilac wave of surmise.

He taught a while in Harlem,
then "Clayton, Chapel, Traub's Schoolhouse, up
to Seisholtzville, all around here."
In Harlem,
the Reverend Johnson came and spoke to the children:

"Bees are like birds. Do you wonder
how that can be? There are some wrens out there
and they leave their homes to their children
and so do bees.
And so do we."

The thought with its pleasant parallels
was for Fox and he remembers it.
His wife
was a Schultz—of Johnson's family,
cousin of Elizabeth Schultz,

neighbor Josephus Gerhard's wife—
a Schwenkfelder.
"She went to church in Palm,
that pretty church there,
while I myself was Lutheran,

but I could sing a hymn
in another church if I had to."
The Schwenkfelders have been slow
marrying
out of the congregation, worrying—

92

they are
individual and chary. Mary
was the first to marry outside. "They're plain,
as they say, but strong,
no formality, the preacher wears no gown,

they use no candles. They're like the Mennonites,
and yet not so different from us
except for the Lord's Prayer.
They use
'debts' and 'debtors.' We use 'trespasses.'

Yes, I met her when I was twenty-one,
and while I was away at school,
we corresponded." Two years later
they joined their lives,
and he moved his twenty-five hives

to her father Benneville's farm
a mile southwest of Hereford
where Mary had been born,
and all
ate together at one table,

the Lutheran heathen included.
So love broke tradition, love
and Mary's willing it,
for she
had a marked obstinacy.

Years later, in church,
asked how many children she had,
"Six," she said. "When we have six more,
we'll have a dozen,"
but as it was, she stopped at nine.

Raising nine is not so easy—
washing, and ever larger servings of food
that Father Fox had to get
not, like his namesake, with cunning,
but with the bees' running

and another running of schoolchildren
when all their voices went to him
and he directed flights of number,
letter,
and the sound from the letter,

and the children, choric and mnemonic,
recited,
each one each day climbing
one step
up the small ladder of the lip.

For doing all he did so well for children,
for seven months of the year
he received a hundred dollars a month.
"In summer
again I turned farmer."

And so the bees came in, traveling plummets
glinting through the grass,
ricocheting from clover to clover,
gold
pendants on the throats of bee balm,

canna robbers, zinnia rapists,
great
hurriers, no small arbutus
getting fewer visits
than the larger cloud of clematis.

"If there is clover and alfalfa,
enough rain and enough sun,
the flow heavy all summer long,
one hive should run
to thirty or forty pounds of honey

you can take off. I've seen it go
to a hundred and twenty, not often,
no. From some hives in a bad year
you may get none.
What do you get in

94

from all that work?
Six or seven hundred dollars. Of course
you get income another way.
In spring
during apple blossoming

you put your hives in the orchards
to pollinate the trees. The pay,
five dollars a hive, or if the hive
is already there,
four dollars, the honey yours."

He thinks how those hastening wings
die every six weeks for him
and by their dying double his school income,
instinct
keeping so its self-respect

beside the intellect. And like a friend
as fast as death, the queen runs with her eggs
to revive the hive
and give him
new thousands of the clover's seraphim.

The queen. For her, he thinks,
how much human thought is needed—
every ten days taking out
the new queen cells
to prevent the swarming of rivals,

for swarming, like most dramatic things,
uses strength—that is, honey—
and its results are unpredictable
like a storm's.
The beekeeper would rather keep it calm.

Yet bees with their unstopping instinct
gather force again,
and mere man at last
tires and neglects a few hives,
and the power tells.

The inch-long cells
where eight or ten new queens have been feeding
on "royal jelly" royally hatch,
and one queen
on a day of collusive sun

calls the swarm
with her for her nuptial flight:
"The drones chase after her
and one mates in the air and dies,
and the other drones

that aren't needed now, they kill."
Outdistancing the swarm, alone
the queen may attract a mockingbird or kingbird
who swallows her. From that
it could happen the hive dies out.

He has seen that trap in the air
catch the young queen. Accident
is always the baffler of instinct
that does not
know any other way around.

"I have sixty hives now, but soon
it may be I can let them go.
The pay for teaching is more now.
It is now
what it should have been long ago.

You know there on Route Twenty-nine
near Hereford they are building
a consolidated school like an O.
It is like a letter O
with a meeting room in the center.

Did you ever see a round schoolhouse?"
He smiles, asking the question,
at the whims of modern architecture.
But,
"I look forward to teaching there."

And, unexpressed, his smile
is at the appropriateness,
that now the children will go
to the old shape of a hive
that was the other part of his life,

and anthropomorphism turn about
and the children look like bees,
running with their shout
and uproar
to the school's open door.

THE MILL

The West Branch of the Perkiomen
flows slowly near Niantic.
White herons stand in groups of three
in the long meadow there,
water-dreaming. The branch
enters the small pond
of the County Line Mill and is channeled from there
to the mill's narrowing penstocks
and overshot wheels. Wheels.
Amos Schultz, the retired miller,
grandson of the Amos who built the mill,
often thinks about the wheels,
disengaged now from the water.
An electric motor grinds in minutes
what used to take a day as the wheels waited,
wide-shelved and drying, hour by hour,
for the water to collect.
"Yes, the wheels go seldom now—or never."
But in the penstocks is the kneeling wave
sliding down yet to the drains
so that the cavern beneath the polished trapdoor
has still great coils of light
rolling along the roof and wall. Amos
speaks well of the new owners, who are "young,"
but he himself likes only the old ways.

He goes to a chair facing a window
looking out on the meadow,
and talks of the "changes" of the mill.

Besides wheat
originally they "ground rye and buckwheat—"
it was "custom trade catering to the farmers."
They had French buhrstones
and later "the short system of rolls"
run by water, always by water,
They shipped "some barrels of flour"
to Baltimore, till the western mills competed.
Then the trade "turned to feeds."
They ground feed from local grain
and hauled feed from Pottstown by wagon
"before the Colebrookdale railroad—
first bran and middlings, later flax meal,
then the ordinary grains."
Later farmers wanted grains mixed,
and for that "we put in a mixer."
So down the years there was "a revolution
as to what the small mills do,
and only those that changed lasted through."
He speaks of his grandfather Amos,
"a great and wonderful man."
Back through the years to him
is a plain record of good work
and the turning of the wheels. "Many ask,
'Is the old stone-ground flour better
or the roller flour?' I don't know. Some said
the stone-ground was better for pies.
I kept one of the old stones when I changed.
A baker who took a lot of flour
asked if I would give him stone-ground.
I said yes, but"—he smiles—
"I told him a lie about that.
I gave him roller flour instead,
then one day I admitted what I'd done.
I told him it was roller flour he'd had.
'Well, I suspected as much,' he said."

98

The locusts sing hotly toward fall,
and the meadow
darkens behind elms. Farms
cling to ropes of roads
that all are fastened here
in the single knot of the mill.
"The new owners
don't want to pull mud out the dam.
My cousin cleaned it out,
but still they won't use the waterwheel.
No, they won't use it anymore.
Too bad—so it stands."

THE FEW WORDS OF
SUSIE DIEFENDERFER

This nine-year-old's jaw
is overlengthened in the crucial line
that curves to her chin,
and her jaw, so slung,
makes her lisp. Nothing seems fair
to her straight-on stare,
but when her grown cousin takes her hand
and lowers his height down
to sweep along even with her, running,
all changes. Her black bangs
beat at her forehead, and joy
goes in her hand that holds his hand.
Out of breath, she stops at the barn gate
and points to the horned cow: "She—
she don't want to be milked, she only pokes"—
the first sentence of her life
to come out without a lisp.

A MEMORY OF TWENTY-NINE

With a child's spontaneous grace
and with nonsense
wrinkling her face,
Annie Fruh sticks two tents
of maple seeds on her nose, trace
of the year's slow-taken evidence
that life is the traveler of eternity;
the ticket seller, Braun's maple tree.

Sitting near Braun, Papa Fruh,
neighbor come for a visit accompanied
by his granddaughter, says: "I see
there was quite a wind last night, wood
all over the ground. Some hail, too.
In twenty-nine I stood
in September in a storm of hail
that was heavy as a rockfall.

"It laid a two-inch mat
everywhere. I had planted
two thousand strawberry plants, sets
doing well, but that hail slanted
into them like you never saw it—
they weren't just dented,
they were knocked right out of the ground.
Yes, everything there was gone.

"It stripped all the leaves off the trees,
and that had a strange effect.
The apple trees on my place
blossomed again, in fact
they were as white as in spring, and bees
came to them again. It nicked
the forsythia so that it bloomed
all yellow again. It was a strange autumn."

Annie, pulling the seed tents off her nose,
says to Braun, "Do you know what
a maple tree is called?" Braun says, "No."
"It's called a nose tree. You forgot,"
and she smiles. Papa Fruh
says, still following his thought,
"You know, the next spring
you could almost count the trees that were blossoming."

FAMILY
(Neighbor talking)

"Henry Benfield has seven sons and daughters,
all married but the one daughter with him.
And all the sons have jobs or farms.
But any day I look over,
I see maybe in one field
a son working with the tractor,
at another field edge a son scything.
Sometimes three working together,
Henry beside. Yes, I've never been there,
there wasn't at least one son home."

THEIR TEMPERAMENT

When the Pennsylvania Germans came in and got land,
that was it.
No second west for them. They built
stone houses and barns to last. A common saying,
"Three movings is one burning," meaning
the same amount of damage.
They stayed where they stopped.
The children stayed too. If away,
they suffered from *heemweh*, "home longing."

Such, the pioneers.

CONRAD WEISER, THE INTERPRETER

"Anno 1696 the 2 November I Conrad Weiser was born
in Europe in the land of Wurtenberg
in the county of Herrenberg the place is called Astät
and baptized at Kupingen nearby
as my father has told me."
When he was fourteen, his mother died:
"Her motto was Jesus I live for thee,
I die for thee, thine am I in life and death."
The same year his father with most of his children
made the usual emigrants' trip:
"June 13, 1710
we came to Anchor at new-york in north America,
and in the same Autumn were settled at lewenstein's Manor"
there "to burn tar and cultivate hemp
for the Queen . . . but it did not work out."
The project cost more than it produced,
and the Palatines were conditionally freed.
Conrad Weiser's father took him to Schenectady.
There, in seventeen twelve, when Conrad was sixteen,
he met a chief of the Mohawks named Qua y nant (Quaynant)
who "visited my Father they agreed
that I should go with quaynant to his country
to learn the Maqua language,"
and become an interpreter
useful to the colonists. The language was
so "Extream hard to be learnt" that it was
"Almost impossible for any to learn it perfectly
except they begin with it when Children."
There was much more to be learned than language.
Conrad found that Mohawks believed
that everything living—animals, perhaps even
grass and trees—was one community
of which man is the head. Their clan names,
Turtle, Turkey, and Wolf,
indicated particular kinship—those in each clan
were brothers and sisters to one another.
The clans made up the tribes, or nations.
The Mohawks were an Iroquois tribe

102

and the Iroquois were a Five-Nations Confederacy,
formidable fighters (he heard) but seldom fighting.
By alliances
they enforced peace, the "Great Peace,"
over an area as large as western Europe,
the clans carrying brotherhood
down to the individual.
They had no slavery.
Captives were not enslaved
but adopted into the tribe
(captured English and German children
made good Indians).
Of their religion, Conrad later wrote:
"The teachings of Christ and his apostles
are more congenial to them than to (us):
for when it is said Owe no man anything
save to love one another Rom 13–8
Be not anxious for the morrow Matth 6:34
He that is greatest among you shall be your servant Matth 23:11 . . .
That is what they actually practice."
True they made war, totally engaged,
numbing in their power, but their intent
was to make and enforce peace.
Tribes who fought
were reinstructed like faulty
children, the Iroquois Confederacy
imposing its discipline at great distances
mercilessly.
And so there was peace. And friendship.
The Iroquois included the colonists
in that friendship, luckily for the colonists:
"Corlaer"—that is, the province of New York—
"is our Brother . . . we suckled him at our Breasts . . .
We will not forsake him,
nor see any Man make War with him without assisting."
That friendship was soon to owe much
to Conrad Weiser.
Conrad at sixteen, when he went to Quaynant,
spent a snowbound winter (he wrote afterward)
in a long house "made of Mats & bark of Trees
together with poles about 3 or 4 yards high."
It was cold. The Indians were "improvident"

and he was sometimes hungry. He made friends
with two boys, Jonathan Cayenquiloquoa
and his brother "Moses, the Song,"
and they were his friends all his life.
Next summer he was back home
with his father now on the Schoharie.
"I had made a good beginning, that is to say
I had learned the greater part of the Mohawk language.
An English mile From my Father's house
there lived several Mohawk families
with the mohawks always around
going out Hunting and coming back
difficulties often cropped up,
so that I had Much interpreting to do
but without pay
there was No one else to be found
among our people who understood,
so that I became Completely master
of the Language, so Far as my Years
and other circumstances permitted."
In the spring of seventeen twenty-three
many of the settlers left, "united
and cut a Way from Schochary
to the SusqueHana River"
and so up and began
the Tulpehocken settlements "in Penn's province."
But Conrad stayed six more years
near his Mohawk friends. He had married
a quiet girl, Ann Eve Feck, "my Ann Eve,"
and with her farmed and began to have children,
but at last, needing more land,
he followed the Germans to Tulpehocken
and settled near Ann Eve's parents.
He put up a square stone house,
much room but little privacy
(like the Indian long house).
Outside, they had a knoll,
a spring and fields and Weiser's Mountain
(as it was to be called) or Eagle Peak
with eagles floating over.
This, for most of the rest of his long life,
was to be home, *heim,* a place to go from

but always, with need, to return to.
The going away soon began.
This is what happened:
In seventeen thirty-one, James Logan
managing the Penn family interests
cast a look at the frontier
and found it threatening. Shawnees,
Delawares, Nanticokes, and Conestogas
had reasons not to be happy. All
were subject to the Six Nations
(the Five Nations had by now become Six
with the inclusion of the Tuscaroras).
Would it not be well, Logan thought,
to formalize by a binding treaty
"pensilvania's" friendship with the Iroquois?
He had Governor Gordon
ask an Oneida, Shickellamy,
to take a message the long distance
to Onondaga in northern New York
to the great Iroquois Council there,
asking the leaders of the Six Nations,
"some of their old wise men of Authority,"
if they would come to Philadelphia
for a conference. Shickellamy
took the winter trip
and on his way back stopped in Tulpehocken
at Conrad Weiser's. Conrad
was considered partly a Mohawk.
"When we adopted him,
we divided him into two equal parts,
one we kept for ourselves
and one we left for You."
After they talked together, Conrad agreed
to be Shickellamy's interpreter.
The choice was logical.
Oneida was close to the Mohawk language,
which Conrad knew, and Conrad as a Mohawk
was an adopted Iroquois. He came now on horseback
in state for his first visit to Philadelphia
with Shickellamy's entourage, the entourage of Indians accompanying
a vice-regent or "half-king"
of the Six-Nations Confederacy.

105

Shickellamy delivered
a small bundle of dressed deerskins
and with Conrad's help
arranged for the visit of the chiefs,
which was to be during the coming summer.
For this too Conrad would be the interpreter.
At the summer meeting,
the delegation, a large one, was headed
by Tyoninhogarao, a Seneca of the wolf clan,
empowered to speak for the Six Nations
with "Brother Onas." *Onas* was the Indian word
for *feather, quill,* or *pen,* so meaning
the Pennsylvania government (Brother Penn).
Both sides made speeches, the Indians
skilled negotiators and diplomats, speaking
as equals, offering friendship but not going
much beyond friendship to commitment.
Still, the Six Nations being there
giving and receiving presents,
becoming acquainted with the colonists, talking
(with Conrad as interpreter),
cleaned "the Chain of Friendship" of rust,
and the Indians showed pleasure
at Brother Onas's saying he would always
keep a fire burning for them
"to sitt down by and take Council together."
It was, the Indians said, "a sure Token
of Brotherly Love towards them." The chiefs
asked that Conrad Weiser and Shickellamy
should "manage" any further conferences,
and Conrad was officially named
"Province Interpreter" and was paid
for his services by the Pennsylvania government.
It was some time before he was used again. Meantime,
this happened.
The Ephrata *Kloster* (Cloister),
that community of Sabbatarians and "dreaming saints,"
was only twelve miles across country
from Tulpehocken. Conrad
was strongly disposed to understand
the *Kloster* and its leader, Conrad Beissel.
He had read the mystics. He was not a ritualist.

106

He defined religion
as "an attraction of the soul to God."
He knew of the Quakers' "inward light."
Then there was the matter of trance.
Beissel had the power
to induce trances in himself, and Weiser
knew about trance from the Indians.
An Indian boy or girl customarily
on reaching a certain age
had to seek a *Manitto*. He or she went away
and by fasting or fatigue
induced a vision: lightning, a bear,
something from the natural world
that would be a personal guardian,
a near representative of the far God.
So when Beissel found Conrad receptive
and a strong figure who could do much
for the Ephrata community,
he recruited him. Conrad
for several years—until disillusioned—
became "a priest of Melchizedek"
wearing a priest's beard and robes,
and spent much time at Ephrata,
though still farming his "plantation"
and keeping himself available to the Indians. For them
he went again to Philadelphia
to help with the negotiations
regarding the Susquehanna River lands:
at this important conference
the chiefs of the Onondaga Council said,
as John Logan reported it,
"they had found Conrad faithful & honest,
that he is a true and good Man,
& had spoke their words & our Words
and not his own . . ." They gave him
"a drest Skin to make him Shoes
& two deer Skins to keep him warm . . ."
But soon there was more trouble, and serious.
The Iroquois had been sending fighting parties
to tame the Catawbas. The colonists
could easily be drawn in. It could be war.
General war. Brother Onas

asked Conrad and Shickellamy in late winter
to go to Onondaga to the Council
to seek peace. On the trip
both men suffered much from hunger and cold
and ice-swollen streams—at one point, Conrad wrote,
"I trembled and shook so much all over, I . . .
sat down under a tree to die,"
but Shickellamy reasoned with him and they went on
and arrived exhausted.
The Indian custom is not to ask questions
until "a stranger . . . has had food set before him,
and his clothes dried, in which things
they did not allow us to want."
At the conference this time
an important armistice was arranged,
the Armistice of Seventeen Thirty-seven,
which brought a period of peace.
They wanted Conrad to stay afterward,
but he wished to get home.
He was much loved now by the Indians.
He would talk with them not officially
but with the interest of a friend.
He helped Moravian missionaries,
teaching them elements of the Mohawk language
after Moravians had settled
at the fork of the Lehigh and Delaware
in a community their leader,
Nicholas Ludwig, Count von Zinzendorf,
named Bethlehem. The Moravians
worked hard with the Indians
and even intermarried. Christian Frederick Post
and Moravians and Indian converts
established Gnaddenhutten (Huts of Grace),
a community some miles up the Lehigh
where they lived together. Conrad
helped the Moravians get land at Nazareth
and helped their missionaries. He was much moved
by their Indian mission at Shecomeco:
"It was as if I beheld a little Flock
of the First Christians together . . .
Their old people sat in the assembly
some on benches and others

for Want of Room on the ground
with great Gravity and devotion
and hearkened to Brother P. [Pyrlaeus]
as if they would hear the Words
out of his very Heart."
But while these acts and persuasions of peace
were going on, the Virginia Indians
were still much provoking the Six Nations.
Again there was
the danger of a general war,
and again Conrad and Shickellamy were sent
to Onondaga. Shickellamy now
knew some English. He could say, for example,
"Lie still." They arrived
at Cachiadachse, a village four miles
from Onondaga, and the Indian children
climbed up on the roofs to see Tarachiawagon,
the Holder of the Heavens (Conrad's Indian name),
with his pale face and Ephrata beard
not yet shaved off, approaching
among the trees. A messenger met him
and told him the Council House itself at Onondaga
was appointed for his and his party's lodging.
On arrival they were given
a dish of dried eels boiled in hominy,
and to amuse them a black-masked comedian
jumped about under plaits of buffalo hair
and corn husks and shook a rattle.
As soon as the Council declared itself "compleat"—
it took some days for the chiefs to assemble—
proceedings began. Conrad
kept an account of them:
"ffirst the Onondagoes
rehearsed the begining of the five Nations
Praised their Grandfathers Wisdom in establishing the Union
or Alliance by which they became
a formidable Body
that they (now living) were but ffools
to their wise ffathers,
yet protected and accompanied
by their ffathers Spirit
and then the discourse was directed

to the Deputies of the several Nations
and to the Messengers from Onas and Assaryquoa"—Virginia—
"then to the Nanticokes to welcome them all
to the council ffire which was now kindled
A string of Wampum was given by Tocanontie
on behalf of the Onondagoes
to wipe off the Sweat from their (the Deputies & Messenger's)
Bodies and God, who had protected them all
against the Evil Spirits in the Woods
who were always doing mischief
to the people traveling to Onondago, was praised
All this was done by way of a Song the Speaker
walking up & down in the House . . .
All those Indian ceremonies
took up that afternoon
Jo-haas from every Nation was given."
This Jo-haa Conrad described
in a later writing: "When any Proposals
are made by them in their Treaties
with the white People, or by the white People to them,
they make the Io-hau, or Shout of Approbation,
which is performed thus: The Speaker after a Pause,
in a slow Tone pronounced the U . . . . huy;
all the other Sachems in perfect silence:
so soon as he stops,
they all with one voice, in exact Time,
begin one general Io, raising & falling their Voices
as the Arch of a Circle,
& then raise it as high as at first, & stop
at the Height at once, in exact time,
& if it is of great Consequence,
the Speaker gives the U . . . . huy thrice,
& they make the Shout as often. It is usual,
when the white People speak to them,
and they give a Belt or String of Wampum,
for the Interpreter to begin the U . . . . huy,
& the Indians make the Shout."
The next day the Council continued
"and Zila Woolien gave me Notice
that they were now ready to hear Onas and Assaryquoa
Speak. . . . Then I took up a Belt of Wampum
and told the Speaker Canassatego a few Words and he proceeded

110

and Spoke in behalf of the Governor of Virginia as follows
—1.— Brethren The United Nations now met in Council
at Sagoghsaanagechtheyky when I heard of the late unhappy
Skirmish that happen'd in my Country
between some of your Warriours and my People
I was Surprized I would not account for it
to my self why such a thing should happen between Brethren
This Belt of Wampum therefore I give
to the ffamilys in Mourning amongst You . . .
to condole with them and moderate their Grief.
The Belt was given and the usual Sound of Approbation
was returned by the whole House
—2.— Then I handed another Belt to the Speaker
and Spoke to him he spoke much the same as before
and desired that the Belt might be given
to the ffamilys in Mourning at Niharuntaquoa
or the Oneidos for the same Use
Thanks was given again by the whole Assembly
with the usual Sound"
The Indians also gave wampum for the white families.
"Brethren the united Nations these strings of Wampum
serve to dispell the Dark Cloud
that overshadowed Us for some Time
that the Sun may shine again and we may be able
to see one another with Pleasure"
The mediation went on with the same moving
ritual of Jo-has and agreement. At last:
"we thank You Brother Assaryquoa
for removing your Hatchet and for burying it
under a heavy Stone
Let this Belt of Wampum serve to remove our Hatchet from You
and not only bury it but we will fling it
into the Bottomless Pitt into the Ocean
there shall be no more Use made of it
In Confirmation of what we say we give You
this Belt of Wampum, after the usual Approbation was given
the Speaker proceeded . . . Brother Assaryquoa
let this String of Wampum serve
to heal the very mark of the Wounds"
Peace was restored and a time was appointed
for a further meeting in Pennsylvania.
So Conrad helped bring

111

colonists and Indians together, using
the instruments of wampum and metaphor
as his own. During the French and Indian War
when the French seemed likely to be the winners,
the Iroquois
kept a guarded neutrality shaded
with their continuing friendship for the English,
not least based on a single man, a German.
The French incited border tribes.
Delawares and some other tribes
under that ex-broom-maker, Teedyuscung,
attacked frontier farms to burn and kill.
Conrad led the defense, appointed
a colonel by the colony,
but he made distinctions among Indians.
When Scaroyady, the Oneida Chief,
visited him with other Indians,
he gave Scaroyady a horse
and went with him to protect him
"for the People were so enraged against all the Indians . . .
I rode before, and in riding along the Road
(and armed Men on both Sides of the Road)
I heard some say, 'Why must we be killed by the Indians
and we not kill them?' " but he carried
Scaroyady and his company to safety
"and so parted in Love and Friendship."
He himself, though an officer, was at times
in danger of being shot by angered Germans,
and when he could give up his army post,
he did. He had opposed scalping bounties:
The scalps most easily taken
were those of friendly Indians.
In seventeen fifty-eight
Thomas Penn wrote him, telling him
that a man "so useful in Indian affairs
should not be exposed to other dangers"
and sending affectionate greetings.
Weiser was still
to strive for justice to the Indians.
That same year
he did much to bring them
away from the French. Teedyuscung

112

came down to Philadelphia to make peace
and said he had given "the halloo . . .
to the Indians of the sunset." They had not heard him.
"The Reason is," he said they said,
"you have not spoak loud enough."
He now was willing to speak loud,
putting both hands to his mouth,
and Conrad encouraged him in this effort.
The effort succeeded. Almost unopposed,
as the Iroquois continued neutral,
General Forbes took Fort Duquesne
and peace was restored to the frontier.
Conrad was to live only two years longer.
July thirteenth, seventeen sixty, a Sunday,
he took sick. He continued
"in a Stupid Condition till night and then expired."
Two weeks before, his son-in-law,
Henry Melchior Muhlenberg, wrote,
he had sung "some hymns with his family
from the depth of his heart . . ."
He was buried by Ann Eve and his children
in a grave by his Tulpehocken house
where he had wanted to be,
and they put up a sandstone slab. They wept.
Later, it is said, several Indians
were buried near him. There are some unmarked stones
The following year
at the opening of "the Treaty" at Easton,
an old friend of his, Chief Seneca George,
said, holding up a belt of wampum:
"Brother Onas: We, the seven Nations, and our cousins
are at a great loss, and air in darkness, as well as you,
by the death of Conrad Weiser, as since his death
we cannot so well understand one another;
By this Belt we cover his Body with Bark."

UNAMI CREEK

The oaks,
ranges of brown along the hills,
become individual here by Unami Creek.
In them
the wind makes a soft sound.

Indian children watched leaves like this one
canoe across the water.

THE MODEL

A legal document, prepared in nineteen twenty-four
and submitted to a New York legislative committee
on behalf of still-surviving Iroquois, says:
"The Iroquois Confederacy was so powerful
and their social order and system of government
so far ahead of anything,
in theory and practice,
that the European had ever known,
that the immigrants to the new world
reported to their respective governments
a mighty nation existed here."

Benjamin Franklin followed
the Iroquois's "united nations" for his project
of a united colonies, later the United States,
and Iroquois to this day claim
that the American Constitution with its balance of powers
was modeled on their six relatively free tribes
meeting in a high council at Onondaga,
a council well known to the constitution-makers
through Conrad Weiser, Franklin's friend.

RALPH BERKY

A German of an old name
who goes back to the old sounds.
Perhaps something Indian in him.

He walks long distances.
He stands still often.

He stands still in a road to listen,
a back road between a field and wood.
A farmer in the field is suspicious.
Anybody who stands still . . .

He knows the sound of the beeches, bird against cone-bur,
hemlock shadows,
the boring, hypnotic drill of the sapsucker,
the variations of wind,
wind in fern, wind in grass,
the approach of rain in the distance.

He is the lover of the place.

DELAWARES HERE

They last in more than place-names.
From the Blue Mountains, forest tracks
skirt the edges of the township fields.
In Rohrbach's backwoods glade
is a boulder bruised by maize,
hollowed where the grinding stone turned,
and the stone is still there.
Faint circles may be guessed on the ground
from which the wigwams' rib poles rose
to crests tied with escaping smoke,
and the spokes of three paths
converge on this wraith encampment yet.
Other camps lie hidden further north, the tents

of Kekerappen, Opekasset,
Taminent, Papanahoal,
sachems of the Fork,
black hair cropped, feather-shadowed:
"Eilhanilhab, noha matappi."
"Greetings, sit down with us."

CREEKS FLOWING

Unami, Perkiomen, Manatawny, Cocalico,
and, echoing west, Cacoosing and Little Swatara,
all the spring "runs" and "sinks," water voices
with the kingbird striking
and that tall bird, the heron,
rising out of the shallows:
names that have lost their Indian meaning,
with only an Indian sound.

THE KIDS

Fred Braun holds the two gray kids
born in the morning, now dry,
shiveringly pleased with their dryness,
but
ma-ah-ah-ing for their mama.
They nudge inside his shirt,
hunting. He lets a finger
into their hard, washboard mouths
and they suck eagerly.
Let down, they are lost again.
They run to the well cover,
ai, to them the world's height,
and first one, then the other,
leaps into the air from bowstring legs.
But again, ma-ah-ah-ah,
we are lost, ah-ah-ah-ah.
"Huh, they are babies, *net?*"

116

THE CHIPMUNK

He throws his rug of stripes
over the pine needles. Goes
sampling the earth with quick paws:
bark, acorn-cup skoals, tamarack cones.
A sawdust drunk,
he slides belly down through the dry-surfaced
litter left by the woodpile, swimming in
an aeon of oaks. Stone walls give him
accessible caves. He runs over them
faster than vision. Illusion
is less quick than he is. On the parade ground
of tree shadow
he astonishes birds with his piccolo throat.
With his slurred note
he scolds boulder and cucumber
and, sitting tranced,
interrupts the attentive slumber
of his wide-open eyes to vanish and reappear
ten feet away.

THE TENANTS

Ralph Berky asks Braun to come with him
to a fountaining lilac bush
that closes off one end of Braun's barn
"Have you seen this?"
Deep in the bush's privacy, a hummingbird's
nest hardly bigger than a thumb.
It shines with lichen and spider web
binding plant-down into a shape
of thimble as implausible as it is
small. And the bird small.
Eye and tail quiver together,
both sticking out and both nervous
in the violated lilac nave.

117

A chained she-goat baas nearby.
"It seems
you have all kinds of tenants
on your property," Ralph says.

ED DRY'S FARM AND ED

Ed Dry's place
is a growth out of the soil,
something the increments of time
have made in steady pearl. Twilight
wraps the buildings in a light that is
the tinge of weather-exposed mortar
in the joints of the walls. Such light
turns unreal and dies. At dawn,
a soap kettle, chained up near the fence, in the wind
creaks like a stunned tongue.

The fence, a few
pointed palings,
is fretted
with the garden's shadow,
netted
with pole-bean tendrils
furling
up the tripods,
curls
of pink and white buds
continually
blossoming up the sticks.
The pods
rise behind the buds,
lengthen,
and make tall tents
green beside the corn.
Dry grows them
with eye upon the succotash,
the old *misickquatash,*
Lenni-Lenape

118

recipe,
a gift behind the years
those tents, those bound poles—
wigwams
of honey for the wife.

Wife—here is his strength,
prospect, memory,
and like a shawl about her throat
the winter guard of love.

Some days he works at Hill Church,
leaving his fields to tend the graves.
His hours of work among these stones carrying
tears of the dead for the dead
are slow, measured with his sickle
in the special grass.
Walking home, he picks
roadside huckleberries, his spade on his shoulder catching
ribbons of the setting sun.

AT THE GRAVE OF MOUNTAIN MARY

From Hill Church, a dirt road goes
along the wooded ridge, winding and opening
into lime-greened fields. It passes
Ed Dry's farm. He knows the genealogies
of Kichlein's Pennsylvania Associators,
Lutz's battalions, and the German saviors
of Long Island. The road keeps forking,
smaller at each fork, past club moss
and juniper and arms of hemlock wavering,
and drops down to a farm
in a single, almost untraveled track.
Perhaps three people go by in a week,
and the voices of those who live here
adjust to solitude. The stone barn,
split by a wide crevice
and propped on the downhill side by beams,

is skirted with the white of hens.
Constant water falls into a trough.
Near the house, a duct of hollowed-out
sapling halves ends in a drip of spring water
into a green stone basin.
Four clay crocks stand beside it.
Winter vines, unbudded, curve their hairlines
over a horsecollar arbor.
The arbor leans. A fence near it drifts
through the sleeping bones of leaves.

This is the Moyer farm: meadow and field
foaming to the ridge, to a windbreak
and a briery square of ground
walled with a stone wall dragged low
by the years. Inside this wall
under the briers, under the windbreak's shadow,
is the grave of Mountain Mary.

    Two centuries ago
near Feuerbach that rises into snow
above Württemberg's Stuttgart,
a peasant child was born, crying hard,
Maria Jung.

She grew. With her family,
or some say without,
but like others desperate and devout
she read word of Penn's Wood, and joined
the western flight.

Her song
their song:
"Wir reisen nach Amerika," words
raised from the pestholes of redemption ships,
boards

on which thousands died,
tithe for the rest, freed
to the fields of *Abend,*
fields promised
to be their own—

fields to own
sown
with solace for the driven sects.
To Menno Simons' followers and Jacob Ammann's
and Caspar Schwenckfeld's, peace.

On the ship's deck
Maria met Theodore Benz,
one with her strength,
one who spoke to her of love
simply

and so, simply, she loved.
With *Landvolk* like themselves
it was a time for quick trust, the leap
of need and tenderness. They had hope
and were young.

At Philadelphia, Theodore
had good offer.
For three years' indenture on an inland farm,
he would get his passage paid
and land besides.

Maria, who must wait,
stayed at the port.
One bid for her,
for three years' household service there,
her passage and some store.

Theodore,
bound man near Oley, *stark*
step by step
cleared and plowed, breathing the new air
everywhere

free of the "lords,"
free of fire and sword,
the deep blackness of ground underfoot
nourished with centuries of trees
instead of blood.

He made one horseback trip
back over the wilderness roads
to Philadelphia to visit Mary.
All else was herds,
fields, and his fealty.

He worked his full three years
and was paid,
the land agreed surveyed—woods, springs,
and spring-fed swale—when, appearing over his ground,
the lords again. He planned

a log cabin,
an opening
in trees heavy with smoke and sun,
a first clearing to meet the sun when—
war!

Far
the muffled throb
of money thrown on the drumhead. Down valleys
from Reading to the sea, volunteers were reaped in rows
from the fields.

Among them
he,
and the need so great in the crisis north,
he had but one day to seek Maria and have wife
and go away.

He met the Hessian spine
advancing in its line
out of the *Europa* he had quit, crop
of starved mercenaries for "Kaiser König" and his kind.
Against them he died.

     Maria loved no more
after the love of Theodore.
She built on his ground the log house he had planned,
sealed
with dried clay.

To live
there must be work.
War's blockade had brought the remedies of herbs,
medicines learned from Indian and the searching knife.
She took these.

Balm of Gilead;
Cockscomb leaves; for typhoid,
Joe-Pye weed or Queen of the Meadow;
pleurisy roots; aconite roots; the pharmacy of the earth read
with eyes low.

Tracks and paths
in the moon's cold and the sun's laths
through aspen brakes, unceasing, numb yet live,
she walked. Births, cures, and ease of deaths
now all her care

all her years.
With her years worn,
old with necessary work,
at last—the work done—
she closed her eyes.

An unmarked headstone
lies in the patch of brier beside a cedar
ringed with sapsucker holes. The wind
of evening goes down from the ridge.
Peace of depth such that to be known
is to be valued even above love
moves in the trees.

MAG

Like many early graves
it had only an unmarked stone to tell
where the field took home its visitant.
Mag Sieberle was her name,

born what year none know or what year died.
All is unknown.
None now touch the iron-fenced end of field,
respecting
a sleep that could be hers and yet their own.

WAR RESISTERS:
FROM THE EMMAUS ARCHIVES

When the American Revolution began,
Emmaus
was a small closed Moravian village
of a hundred or so inhabitants—
an offshoot of Bethlehem. In seventeen seventy-five,
the Moravian *Oeconomats-Conferenz*
sent a cautiously unsigned letter to their congregations:
"Under the present turbulent conditions
prevailing in the land in which
the Lord has placed us . . ." it becomes the concern
of "all our congregations and their members
so to deport themselves in this crisis
as befits the character of the Lord's people."
The Brethren had been granted
immunity from military service
by an act of British Parliament,
seventeen forty-nine.
But now, June, seventeen seventy-six,
came an "address"
from the "Provincial Conference" in Philadelphia
to the Pennsylvania "Associators"
(to "associate" meant come together
with guns ready to do battle):
"It is . . . in your power to immortalize your names,"
establishing
"the liberties of one quarter of the globe . . .
Remember the *name* of Pennsylvania."
Pennsylvania's
later German immigration,
which had come near and around Emmaus,

had been not so much plain-sect as high church,
Lutheran and Reformed. Even Catholics
had been allowed in and had come in numbers,
often sharing the ship with Protestants.
These all found their religion compatible
with war and revolution. And now,
bearing out the popular feeling,
came a "test oath":
"I . . . do declare that I do not
hold myself bound to bear allegiance
to George the Third, King of Great Britain, Etc,
and that I will not, by any means,
directly or indirectly,
oppose the establishment of a free government
in this province." Moravians
were strictly forbidden to take any oath.
This was "the character of the Lord's people."
No oaths, and obedience to a God
Who with His New Testament voice
asked men not to kill. Emmaus's
Northampton County had to raise
three hundred forty-six men
as its part of Pennsylvania's six thousand
for the newly forming militia.
The Emmaus Brethren refused to enlist.
At first reprisals were moderate,
merely fines. Every male
between sixteen and fifty
who did not enroll in the militia
must pay twenty shillings a month
every month he was not enrolled.
He must also pay a monthy tax
on the value of his "estate"—
this was purported to be to support
the families of "poor associators." The Brethren
paid the levy, but not happily.
From the Diarium of the Emmaus church,
seventeen seventy-seven:
"July 8. This afternoon our neighbor Blank,
who is the collector, came
together with six men of the militia
to collect the fines imposed

125

for not yielding to the draft."
The Brethren did not pay willingly.
"The collector added another penalty
of 5 shillings for costs."
He collected six pounds five shillings.
Later "official penalties"
became at times extortionary.
Emmaus was put under other pressures.
Its parent town Bethlehem
in seventeen seventy-seven
was commandeered
to help the Revolutionary Army
as a hospital. When Bethlehem and Allentown
overflowed, seventy wounded
were sent to Emmaus. Then, October 18:
"Some more sick and wounded soldiers
were brought here from Allentown.
In the evening a wagonful
came direct from camp, so that we now have
in our village and in a neighbor's house
132 men."
The Emmaus minister, Franz Boehler,
and the congregation in their limited space
cared for the soldiers and "won their gratitude."
Boehler even preached to them "in English."
Yet this occured:
"December 2. Brother Giering
was out all day procuring things
for the hospital, on returning home
stopped toward evening in a house
about a mile from here to warm himself.
While there he was attacked, roughly treated
and beaten by a certain Peter Lauer
from Goschenhoppen, although
he had had no words with him.
This Peter Lauer took him to be a Tory."
Throughout the war,
the Moravians were much "belittled" and scorned.
In seventeen seventy-eight
scorn turned to malice. A certain John Wetzel,
county lieutenant and a "former Moravian"—
always the rejecter is the hater—

126

ordered twelve Emmaus Brethren arrested.
With a show of guards, slowly
he had them marched like common criminals
through Bethlehem to Easton to jail.
There they were asked to take the test oath.
They refused. Wetzel
and a Jacob Miller appeared
and swore they were "dangerous enemies of the state,"
and they were "bound over." Summoned
before Squire Morey, at Allentown,
they were again asked to take the oath.
"Eventually most of them
were worried into doing so." Some
were threatened with the confiscation
of all their property. Franz Boehler said
"we were not the people against whom
they should be executing the laws
with such severity." In the town archives
is no record of any Emmaus brother
who was recruited by the militia,
yet later
names of some villagers were, it was said,
found in militia rolls.
If so, there is no record
that any of them was killed.

HOW TO BE A SPY
(From various depositions)

On August 6, 1777,
Henry Funk, a nonviolent religionist,
had certain things happen to him
when he had gone from his home.
He went first to Michael Smith
and "pay'd some money unto him
for wheat which I had bought . . .
from there I went unto one Nicholas Klotz
a black Smith" to enquire if a wagon
that he had ordered was "done or not . . .

From there I went back again
with an intent to go home.
But when I was come about half a mile
back to a Tavern" and was passing by,
"Philip Walter seeing me through the window
called me to stop. . . . I stopt"
and Walter said: " 'Have you a pass?'
I said no! Then said he:
'You are my prisoner.'
'For what do you take me up what is the Reason'
'You will not take the oath of allegiance,
and therefore it is our Duty
to take such People up.' "
Funk was then brought before
Mr. Limbach to whom
Walter and others declared
that they "had some mistrust upon me
because I would not take the Oath
not today . . . nor tomorrow neither
if I could not be better convinced.
Mr. Limbach asked me: why I could not take it?
I said: It is against my Conscience,
because we shall be at Peace
with everybody and forgive all Men,
etc.: Mr. Limbach asked these men . . .
whether I had spoken any Thing
against the State, They answered No!"
Funk was given time to reconsider,
and when they met again,
Limbach asked "what I would do now.
I said I had considered the matter well
. . . and the more I consider it
the less Liberty I can find
in my Conscience to take that Test."
Mr. Limbach asked Walter and John Lamb
if they could swear they were convinced
"in their hearts and consciences
that they mistrust me to be a Spy.
He asked them what Reason they had
for such a Suspicion. They said:
because he travels forwards and backwards

and for refusing to take the oath.
Then Mr. Limbach Swore them
upon the holy Evangelists
of Almighty God and after
they had Sworn Mr. Limbach said:
now you are Qalified to say
the Truth the whole Truth
and Nothing but the Truth.
What reason have you to supose
that Henry Funk is a Spy.
They made the same answer as before
for traveling forwards and backwards.
Then Mr. Limbach asked them again:
If they were convinced in their Conscience
that Henry Funk might be a Spy,
they said Yes. Then Mr. Limbach
asked . . . If they had any other thing
to say against Mr. Funk,
they said no, upon this
Mr. Limbach committed me to Gaol.
This is the Substance of my trial
before Mr. Limbach.

       Henry Funk"

THE CONVENTION HESSIANS

From the beginning of the Revolution to the end,
about thirty thousand German mercenaries
were used by "the British king."
More than half were hired
from the Prince of Hesse-Cassel
(who received thirty dollars a man)
and so the term "Hessians." These troops
were promised easy plundering:
Americans by rebelling had forfeited
"all the rich and fertile country"

which they, the Germans, could have by only
"taking the trifling trouble
to drive out the possessors" thereof.
It did not happen that way.

Americans captured them by the thousands.
About half of Burgoyne's expedition were Hessians who,
taken prisoner, were sent by forced march
first to Boston, then to Virginia,
and were kept there for two years.
They were called "Convention Hessians"
because by a signed convention they were to be
repatriated after the war.
When the British attacked in Virginia,
these prisoners were shifted to Pennsylvania, to Lancaster,
and then some thousand and fifty Germans
arrived in Reading under guard.
Prisoners were not ·asy to have
in a community not prepared for them,
and they at that time outnumbered
the males of Reading two to one. But
"the prisoners since their arrival here
have behaved themselves very orderly
and Peaceably." A few
had brought women with them, either
wives from Europe or women
married in Virginia. Most were single.
What to do with them then, these reputedly
well-behaved German prisoners?
They could have been put behind stockades
(no word angrier than Hess),
but instead it was decided to "hut" them
on an open tract, and keep them only
technically under guard.
After some indecision,
a piece of land running
roughly parallel to today's Hill Road
was chosen. It was pleasant and looked out
to the morning sun, toward the valley.
The prisoners, supplied with "Public Tools,"
in three months put up
some hundred and fifty huts constituting

130

a village larger than Reading itself.
They cut trees, gathered stone
(dismantled later and used in Reading),
mixed clay mortar,
mortised logs, built chimneys,
fitted roofs of overlapping boards,
and at last had everything ready
ahead of cold weather, all sealed
and made reasonably comfortable.
For a time the men
were on "short rations," but with spring
they cleared a large plot of ground,
dividing it into seven terraces,
and planted vegetables. So they lived,
caring for themselves:
had their own kitchens, their own cooks,
doctors, and chaplains. It was communal,
a group with an inward life
and a curious quiet waiting. Meanwhile
some Hessians elsewhere were now fighting for the rebellion.
When German troops were captured at Trenton,
the Pennsylvania Council of Safety said:
"It is General Washington's earnest wish
that the prisoners be well treated. . . .
They have no enmity with us . . .
they were dragged from their native country
and sold to a foreign monarch. . . .
From the moment they are rescued
from the authority of the British officers
we ought no longer to regard them as our enemies   "
Instead, we should "weaken" the British force
"by making their auxiliaries our friends."
A Frenchman, Charles Armand Tufin,
Marquis de la Rourie, commanded two squadrons
"four hundred strong,
composed entirely of German deserters,"
and in early seventeen eighty
these troops passed through Reading. Almost surely
Reading Hessians could have been recruited,
but their status as "conventioners" was respected.
When the war was over
and prisoners were to be repatriated,

131

German monarchs made no great issue
of getting back these freedom-infected troops.
Seven thousand or more Germans
stayed on in America, including
most of the Reading "Hesses."
Even if their *Deitsch* was different,
they blended in. Some married Reading girls,
some spread into the farms around.

The huts of course, were abandoned,
and grasses, ferns, and shrubbery sprang up
and covered the ground.
Trees grew, cedar and pine,
and crossbills flew in
and wild pigeons whistled by
in their immense yearly migrations.
Of the "hutting" only
traces remained, a few foundations,
the circle of a pit.

GREAT AGE

A grandmother among her children,
old and dying too slow,
she sits confined, her chair
the miserable end of the world.
She got up one morning early,
wanting to go to the privy,
and closed the house door on an untied shoelace.
She was thrown headlong down
and has not walked since.
She sometimes complains, "My ass hurts,"
as the long days irk her.
Toward night in a chair of darkness
she dreams of being loved,
a pillow of the softest hour
under her as the prison fades.

LESTER KEMP

He climbs Crow Hill,
a boy in summer, greeting earth and air
whose jubilee he is—in one hand
the rustling staff of a green cornstalk,
and in the other hand a bouquet.

EMMAUS'S BEGINNING

This is the story of an experiment.
Somewhere near seventeen fifty
two Moravian brethren gave the Emmaus *Gemein*
(or Congregation) a hundred acres
to be a "closed village" lived in
only by members of the Unitas Fratrum,
to keep them from
"dangerous and hurtful worldly connections."
They then built
a church with a *Gottes Acker* (cemetery),
and a patch of woodland reserved
for the pastor's use. The rest of the sloping tract
was measured off for the building lots, called "in-lots,"
and for larger, several-acre plots
of garden and orchard, called "out-lots,"
one out-lot for each in-lot.
The land was never to be sold,
its fixed moderate rents going
to help support the church. Houses
could be sold, but only to church members.
So the *Gemein* was to be preserved,
and so for many years it was preserved
in the brotherhood of God. Still,
change comes. Father Theodore Schneider,
the Jesuit missionary, walked from Churchville
(later Bally) to the few outlying Catholics
in the neighborhood of Emmaus, bringing

recollections of the state church, that shadow.
The Revolutionary War passed by.
Some proselytizing Methodists,
Fremden (outsiders), talked
to the Emmaus *Geschwister* (sisters). "Strangers"
visited the Moravian church
and, liking the services,
leased land and bought houses
on the promise of joining the church,
but not all kept the promise.
Not as often now as earlier
the village "regulations" were read.
By eighteen twenty-seven,
Pastor Paul Weiss wrote in that year's
church "Memorabilia":
"All loyal members . . . must notice . . .
that the purpose of our unity
is so little being taken to heart
by many among us . . . that
things are beginning to intrude themselves
upon us, which are entirely contrary
to our rules and regulations.
Especially does this concern our children and young people,
who are in greater danger of becoming ensnared
by soul-destructive forces."
In the church diary for eighteen thirty:
"We complain about the frolics in the tavern."
In eighteen thirty-four,
a new church was built. Curiously
the building of this church, with its expenses,
hastened the end of the closed village.
Debts incurred required more income.
Some tenants, otherwise good church members,
had stopped paying the land rent, though small.
Others complained about the rent.
The "greed" of still others was noted,
who capitalized on their low, unchanging ground rent
in selling their buildings. The solution,
all could see,
was to sell the lease land, but this meant
giving up closeness,
the pure communal *Gemein* they had.

134

Still, members by now
were unwilling to make the sacrifices
that would keep the *Gemein* going.
They would not or could not
buy out the outsiders. So
the Moravian administration
in Bethlehem authorized selling the lease land,
and when that happened,
lot after lot was sold, and though each sale
was carefully voted on and though
the end of leasing was slow,
it finally was reached.
The conformity or nonconformity
of the advancing Republic triumphed
and Emmaus became
a town like any other. Today only ghosts
of in-lots and out-lots remain,
church records telling a few their past.
Dr. Preston A. Barba knows
he is on Lot # 1 of the old village,
and others know their sites. Streets
follow the old tracks into the hills.
Memory has its grace: Archives,
diaries, and letters lead back
to the old *Gemein* and its brotherhood,
its good intent. The documents,
after this good start,
mention failures, sicknesses, defections,
"pain and sadness,"
but at least at one time—
and for almost a hundred years—
one group of American settlers maintained
a commune of unowned land.

AMERIKA

The aging Goethe wrote:
"Amerika! Du hast es besser
als unser Kontinent, der alte;
hast keine verfallenen Burgen und Schloesser
und keine Basalte . . ."
"America! You have it better
than our old continent;
you have no ruined forts and castles
and no basalt . . ."
There was much to be said for the modesty
of Emmaus, for its gardens and orchards
under no gateways of stone,
for its years written out
in a parish diary. But Emmaus changed,
and other change
lay ahead in this new land.

PART TWO

FORMS

Upended on a wall, a flat stone
has on it three bands of red barn paint:
two eyes and a crescent mouth.
Comedy directed the hands
that set this stone on end and painted it,
and masks of comedy and sadness
haunt the unpainted ones too
with black holes of lichen eyes
and lips of creeper pointed up and down.
Here is a silhouette of dew,
there a heart where the indented stone
bleeds from the arrow weed, and all
take form in the observer's gaze
according to his agony or ease.

MAN AND CHILDREN

All in some way comes to one moment,
comes to this evening
as John Simmons, living on Route 100
just outside of Bally,
gets up from the table, yes, gets up,
taking his sons and two small daughters with him,
and haws his horse and flat plank wagon
out to the potato field. It is sunset.
He likes the fire on the hilltops. As he drives
along the aisles of filled potato crates,
the boys swing them up to him,
stepping between the wheels rhythmically
in and out as the wagon slows
to his repeated "whoa," the horse stopping and starting
with even plunges. Boys, horse, and man
work as one being, caged in twilight.
He sets the crates. When the weight grows,
the horse's red haunches straighten and swell

139

from the ground up. In the sky
the final color has come.
A new moon cuts the clouds
raked out like broken windrows of grass.
The wind is warm and the horse snuffles it.
The two girls race down the field
and one calls, "Anna, nah the horse turns.
Look aht!" Dot, swerving,
pretends to be afraid. Conspiracy
infects the two as they run and laugh.

While the boys dump the potatoes
from the crates down a barn chute
in a drumming roar, Simmons
takes a chlorine pump to spray the hens,
sick again. He walks through the apple orchard,
the girls after him as if hitch-lined
to his waist, silent, attendant
in a flow of long dresses. Night has come
in a pool that fills the trees.
"The chickens have come oaf the trees,"
Anna says. A coop looms in the blackness.
Simmons enters, saying, "Stand back." He pumps
white burning clouds into the air,
and more-than-human sneezes and coughs
retch from the chickens. "Enough."
Now a second coop bulks up.
The girls run to the netting and call out,
"Something white is on the floor, Papa."
"Yeah," he says, unlatching the door, "it's a hen. It died."
Anna lifts the white body
already stiffening: "Yeah, it's dead.
It died." She drops it to the ground
and all the unrest and joy,
all the evening's conspiracy
sinks in her arms and in her eyes.

A bat overhead, zigzagging,
flaps downward toward the girls' hair.
Another night they might run and scare,
but tonight they have no fear.

BECHTELS' STORE IN BALLY

The two front windows of the store
reflect the shaft of the Catholic Church
across low ground. Bees buzz
in storeside hollyhocks. Inside,
a customer writes a check to M. A. Bechtel,
not knowing whose the initials are.

The History of Berks County (with illustrations),
published in eighteen eighty-six, says
that opposite a public house in then-called Churchville
"is a general store carried on
by William Bechtel since eighteen sixty-nine."
Dr. Oswin Berky adds to this
as his own memory
that William Bechtel was "a well-built man,
and had a long beard, about so."
In October, eighteen eighty-three
he "brought the Post Office here,
renamed Bally then to honor the priest.
The Post Office was in the store,
and it gave the store a character."
Calico twenty-five cents a yard.
Eggs eight cents a dozen.
Molasses thirty-seven cents a quart.
"The store kept open till eleven at night—"

William's son, Irvin H. Bechtel,
In "the great Centennial year"
married Mary Ava Latshaw,
"the mill-owner's daughter," and the couple
on their honeymoon
walked through "the wonderful stalls"
where Philadelphia had made itself
America's exhibit to the world.
They saw "the agricultural displays,"
and looked at sewing machines and drainpipe.

That year Irvin took the store.
His son Stanley was born five years later.
In nineteen two, Mary was carrying Russell
when her husband died. Two months later,
her husband's father, William, also died.
So Mary Ava Bechtel
was left with a store
and one child born and one to come,
but "Mother had a great spirit,"
Russell says. "She wasn't discouraged.
She herself ran the store."

"In nineteen twelve, in mid-April," Stanley says,
"the day after the *Titanic* sank,
I was flying a kite in a field
when a boy called, 'Look at the barn,' "
meaning the barn behind the store.
Smoke was pouring out of a gable.
"Then it was just a matter of minutes
till it was in flames."
At Pottstown
a fire engine was loaded on a flat car
on the Colebrookdale Railroad,
and Harry Pyott, the engineer,
took the car in only twelve minutes
by "the winding line" to Barto,
the firemen clinging to the sides.
There Nick Schwoyer waited with six horses,
two teams of his own and one of Nick Melcher's,
hitched them up to the fire engine,
and whipped the horses up the Barto hill.
The flames now had caught the store itself
and licked at the house. Mary ordered
the household goods put out on the lawn.
At the well, one man pumped,
filling buckets that helping hands
passed through the house stairs to side windows
where they wetted the house down.
When the Pottstown engine arrived
and ran its rescuing hose out,
it saved the house, not the store.

Mary Ava
used the house as store while rebuilding.
"Yes, she would not give in at all.
She even refused to cut down
a linden tree the fire had burned,
but left it with its scars." So
she kept the store till her sons
grew up and took charge.

Russell's wife, Marian,
sitting in the twilight, says,
"Grandma Bechtel used to come often
to visit her granddaughter, Carole Ann,
repeating always,
'Bless her little baby heart.' Grandma once
asked me to read from the Bible
and when I stopped,
Carole Ann took the Book."
Pretending to read, she babbled baby words
to Him who binds the unicorn,
harrowing in the valleys.

Now when a new customer,
paying a bill,
asks to whom he shall write the check,
"Why," Russell says, "you shall write it
to M. A. Bechtel."
"Thanks."

PORTRAIT OF CAROLE ANN
A YEAR AFTER GRANDMA BECHTEL DIED

She sits in a little chair,
one braid a crown, the other a tail.
With wide cheeks, eyes
like a chipmunk's.
Can sing "Holy Nighd."
"I trow dis button trough de vindow—

it don't hurt de vindow, it comes righd back.
See? Like dis. Goes far avay,
comes back. You vant me to make
a monguey?"

FIRE

Val Duheim Gehman
hurries to the house door, smelling smoke.
A rope of blue is unraveling
from some downhill roadside brush.
He calls to his sons, "Fire.
Get brooms, quick!"
They run to where flame crawls
through a patch of dead weeds toward a tree
that, fallen, has been quartered and sectioned
with its litter around it. The blaze
sucks at the tinder.
"Keep it checked at the edges!" he calls,
and the brooms beat.

Twelve years ago a live coal
fell one night from the kitchen stove,
nudged by some freak pocket of gas
through the open damper. Gehman
and his wife, Katherine, and the boys
only just got out. Nothing was saved.
The slate roof dropped to the cellar.
The marriage bed and all their homemade linen
with seamed hems like boxed clouds, all went down
in the moaning pillar of fire.

When the brush fire is out,
all cools. Black and bare,
the cut tree-sections lie like beams or rafters
on the ground, smoking a little.
The brooms rest. Tufts of green
loosen from black ash. "It's out,"
one of the sons says.

144

"It seems to be," Gehman says,
but stays uneasy. "But I'll watch it awhile.
Best keep an eye on it.
You can't trust a fire."

THE WASP

Vul Gehman
six days after Fred Schoepf's sister's funeral
had just parked his car at Saunders' Tavern when Schoepf
drove up in his rattling sulky,
one of the few still on the road. Gehman,
watching him tie his horse, said,
"I was sorry to hear about your sister."
Schoepf answered, "Yeah," and took a basket
from the sulky, and went with Gehman
into the bar and was going on through
to get groceries in Saunders' store
when Gehman asked him would he have a drink,
then remembered that he never drank.
To his surprise, Schoepf said, "All right, why not?"
and had a drink with him,
then went on with his basket.

One standing at the bar said to another:
"You see that man just went in the store?
He once killed a man. . . . You didn't know?
Twenty or more years ago it happened.
Him and his sister Laura that lived with him,
that died just nah, they was invited
to a big wedding—it was there somewheres
over by Heydt's Schoolhouse.
At the wedding there was drinking
and some dummkup who'd had one too many
thought Laura had give him a sign.
So that night he come to Schoepf's farm
and tried to get in at a window.
Fred called aht. The man, half in the window,
kept on crawling through.

145

Fred fired one shot.
The man got back aht the house,
but fell on the lawn." "Well,
Schoepf's free now, it looks."
"He never went to jail.
At the trial he told his story
and was acquitted." A tall man
said from behind a beer:
"Well, he done right so!
I wouldn't let nobody climb in after my sister."
"But you wouldn't kill the man."
"Yes, I would kill him so."

In the weeks after Laura's death
there was a noticeable change in Schoepf.
On his face the beard grew.
His blue eyes weakened and he took to driving
afternoon after afternoon
along the dusty roads of early autumn.
Gehman felt sympathy.
Though they had not particularly been friends,
he would stop by Schoepf's to talk.
Once they stood on the lawn by a tree
where some overripe pears had fallen.
One pear had a crack across it
and at the crack a wasp has fastened,
drinking the fermenting juice.
Schoepf jogged the pear with his foot
so that the wasp fell off.
He started to crush it, but stopped.
"*Ja*, even wasps get drunk.
It is no crime, is it?
Why should I kill it, so?"
The wasp staggered off through the grass.

IN A DISTANT BARN

Benson Dorfman stands in the shadow
under a low beam that drips hay.
His teen-age son runs past with a big withe basket
and dumps mash into the cow troughs.
Benson has come a long distance
and now watches. The farmer, a renter, milks.
"You ain't paid the boy no wages," Benson says.

"You didn't arrange no wages," the renter says;
"you didn't come."

"It was agreed he'd get wages,
ten dollars a month at least."

"You didn't come," the renter says.

"I ain't had time to come.
Still, you owe him the back wages."

"He didn't do the work of a man."

"He earned the wages," Benson says.
"He worked from dawn to dark. I got his letters.
You owe him now for five months."

"I don't owe nothing." Milk hisses into the pail,
and the boy runs,
doing his work quick and silent
as if his father was not there.

LOST

In the six-acre field,
Heimbacher's smallest children
work like men among the grain.
Each has a sharpened sickle
and each swings at the wild mustard
that blazes fitfully from the green.
They are no higher than the paper flame
of the weed they bend to cut.
No, they might not be there at all
but that one sees the flames go out.

THE EARLY LIFE OF RAYM KLINE

Raym Kline has built houses and handled looms
with their shuttling threads. He has raised children,
and now those children are raising children.
He is at the loom yet.

He was born a mile from Saylor's mill,
" 'the first baby in the new house,'
that's what my grandmother used to say."
"The new house" was the frame one
put up after the log house,
so he just missed a log-house birthing.
After "maybe only a year in it,"
his mother went to Royersford with his dad
and there parted from him. "My grandparents
took me in then." From then on:
"We lived in Barto, Long Swamp, Oley,
Mertztown, Breinigsville, Shamrock,
all around here." About Dale:
"I went up the hills from the creek there,
hunting with a dog and cat.
Yes, the cat followed me like the dog.
It would be still, then it would run ahead."

In the house by the big hole near the Krum place,
where Louis Kuhns, the plasterer, lives,
Raym's great-grandfather died:
"He was the first one I saw dead,"
one who had had such a light foot in life,
so agile. "Charlie Keisel, the circus clown.
He was so light he told me he could dance
on a mirror and not break it.
I never see him do that,
but he done so many other tricks
I believed him. He could turn a somersault
out of a barrel. I see that.
He could turn three somersaults in the air
before he come back to the ground. I see that.
He was small like me.
People used to call him *'Shtehkeitzel.'*
That made him mad—a *Shtehkeitzel*
is a little owl that lives around the barn.

"I knew when we had only
molasses and bread and coffee
besides only some potatoes and flitch—
flitch we called 'the Irish bacon.' "
Between terms of schooling, he had jobs.
At ten, living at Farmington,
he worked at the mine "washery" there,
twenty-five cents his pay for eleven hours.
"There was no labor laws then,
and all could work." So he did work,
his hands in the water all day long
in the trough
cold and sore and bleeding
"We separated ore from the stone.
If there was more ore,
we picked out the stone. If there was more stone,
we picked out the ore. I worked
right at the end of the washery
near Uney Eck. I wore an apron,
but that did not keep the cold water out."

The men
made up a poem about the engineer:
"Der Willie Reinert ist der engineer.
Er shpringed do rum wie ein wildes deer,
un wun mer en froagt for was ers tut,
saagt er es kumt seim gelt sock gut."
"Willie Reinert is the engineer.
He runs around like a wild deer,
and when we asked him why he did it,
he said it did his money bag good."

Another memory he has of the mine:
"I used to have home six-cornered stones
like the crystals that hung from the lamps.
These I got from the washery.
Yes, they dug them out of the ground,
and they were nice as if they were cut.
They had just one rough end on them.
I kept many of them. None believed
they come just so from the ground."

So in the washery, working,
in eight days of eleven hours
he earned the sum needed
for a month's rent of the house
he lived in with his grandparents.
"It was not so bad a house.
It had no well, we used cistern water."
The sky provided where the landlord failed.

At fifteen, school days done,
he started to "work steady,"
and so grew from the ore trough to the loom.

150

PATRICK GIAGNOCAVO

The name is too much for the neighbors.
They call him Pat Janocky or Janockeo,
and the years have agreed to it.
Past Indian Rock, his farm on Crow Hill
is German in its care. No "buon giorno"
comes from his mouth—
he has learned to be still in that language,
but over a fence post
he has put a goat's skull, and in his garden
he has managed to grow a fig tree.
He sings to Fox, his red horse, in the morning
and his dog sits on his haunches pointed toward him,
ready to run or stay. His house
is out of sight from the Dale road,
but can be seen from afar in the sun,
like a lighthouse flickering—alien, all think.
What made him, an Italian,
and across the road from him, two Swedes
wander into this German world?
His dog does not care
and what does the sky care, the same blue
over Montefalcone, over Moheda,
or here on a clear day?

His face is
humor and sorrow
in double furrow
at the mouth edge.
The mouth a rock ledge
broken toward the middle.
Cheeks sunk
and up from them, deeply set in,
eyes of journey,
of doubt without
object. Lines
around his eyes smile,
and from the tonsure

over his eyes,
black hair
comes down like cord
to tie his ears.

"The language not always easy.
When young,
I work at the Pottstown furnace.
One day get sick to the stomach, get sick
few minutes, then all right.
Was near the heat at that time.
The foreman say, 'Why you stay near the heat?'
When I explain how I was sick, he say,
'You better git out to the cold air quick.
It's gas. They mix gas with the coal,
and the mine gas you can not smell.'
I get my time card and punch it,
and I begin to fall. Man catch me
and I remember I say, 'Thank you.'
I can not remember
what become the time card.
That night I go back to work,
tell the foreman I can not find the time card,
and tell about what happen in the morning.
'Du warst grank,' the foreman say.
'No, now I was not drunk,'
I say, and want to quit the work.
Man caught me when I fall was there,
and tell me I must not quit—
'grank' mean 'sick,' their way,
and the foreman mean that I was sick.
I say, 'Scuse me. Please,
is not always easy, the language.'"

GIAGNOCAVO AT CHURCH

Giagnocavo, convert to the brotherhood
and faith of Menno Simons,
dressed in his Sunday black—white
tieless collar drawing him

close to the simple elevation
of deacons and minister—
walks down the Bally chapel's men's side
to the front to hear.
The air is still. Old Mennonites
gather: on one side,
the dark suits of men
and on the other, the white
head coverings of women.
As the pews fill, babies
are comforted though a few still cry
in the plain church of plaster walls
and plaster ceiling. Giagnocavo
sits straight and waits

The first hymn, voices
unaccompanied, two banks of sound,
the women's and the men's,
answering as clear as birds.
A pulpit box fronts the pews.
Reverend Elias Kulp sits in the middle
in white shirt and white suspenders,
and on one side, two dark coats,
and two dark coats on the other,
five in all, the leadership
of the church of plain men

"Now, considering whatever
we need,
the needs of others, the communion with God,
we will have a minute of silent prayer."
All kneel,
laying their arms on the church benches.
Giagnocavo bows his head
into his arms and silence.

"Today we have the bishop with us.
This is a rare privilege.
He cannot come often, though he loves
the church. I will not take his time,
but let him talk to you."

153

"Brethren and sistern,
today is baptismal day.
There is only one to be baptized,
a precious sister, yes, only one,
but we are glad for the one.
Baptism is regeneration.
Jesus said, Except ye be born again—
well now, what does that mean?
That was not understood, you know,
no, it was not understood when he said it.
Does it mean be reborn physically?
No, the meaning is spiritual.
I'll tell you what it means.
It means now a new element.
You have gone fishing. I have too.
Yes, I am a fisher of men.
The line pulls the fish out,
throws the fish out on land,
then in a few minutes it dies.
It is in a new element.
If it is to live there, yes,
the gills must become lungs,
the fins must become wings,
the scales must become feathers.
So at the rebirth, yes,
all must change, all become different,
so that the new life begins."
A girl in a short white dress comes up
to be laved by the old man's hand, the water
the symbol of her change. Giagnocavo
remembers, in Montefalcone,
how he fished for little carp.
As the service ends,
in the white-painted vestibule
he clasps German hands
and receives on his cheek the kiss of brotherhood
he has found and wants.

154

THE OLD MENNONITES'
FOOT WASHING
(Lou Kintner speaking)

"Next Sunday they'll wash feet in church.
Not much good in that.
Everybody'll wash first
to home, you know that.
There was once a dinner
people come to tired and dirty.
Christ washed the feet of them
that needed. Once years ago
I was coming home from work,
and I was in an accident.
Attendant at the hospital
said, 'Wash your feet.'
I leaned over and tried,
but I near fainted.
A girl nurse looked at me
and said, 'This man's hurt
and he can't wash his own feet.'
So she washed my dirty feet. I guess
that's what Christ had in mind, *net?*"

THE OLD MENNONITE CHURCH

It is a small church set back from the street
that goes through the center of Bally. In it
are no decorations, no "images," the walls plain,
obeying Him who clothes the lilies
and gives as raiment to men
an equal glory and unconcern.
Such a church is like a house.
The service had once been
in one or another of the members' homes.

THE MENNONITES:
ACCORDING TO HER

Laura Hertz stands by the door
in plain shoes, plain dress,
and the devotional covering
with its whiteness

falling backward on her hair:
•"For this cause," Paul said,
that woman was made "for the man,"
ought she to cover her head,

and yet "have power on her head
because of the angels." Mrs. Hertz
has in her eyes the quietness
of Catharists and Waldenses. She thinks:

Why did the church divide?
The faith of Menno we still share,
but the reformed ones rebelled,
the women rebelled against the wear

that held their level under man's
though God's word spoke
clearly for the covering,
apostle Paul's yoke.

The men rebelled too, won't kiss
one another as ours do, though we both
are still against state and war.
Both care as before.

ACCORDING TO HIM

Elias Kulp sits considering,
communing
in the night,
minister of the Old Flock
with Pentecostal tongues.

Mine the given duty, plain—
chosen by the lot
that leaves room only for God—
to hold the church
strong

in oneness. "Thanks
alway to God for you,
brethren beloved of the Lord."
His raised fingertips
touched with the hue of fire

point his thought.
Father,
the early Christians endured
persecution, martyrdom,
everything rather

than deny Thy truth.
Yet, upheld by Constantine,
the church took power and left,
with its old simple ways,
the divine.

The centuries have come and gone,
but Thy word remains,
which any can study as I do.
My authority is one,
only Thine own.

So it is my privilege to keep
steadfastly true.
My ministry is easy,
for I please not men,
but Thee

as I am given to know.
In the division of the church
and change of doctrine
the new Mennonites draw away
though God beseech

in His own read word to stay.
Why? Ours is the truth,
ours God's whole love,
ours the return to the one
unity.

By that return, did we not
resurrect the first church,
wash feet, kiss in the love
of brother for brother,
sister for sister,

and become as the first Christians?
Some change is good, but not
that which the world makes
so that again
the old truth of Thy word

is dimmed.
Thou art the one God. We stay
confident that in our plain room
Thou and Thy presence remain
the one flame.

THE FAITH AND CONSTANTINE

Until Constantine,
Christianity meant conviction;
the Christian Word
persuaded others to belief. The baptized were believers,
none but believers. They were not
a "sacral society." They were in society
but not of it. *The Epistle to Diognetus* said:
"Christians are not distinct from the rest of men
in country or language or customs.
For neither do they dwell anywhere in special cities
nor do they use a different language. . . .
Every foreign country is to them a fatherland
and every fatherland a foreign country. . . ."
Christians were persecuted, but they offered
faith.
A servant might convert a master
or more likely, a master's wife or child. As Jesus said,
"A man's foes shall be those of his own household."
A society was to be composite,
for not all could or would believe.

Then Constantine
felt the power of the Word,
felt it—who is to say exactly—
as a political force.
The story is:
On October twenty-seventh, three twelve,
at Saxa Rubra, nine miles from Rome,
he saw a flaming cross on the sky
with the Greek words *en toutoi nika,*
"in this sign conquer." He had his soldiers
mark on their shields an X
and through it a vertical line curved at the top,
the Greek "chr" or symbol
for Christ. With this sign,
the letters of the crucified Prince of Peace,
and with the cross itself,
he and his soldiers went into battle

159

and won. The victory
made him sole emperor of the West.
He gave Christians first
toleration, next, preference, and at last,
the status of state church.

Now all changed. Now pagans were the ones persecuted.
True, some were indifferent to the old gods
and went casually and easily
to catechism classes and prepared
for baptism. But others held to the past
one way or another and, discovered,
were killed or severely penalized.
Eventually all, since they had to—
merchants, princes, generals, even the apathetic
and actively unethical—
joined the church.
It was not necessary to believe, only to join.
The Church then arranged for "just wars."
It made statements like:
"As, in a mystery,
the human nature and the divine flow together in Christ
so, likewise in a mystery,
do the rule of the magistrate and that of the priesthood
flow together."
The Church was the state. Down the centuries
the change was so all-inclusive
that even monks and nuns who branched off
into communities of their own
were regarded with suspicion.

Believers now were "Restitutionists,"
heretics who subversively wanted
to go back to the early church.
All over medieval Europe, the official Church
eagerly hunted them down.
In the outcry against them,
one means of identification
was if they lived a "comely life,"
if they emphasized
"fruits worthy of repentance."
Heretics spent time in hiding

and so were "pale." They came out
mostly at night, and in France
and elsewhere were called *"turlupins,"*
wolf-people.
Though they seeded the Reformation,
Luther's followers could say about them,
"Like the Donatists of long ago,
they seek to rend the Church
because we allow evil men in the Church
and wherever that is undertaken
the public order is sure to be overthrown   "
Neither Lutherans nor Catholics
tolerated the Anabaptists
or, later, the Mennonites,
heirs of the Restitutionists,
but despised and martyred them:
Anabaptists wanted not to war, not to kill.
They wanted to live by what the Gospels said.
They wanted to do what Christ commanded.
No state church could countenance that.

Elias Kulp
is one of those people
who to this day continue
to disconcert the world with their acceptance
of Jesus's instruction, to love.

LOCAL ECUMENISM

In the early seventeen hundreds,
Jesuits and Mennonites
appeared together in the heavy woods.
The Mennonites liked the first Father,
Theodore Schneider, and volunteered their labor
to help him build his church. Father Schneider
then gave them an acre of the Jesuit tract
as the site for their own first chapel.
True, the Father watched his own
with a coercion that, benevolent or not,

Mennonites and Schwenkfelders would have nothing of,
but when Catholics sing for their dead
the *Dies Irae*—the Mass that throbs from the throats
of a line of hidden choirboys,
iterant, on and on,
throb that almost justifies death—
Mennonites may be in the church
listening and grieving too
and be consoled, and Catholics in turn
go to be with their friends
at Mennonite funerals. Catholic
Raym Kline invites Fred Braun,
a Reformed Mennonite,
to visit Raym's family graves
in the Catholic graveyard.
The Reverend Johnson has as his good friend
Father Sherf, the present Father
of the Bally Catholic church.
The likeness goes beyond the differences,
but of course privately each one
thinks his own is the true church.

THE MAYOR

Ralph Berky, that airy radical,
tells a Bally newcomer (the truth)
that Bally once elected
an atheist as its mayor.
This atheist
was of course neither Mennonite nor Catholic
and could receive the votes of both.

ORDERING LIME

"The farm program? Yes,
I want lime,
but don't tell my farmer now
it comes from the government.
He's a Mennonite, an old one,
and don't bend none.
You have others like that?
All fields God's fields?
When you bring the lime,
unload and say nothing.
That way I'll keep my farmer."

THE REVEREND JOHNSON IN GERMANY

"Some wonder that here in Bally
I have as a friend the local priest
and that I have the privilege
of going anywhere in the Catholic church,
that shrine of Pennsylvania Catholics

"When I first went to Germany
to do research on Caspar Schwenckfeld
and to help get Schwenckfeld's writings published
in a complete edition—
all is published now, in fifteen volumes
I was most afraid of the Catholic hierarchy.
I feared they would block my labors
by closing to me the doors to documents,
preventing me from finding needed facts.

"It was with this fear I went to Breslau,
to Cardinal Bertram, then archbishop, young,
two years younger than I,
a most learned Catholic scholar.
I said, 'I'm a Schwenkfelder, from Pennsylvania,

residing in Wolfenbüttel,'
and so I gave him my credentials.
Immediately he opened to me
the Episcopal Archives with its documents,
letting all know I was to use them.
The Privy Councilor, Canon Jungnitz,
said, 'Thrice welcome, thrice welcome,'
and there was assigned, to help me,
a priest named Griepenkerl,
a man of a beautiful character
who devoted himself to me.
So I remained three weeks
and it gave me insights unknown before.
The priest Griepenkerl is dead,
the Privy Councilor is dead,
and Cardinal Bertram is dead,
but the memory is not dead.
In the years following, while Cardinal Bertram
still lived, a bond sprang up
between me and that Catholic,
a fellowship in bond so thick
that it lasts yet.
He wrote once a line in a book for me:
'Der Zweck all unsers Forschen
muss die Wahrheit sein.'
'The purpose of all our research
must be to find the truth.'

"Then I went to Bavaria,
so full of Catholics, the place
of Schwenckfeld's exile for thirty-nine years.
From Ulm, one day, I was to go to a certain village.
Soon after dawn, I took a train to Erbach,
then walked six hours westward
on the north bank of the Danube, close to the river,
and came to the little village of Oepfingen.
When I reached it,
it was empty, chickens and pigeons the only life,
not a soul to be seen.
I went toward the church, which stood
high above the Danube's sweep—
I can hear its rustling yet—

164

and a woman and a boy appeared
obviously on the way to the church
to receive the priest's closing blessing.
The woman said, *'Gesegnet sei Jesus Christus.'*
Soon after, the whole village
dropped out of the church and I stepped aside,
not to disturb them, then went to the parish house.
A sister fetched the 'Father.'
He stood in his cloak with folded arms.
'What can I do for you?' he said.
I said I was a Schwenkfelder from Pennsylvania
and he said, ' Then I know what you want,'
and took me to the church altar
and said, 'Behind that altar—'
I interrupted him: 'You would say,
"Behind that altar stands Schwenckfeld,"
I said, 'but it is not so.'
I drew out then a pen sketch I had
of a handsome black marble statue
of Schwenckfeld's most eminent patron,
Lutz von Freyberg. It was the statue.
The priest admitted the error,
and so we began to talk.
He invited me to dinner,
but I said my time was limited
and I must continue on my way.
He then refused to leave me.
He walked two hours in his gown.
When I said his soup was getting cold,
he said, 'My soup I can eat tomorrow.
You I can have only now.'
When at last we parted, he stood watching me
with his hand raised in farewell,
and as long as I was in sight,
his hand was raised.

"Another priest, from the village of Justingen,
took me to see the ruins
of von Freyberg's castle, which Wallenstein
destroyed in sixteen twenty-six,
at the same time, it may be,
destroying Schwenckfeld's library.

The ruins were on a rocky cliff
in an immense park now a cow pasture.
We could see fragments of wall,
trees that were once ornamental trees,
traces of roads and paths.
We sat on the ruins, among walls and arches,
and watched the sun go down.
Below in the tops of trees
we could see the outline of the railroad
on which I must return. Night came.
We talked together till midnight
of religion, church history, such things
as would come to us on such a night,
then the priest took my hand
and led me by the light only of stars
down the precipice to the meadow below,
taking care that I should be safe. Then:
'Here our ways part. Mine goes back up the mountain
to my village and my people—
yours goes toward the light and the railroad station
and at last home to your Schwenkfelder people.
It may be our ways will never again
cross, but I am convinced
we will meet in the life hereafter.'

"The Catholics sometimes said to me,
about Schwenckfeld,
'We can never make up for what we did to him.
He condemned our errors, not our church.'

"In all religions is a common something—
what it is exactly I do not know—
but it is greater than the differences.
Unless I believed that, I would believe nothing.
Although for years I have held in Bally
the pastorate of the Reformed Mennonite Church,
I never united with that church,
but stayed, as before, a Schwenkfelder,
believing it to be the right thing.
What my mother and my people taught
was in my heart, so I kept to it.
Others keep to their own."

JIM FROMM TELLS OF
THE SIX SCENES OF THE PUTZ

"Yes, the six scenes of the Christmas *putz*,
now that was a great thing once,
and a good thing. In my day, in my childhood,
older people had a way
to show the children the Christmas story
The grandfather went out and got a tree stump
and hollowed the side into a cave
for the scene of the nativity.
The figures were carved of wood;
the shepherds, the camels, the star,
the heavenly host—four or five,
maybe half a dozen little angels
hanging from a blue night sky
by blue threads. Then was the stable,
the city of Bethlehem, and last,
the flight into Egypt—six scenes in all.
That was something now to make wonder
the eyes of the littlest children.
On Christmas Eve, a basket of moss
was brought in and spread on the floor
around the sheep and shepherds. Yes, the smell
when the moss was sprinkled was sweet.
Then in the morning the little ones,
before dawn, came carrying beeswax candles
so the light fell on that stump
with the Holy Child and on all
that had been made, but more
it lighted up the children's eyes.

"*Putz*, yes, that had a special meaning. The word
comes from 'putzen,' 'to polish.'
All year it meant that,
but at the Christmas season the meaning changed,
then it meant to decorate,
to make such scenes for the children.
It was surely a great thing then,
a special happiness."

THE CATHOLIC CHURCH

The church stands, a shaft of white
like a finger with the nail of steeple
holding the center of heaven pinned.
Sheds, parochial school, cemetery
bow away, subdued.
The ring of hills even
seems low against that central shaft.

FATHER SHERF SHOWS
THE CHURCH IN BALLY

Father Aloysius Sherf
comes to the rectory door
in his black garments, moist
from a hot day
that should have kept visitors away.

"You want to see the old church. All right,
I'll get me slippers. Just wait a minute here.
I was reading in the Psalms, yes—
we must read
so much each day, but me eyes are getting poor,

and the hour and twenty minutes required is hard.
Just wait for me, yes. Take a chair.
The dog won't trouble you—he's getting old.
He's bad.
First he wants to come in, then wants to go out,

like anybody who's old and restless.
A warm day like this the best place for him
is on the cool linoleum. Just wait."
He goes
to an inside room and removes his shoes

168

and comes back in his large slippers.
His face, silver with autumn sweat,
glistens all over. His body, tall,
fills out his wide black pants
and the shirt that under the pectoral

wrinkles with wear.
Eyes of the guarded faith
and security of an aged power
moving
easily, knowing the understood

understand, and that the Church can change
its seemingly fixed canon law
and still remain.
"This way.
This is a good time of day

to come. The light now, this time of afternoon,
shows up the old glass well.
Yes, a few steps down
and to the right—"
He brings the visitor sight

of the windows, and of two centuries of heavy robes,
gold thread, damask, pearl,
sewn for the sacraments—
so they enter a room
in the likeness of a tomb,

something of a saturated glaze
in its walls: walls
bent on two sides to altar wings,
panels hung
with rich paintings, each as if on a rung.

"That's an old painting, the one up there
by the image. The candlesticks—old too.
And that other painting,
of Saint Francis Xavier
who christianized the Japanese, was given early.

"The Cardinal has asked us for it.
He hints at the danger of fire,
but we don't want to lose these things,
and they're insured.
Yes, all belong here."

The visitor looks down.
"The tombstones you see embedded in the floor
are three priests of the church, two buried here
and one
I found outside and had brought in.

"I take an interest in the old things,
records, such—but much of value
the Jesuits packed when they left
and took away.
I want to go to their college some day, yes—

it would be worth the trip to see.
They have writings preserved there,
and especially they have an old missal. Well,
that's a dream. That's for me prayers.
Now follow me upstairs

and you'll see a bell
fifty years older than the Liberty Bell.
Watch your step—the stairs are steep.
There,
now you can look up from here, through the beams,

and see it. It was made in France
in seventeen four and has French writing on it.
Pull the rope." The clapper hits once
and one note
rolls from the throat

dully. "It isn't used now, no—
we have three new bells now.
This is just for visitors to play with:
now we'll go down."
The bell note ends

170

and there is only
the sound of their steps climbing down.
"I haven't felt so well the past year.
Some complaint . . .
Dr. Hottenstein

takes care of me and says more exercise
is what I need—yes, no medicine
for me, he says,
but exercise.
There's a weakness now in me eyes.

"This way. You'd like to see the outside.
The church
was built on low ground,
I don't know why.
The higher ground, there above the cemetery,

would have been a good place for the church,
I often think, not this low ground.
But I notice it shows well from the hills."
His slippers
cross the ground like calipers

as he walks
easily along the buttresses
outside the building, along the half-drooped wings of stone.
"Here,
behind the old church where

the original wall is, is a grotto
of our Lady of Lourdes
Notice the wire-enclosed space there.
Buried there
are two soldiers of the Revolutionary War,

and those are two flags I put there for them.
One, Isaac Jones, was a Negro.
There are few Negroes through here—
the Germans
had few slaves, or none.

"Now down here is a housekeeper's grave
all alone under a tree,
and she deserves the large stone, yes,
she
served three incumbents gratuitously."

The grave stands like a mortar box
holding a bucket of flowers.
The stone says, "Pray for her soul."
He paces
back into the church where a window raises

over his heated, dewy head
the Lord of the parable of lilies
shining in glass that, as he said, the afternoon light
shows well.
He lifts his hand, and the glass distils

the Master for him,
a stillness and a coolness,
and in that steady light he has a thought
or afterthought:
"The Church is greater than its servants, *net?*"

A PARTICULAR MEMORY
OF HENRY URFFER

"I remember my grandfather," Marian Bechtel says.
"He encouraged me with my music.
You know, he and Edwin Kraus
were organ builders: Part of the organ
in the Bally Catholic Church
was built by them. But about the music—
he used to come often to the house.
There was a chair there near the piano
and whenever I would practice,
at the first note he heard me play,
he would seat himself in that chair.

He wouldn't criticize,
but just sit there quietly
till I finished, then he would say,
'Fergessen net deine musik, Maudlie.'
'Don't forget your music, Maudlie.'
That was what he always said,
'Fergessen net deine musik, Maudlie.' "

THE LUTE

Before he went to Germany,
the Reverend Johnson read "all the lyrics"
of Goethe—the walk to Tiefurt,
the façade of the Opera House—
love, splendor, dream.
Who knows if, in a lyric pause,
the young Johnson thought of Menno Simons
who wrote about such as himself:
"Called hedge preachers and heretics,
our recompense is fire, the sword, and death.
When others are entertained with the lute,
we fear that the catchpolls are at hand,
hearing the dogs bark." The reproach stays,
but the pear-shaped box whose bent handle
drapes over the player's shoulder
is strong in its thin strings.
The singer to it has the world in him.
Goethe's Faust says,
"Do I not still feel her anguish? Am I not
the fugitive? The unhoused?" The dogs' barking,
the moan from the ditches,
the smoke of hell seeps back
to that music.

THE OLD SPRUCE

Seen from a distance, it draws a wrapper
of blue-green light around itself. But, close,
it winds a staircase of black steps
up a tower where at the top,
breaking through the ruined roof,
it continues in the sky.

THE LIFE OF SALLY URFFER
(Marian Bechtel's mother)

Born Sally Kriebel. Born in Hereford,
April seventeenth,
eighteen seventy-five,
daughter of Elizabeth and Henry Kriebel,
her mother a Griesemer. "We farmed
and my dad had a mill by a dam
in the Perkiomen, had a grist and oil mill.
Made linseed oil.
We went over to the Delaware
with a four-horse covered wagon
to get seed." The farm big,
over a hundred acres, and cows:
"Often people would come to see the cows,
full-bred Holsteins. They came from everywhere
to see them, and the trout."
The trout were a hobby. "Father had a trough
maybe as long as from here to there,
and sand in it. He caught the trout
and stripped the eggs out, the eggs
as big as those berries there,
and bred them in the sand, water
all the time running through,
so they hatched out like little minnows.
Once he lost a five-dollar gold piece
in the spring and could never find it."

174

The glitter gone into the sand's glitter.
"Mostly, with a big farm, it was work.
Good they made us work.
If you don't, you get sick and unconcerned.
I'm eighty-two and I work yet.
Some days it's hard, but I get over it."
There was her father's and mother's strictness—
then once:
"You know we kids used to follow the corn planting
and see that the seed wasn't exposed.
So I was going behind Father
when he fell. It was a sunstroke.
I was alone there with him
and took his head in my legs and screamed.
The farmer next to us heard me
and came running and carried him to the house.
But it wasn't as bad as I thought."

Her father was a Schwenkfelder.
"Mother belonged to the Reformed Church,
and when I was fifteen,
it was agreed that I should go to the Reformed"—
smiling—"not that I know if I'm reformed,
but I belong to that church."

She went to school at Hereford.
"I studied physiology,
I hated grammar! We did recitations
and dialogs. That one-room schoolhouse
called the Hereford Academy—
many that were distinguished later
came from that little school
An older cousin of mine, Oscar Kriebel,
went from there to Oberlin.
He was the one who made
the Perkiomen Seminary go,
giving the best years of his life to it."
At fourteen she was through school
and worked now like a full-grown woman.
"At sixteen,
Mother made me start singing school
and there I met Adam Urffer.

Those Urffers were musical,
and Pop"—so she calls her husband, looking back—
"took singing lessons too."
Indignantly she says,
"You know, I wasn't supposed to see him
but every two weeks, and now
you can see a boy every night."
For three years, so, she saw him,
then her father died. To settle the estate:
"Everything was sold.
Father had given me and my sister
a little calf. It was sold." Auctioned,
everything cleared off.
In the shock and grief
of the family breaking up,
Adam was her salvation.
Yes, it seemed less dreadful
because of him,
and out of it came their marriage.
"We wanted it to happen sometime,
so we said
we might as well do it now,"
so they did. That started
that sense of steadfastness beside her,
Pop. She remembers: "The old farm
my brother Calvin bought and kept it Kriebel,
and Al Albitz worked for him there,
who was later the miner." Her mind returns
to those times. Yes, at night:
"The other night I thought of something.
I didn't dream, you lie and think and think.
I thought of my cousin, the Reverend Kriebel,
the time when he was preaching
and brought in about this man:
If you have a coat and another doesn't,
give him the coat. I thought of that
because the other day my daughter and I gave
two blankets to a man up the hill.
It's so cold
and he didn't have any blankets.
Pop was much better even
than I to remember such things."

176

VIRTUE

Heimbacher's horse breaks loose
and starts down the hill, neighing and tossing,
knowing Heimbacher must follow.
"Horse gets smart when he don't work.
Two days' hard work is what he needs.
Yeah, after two days' work
you can handle any horse."

MOMMY STAUFFER

Andros Stauffer's wife, Mommy Stauffer,
was one reputed hard to figure out, one that kept a straight
        face
and said things that could be taken two ways, often.
Along her garden edge
she planted some sour cherry trees and some sweet.
One summer they bore, the cherries ripened,
        and then one morning the ripe fruit disappeared.
Billy Dietz
who lived on the other side of the hill from Mommy
came by and said,
"I understand somebody stole your cherries."
"Yes, well," she said, "they just went up over the hill"—
this was a local expression for something mysteriously
        disappearing, and of course
        Billy couldn't take offense.

THE DESCENT

Ralph Berky says,
"Hans Ulrich Bergi was the first
emigrant to America, the one
the Berkys are all descended from.
Bergi meant 'little hill'—I'm proud of that.
The first one in Berks County
to spell it Berky was a blacksmith, and since him
six generations have spelled it that way.
Figure thirty years to a generation,
that makes a hundred eighty years."

FATHER AND MOTHER

Andrew Stauffer Berky was born
April fourteenth, eighteen fifty-five.
His sons later thought
something in him "started away
from the conventions of the community."
Hard to call it nonconformity,
but he had a talent
for finding things out for himself.
Prevented from getting advanced schooling
except a Chautauqua correspondence course,
he still determined to teach.
Hired at seventeen,
he taught at first "at so much a head,"
and one of his first schools
was the one in Clayton, behind the tollhouse.
During the long summer school-closings
he did house painting,
was an expert wood grainer
and furniture finisher
(an "interior decorator"
of the plain rooms of those days),
and during the haymaking and harvest

178

he helped Josephus Gerhard
to whom, in the scales of his soul,
he felt a lifelong debt. The debt, Amanda.
When he was about twenty,
at the farm across from the Gerhards',
at Abe Clemmer's, a girl came to work—
Amanda Weller. Small, slender, fine-boned,
"the nimble type," quick in spirit.
Blue eyes. Fair brown hair parted
in a silver ray at the middle.
A face appealing and thin too, lips
"always ready with a verbal dart."
An early picture shows that face
smiling beside Andrew's big black beard.
Her eyes would lift to him
with possession.
She came from the hills, born
in a weatherboarded log cabin.
On her mother's side a Houck. The girls—
Amanda and her many sisters—
used to shake the snow
off the featherbeds in the attic
when they got up of a winter morning.
She came down deliberately to the valley, and there
she and Andrew, working near each other,
fell in love. Ralph says,
"The easier, irresistible part
of that falling in love
must have been my father's part,
for Mother was beautiful." Soon
they were married
in the low-roofed and low-doored Hill Church,
Josephus Gerhard then
lived in an ell-shaped stone house
and had another house called a "tenant's house—
so close you could almost go through."
This house
he rented to the new couple.
There, as they started housekeeping,
it must have been comforting for Amanda to have
Elizabeth Gerhard
just across the windowsill.

In that tenant house
Oswin, Alice, and Darius were born.
In the eighteen eighties, needing more room,
they moved to a tall, square house
built by Manasses Ziegler, the cobbler,
further down the road toward Bally.
In this house,
Clara, Frederick,
Herbert, and Ralph were born.
Ralph was born September twenty-first,
eighteen ninety. Oddly,
three of the Berky boys had birthdays
on successive days in September,
Ralph on the twenty-first,
Oswin, the twenty-second,
and Herbert, the twenty-third.
Ralph was the last child. When he was three,
a family picture was taken.
He was still "the baby"
and wore a skirt as boys did then
and "he didn't get off Mother's lap, wouldn't,"
Herbert says. In the photo
she looks over Ralph's head
straight at the camera. Andrew
is serious, already known
as one of the most enterprising men
in the community, the "inspiring" founder
of the Hereford Literary Society
that still ran Homeric debates
in the Clayton schoolhouse. His exuberance,
his wit, brought to the Society
much of its stir. In public school
he introduced subjects unheard-of then:
Latin and algebra. His sons,
who took after him, were called
"dinde Schlecker," "ink dudes,"
and they were. Three went to college.
Oswin became a doctor.
Herbert became a professor and helped found
Bluffton Mennonite College, in Ohio,
where he taught and guided
many future scientists. Darius

180

finished Franklin and Marshall College
as salutatorian and became
one of the world's great geophysicists, reorienting
the maps of the continents.

When, in nineteen fourteen, Andrew
died of a cerebral hemorrhage, Amanda
did not adjust to the loss.
She who had prayed to God
during her children's illnesses
that He would spare her "stems" (three died)
was unable now to pray.
All felt she should not be alone.
Ralph, the only one remaining home
unmarried, said
that he would stay as long as he was needed.
It proved to be as long as "Mother" lived.
Keeping the home going, he worked
just enough to get by.
He called it "getting contentment."
Otherwise he took to the roads, the woods.
Walked long distances.
Stood still, listened.
Found an intimacy
in the *"Mach faat"* of the bobolink,
in the gun song of the lark,
in rain.
He began to write poems
on odd pieces of paper
and would drop them here and there.
He wrote lines called "In Passing"
in his letters, or scribbled rhymes
in daybooks after notations
on the day's weather. He wrote several hymns,
tinkling out the tunes on a piano, hymns
still sung in local churches.
He stayed faithful,
studying the naturalists and the trees, the unfolding
of fern, safeguard
against the wilderness within.

BERKIANA

Mary Gehman says:
"Ralph Berky's mother—her name was Amanda.
As a little girl
I used to go to see her
in the house there on Route One Hundred
across from the Shuhlers.
She and Ralph lived simply
and once had only
lettuce and potatoes to eat.
She said, 'For variety
one day I have lettuce and potatoes
and the next day I have potatoes and lettuce.'
In the rush season
Ralph used to work for my father,
husking corn, digging potatoes. Once
we were bringing corn from the field,
and Ralph was singing
'Carry Me Back to Old Virginny.'
He had his mouth shaped
as if he was whistling,
as if he had a trumpet or a flute
and was playing. It was so beautiful—"

LARKLAND

Ralph says,
"Mother one day was combing out her hair
under the grape arbor. She noticed
a Baltimore oriole snatch up several strands
from her combings. From then on
she hung her combings for it on a grape twig,
and as she liked to tend her fine long hair,
the orioles built themselves a nest from it

on the end of an apple bough.
That fall, when they had raised their babies,
I climbed a stepladder
and cut the nest down. I still have it."

Eventually, after Amanda's death,
he created a place called "Larkland," a tract
overlooking the Huff Church road,
a thick hover of boughs of trees:
oak, hemlock, beech, arms of spruce
with bluish branch tips like fingers,
tulip trees, sassafras, cedars.
He made almost invisible paths
that would come out from behind a hemlock
into a growth of myrtle, birds
flying through the understory.
He called it all his "arboretum."
In an oak's shade
he would plant arbutus, solitary that
keeps its white note to itself,
and in a nearby hollow he would transplant
different kinds of fern,
identifying them with small signs.
Rock specimens, marked,
glinted like sulfur or blood
in the damp of moss. He would set
an inverted turtle shell in moss
as a drinking fountain for birds.
Summer and winter
he fed the birds. He made feeding stations
of cracks in the bark of trees and stumps, wedging them
with peanuts and pieces of suet. In summer
he laid small trails of birdseed
out from the corners of the wood
into the fields. Back in the wood
as in an unobtrusive gallery,
he watched the feeders come. A flick of wings
and a cardinal was on the ground
or the lark itself was there,
dragging its long spurs, down
from its sky gallop.

Larkland is now part of the community.
Once a year in the twilight and dark
of a late summer day, all Bally
comes to Larkland for a cookout,
gathering at a central campfire
where trees make a larger circle
around a circle of stone.
The Reverend Johnson asks the blessing.
Russell Bechtel's voice joins Ralph's
and perhaps John Simmons's and Ed Kulp's
in rites of fire, singing.
Children in firelight masks
point their marshmallow sticks down
into the flames as their parents talk. The trees
are heavy with light.
All at the fireside feel the ease,
the sumptuousness of the summer night.

SWINGING OFF SWAMP CREEK

First, Joe-Pye weed with its crazy, orderly face shining up
   over the meadow, a chorus all alone.
It leans on some poke, its face under a froth of lavender
   a "Kilroy was here." It manages memories of Indians, it
   blows some runs of Indian healing through the backyards
   of the hills.
Under the pale willow light, how powerful it is on its long
   stalk! How it sucks up the rain in this wet summer, how
   it shampoos its hair in dark drizzles!
How the notes of the tufted titmice, *peter peter peter,*
   circle the Larkland oak. Ralph left his wool hat covered
   with birdseed, and those white breasts floated down to
   it, they got used to going to it.
Now they eat from the hat on his head, they eat from his lips,
   they give him kisses of white rapture with rose suffusions
   down their flanks. They are in love with him. They say,
   Terpee, terpee, terpee.
The quarry's cave calls and dry footprints follow the trees

184

in bracken gone sallow from the heat, in a fern of
loneliness writhing in the afterglow.
The hickory turns yellow where the understory dies. Two-lobed
leaves cover the tulip tree. In Larkland
at the foot of night, a special stone choruses. Al Gemmel
put it there and labeled it. It is Franklinite drenched
with blood, breathing quartz and iron in the kneeholes
of the roots. Al fell dead afterward.
Small stone, arrange some crimson cracks in a lettering of mist.
Morning goes wild again with roads that cut the first-growth
woods up toward Hugo Zintner's. Raccoons with ringed
tails and living masks lurk in the unhunted ditches.
Clara arms herself against them. She had two pullets and lost
one. To the other one: "They got your sister. You be
careful." Eight seraphs with cross-back wings marked with
stubs of feathers, peeps she hatched in the electric frying
pan after the broody mother died—now she is the mother.
They run to her, automatons of love, and she tends their two-
inch cries, their helplessness stepping all over her heart
in the bypasses of the lilacs.
Some screams of alfalfa lift life like a rocket. Crickets hurry
toward the evening's sill as twilight taps a deathly ruffle.
The creek is washing heavily down, ready for the last chord
distorted with fatigue. Herons have had their solo turn
in the shiver that descends across the pool.
Queen of blue hair, meadow spy,
acknowledge them, please,
before you go.

THE FARM ORCHESTRA
(Ralph Berky speaking at the old house)

"Father directed it and played the first fiddle.
Lillian was organist, and Herbert
was assistant organist and pianist.
When he wasn't called upon to do that,
he played the second fiddle. I played the mandolin.
Down on that farm was Alfred Stauffer.

He played the first fiddle too.
Elias Stauffer played flute.
On that hill beyond Clayton
was another Stauffer family
and the two boys played the violoncello,
the small big fiddle about this high,
and at another farm
about a mile to the east, toward Bally,
the Pennypacker farm, was Ulysses Moyer—
he played the cornet. My older brother,
Oswin the doctor, played the cornet
if he wasn't too busy at the office.
Well, we practiced at different houses
on Wednesday nights, sometimes it was here,
sometimes down there or up on the hill—
boy, it's a wonder this house
is still standing, the noise we made."

EXAMINATION OF APPLICANTS
FOR TEACHING

Concerning the time
when Andrew Berky, Aaron Rohrbach, and others
were entering the teaching profession
in the last century,
the Honorable D. B. Brunner
has this recollection: "In those days
there were no county superintendents,
and the directors themselves
used to examine the applicants.
Three questions were usually put to each candidate:
'Kannscht du lesa? schreiwa? rechla?'
('Can you read? write? figure?')
The answer would naturally be Yes,
and that closed the examination.
Later a fourth question was added
that a certain director put this way:
'Verstehscht du jogger?' meaning geography—"

Again, of course, the answer was Yes, and again
the applicant was accepted.
This examination, it seems,
worked well for those days. All were honest
and some of the best of their generation
in those days became teachers.

THE HEREFORD LITERARY SOCIETY

It had its beginnings in a nameless
Sprechschul (speaking school) that met
in the eighteen fifties
in the old Treichlersville schoolhouse
(Treichlersville, now Hereford).
Then came the Hereford Debating Club
that met first in a barroom
and then on the second floor of a shed
that had an outside stairs to the upper door.
Henry A. Schuler says,
". . . debate was excellently conducted.
There was no digression worth notice,
not one unbecoming or bitter remark."
After two years this club dissolved *(sine die)*
and when revived,
largely "inspired" by Andrew Berky,
it took the name
of the Hereford Literary Society,
though it was still a group for debating.
Among the founders, besides Andrew,
were Henry Schuler, teacher and reporter
on the *Allentown Morning Call,*
H. W. Kriebel, Oscar Kriebel,
Benneville Schultz, and Josephus Gerhard.
The necessary season for debates—
which required "close reasoning,
the clear and impressive setting forth"
of the "arguments and illustrations,"
and a trigger-quick adjustment of eloquence
to intellect—was winter,

winter when the long hours of the fields
let up and the mind was fresh.
The initial question debated was always:
"Which deserves the greater honor,
Washington for liberating this country,
or Columbus for discovering it?"
Then might come:
"With which foot did Julius Caesar enter Gaul?"
"Before the Civil War,
who had the greater cause for complaint,
the Indian or the Negro?"
"Which is more useful to society,
the farmer or the mechanic?" It was even
"Resolved, that the school term of Hereford
be lengthened." This threatened to take
children from the farm.
Decision on this one: No.
Debate was usually orderly, but sometimes
in later days
informality went far. Jack Gery
became so hot one evening
he said, *'Ich hab schon g'herdt*
fon leit des so dief in die bottle
g'schnauft hen des sie nimmy gewisst
hen was sie sawge." ("I've heard
of people who breathed so deeply into a bottle
they did not know what they were saying.")
This was aimed at his opponent,
James W. Sallade, but unfortunately
Gery himself was vulnerable.
He had bought a hat in Macungie, so the story went,
and to avoid paying for it,
had changed his name in charging it.
Sallade had only to say,
"I don't breathe so deeply into a bottle
I can't remember my own name,"
to win the round. After all the heat
and the arguing,
the audience had the last say.
Debate was thrown open to the floor,
and the popular vote then
might reverse the judges' decision.

Early in the society's existence,
a young girl, Ida E. Sallade,
sister of James, became a member
and debated along with the men.
She walked "all alone at night" several miles
to attend the meetings, and in time became
the recording secretary. Later
Mary A. Bechtel was secretary.
For all the debaters
their first participation was hard.
Jacob M. Gery said
when he first spoke, he felt
"as though I had a veil on my face;
another member told me
that he too saw no man,
when he spoke for the first time."
But speak they did
and the society grew.
It had, over its whole history,
two hundred fifty-five members.
The Reverend Kriebel was to say,
at the first reunion of the society
in nineteen three, that "he had heard
debates by college men, but these were not
in his opinion the equals
of the old-time debaters
of the Hereford Literary Society."
At the reunion
Andrew Berky also was called on
to say a few words.
His recollections, he said, went back
to the winter of seventy-five to seventy-six,
and in that first term, he admitted,
he had been as nervous as any.
One of the speakers today
had "mentioned the disappearance
of the old schoolhouse at Clayton
in which the society used to meet.
I myself regret much more
the destruction of a fine ash tree
that stood for decades in the schoolhouse yard."
Now, another speaker said,

189

many of the great debaters were gone. Many
who had grown in "intellectual struggle"
had crossed the dark river. Times had changed.
There were now many advantages—
colleges, libraries,
"the telephone and trolley car"—so
the old society meetings were being
undervalued, meetings
that had lit up lonely winters,
that had been looked forward to
for their "contact with congenial minds."
How much the debating clubs
were a sign of freedom!
The statement was made
that "state legislatures and Congress itself
were but debating schools on a larger scale."
The society had done enough to be part
of the history of its time.

THE RAINBOW

Herbert Berky tells this story:
When he was a boy, he used to work
in two hill fields Josephus Gerhard
had given his father.
"You went up a lane that started
between the Borneman place and Uncle John's,
and made a left turn past a tenant house,
and then up past Mommy Stauffer's."
She was married
to his great-uncle Andros
and "there were some special springs there
and we always stopped to have a drink."
Beyond Mommy's were the two fields.
One day he was working "in the onion patch,"
when in a nearby field
down the hill slope at an angle
a neighbor named Stengel
came plowing with a two-horse plow.

190

Just then a shower
traveled lightly over the valley
and there was "a most beautiful bow.
I had always thought bows were far away,
but when Stengel that day came
to where the end of the bow was,
he and the horses went right through it.
The colors washed right over team and man."

HIDING

"Yes," Ralph says,
"my brother Herbert when he was a boy
had rich red hair, dark red. Well, one day
when he was four,
he stole away from Mother when she was visiting
Uncle John, and in Uncle John's truck patch
he tried to hide behind a cabbage head.
It was no use, with that hair."

TINA

Single-handed, while teaching college,
Herbert Berky built a stone house
in Bluffton, Ohio, cutting
practically a quarry of limestone,
scattering stone all over. For months
the planned house hovered over rubble.
He described it later to Tina,
his granddaughter, who said,
"Did you have a nervous wreckdown, Grampa?"
He said that he nearly did. Now
she goes to Bluffton High School.
At seventeen
she is slim and tall and has
hair as red as Herbert's once was.

She writes poetry:
"If I fly now
before spring comes
before you laugh again
remember
the dowdy sparrows
who used to steal corn
from Uncle Ralph's hand."
She is sitting in her grandfather's living room,
that long room overlooking a garden
down in a hollow: "You want to know
about the volunteer work?
That I did last summer? I liked it.
I volunteered with some other high school kids
to work in the state hospitals."
First they studied to get "concepts for teaching,"
working with lab rats, "getting them to depress levers—
after that the good stuff started.
We went to the Fort Custer State Home
for retarded children.
They had IQs below thirty.
That's pretty retarded, you know.
I worked in a language-acquisition program.
We were supposed to use
the Skinner psychology of rewards.
Like take this kid, sit him down,
and say that I was going to teach him
how to give me two things: toy, hat, ball, card, two of them.
'Give me the hat and the ball.'
If he does, I get all excited and say"—
and her voice gets high and excited—
" 'Oh, you did it, you did it!'
I give him a checker and if he gets four,
I give him what he wants. This kid
loved ice cream, so we gave him that.
Another turned in his tokens
(he had to have a lot)
to go outside and swing, and another
got to do coloring.
One kid we taught to make vowel sounds,
a kid who couldn't talk at all, David.
David was eleven and looked like seven.

192

Wasn't toilet-trained.
He just sat around and smiled,
didn't respond emotionally to anything.
Didn't make any sound.
We played with him to see if he liked anything
and found if we tickled him, he made a sound.
We put his hand on our throat—he liked that.
We tickled him and he made the sound. Then
about seventy percent of the time
he made the sound without touching.
Getting him to do that was so great,
I almost cried.
Getting him to where he could laugh,
that's communication.
And ecolalia, repeating mechanically
what you say—getting a kid to stop that.
Like one kid, I said, 'You can't go out, it's raining—'
and I let him get some rain on his arm
and he said, 'Rain?' and then later
he said, 'It's raining outside.'
Getting a kid to say that
is almost more than you can stand.
Just putting people away
like they just exist and that's enough—
it isn't enough. You have to do something.
Don't you?"
Her poem says:
"I would walk
to the place
where last
we understood each other
and build an altar there
of flowers in rain."

THE LIE

Ralph Berky, his summer cap in hand,
knocks on the front screen door
of Lillian Schwenk in Souderton.
She comes to the door,
a woman about his own age
wearing a plain dress and long skirt.
"Come in." "It won't be any trouble?"
She smiles. "What brings you to Souderton?
It's so long that we haven't seen you."
He says he had a ride over
and took the chance to see her and Elsie.
"Of course—she will want to see you."
They go into a cool downstairs room
that was once the dining room.
Now it is a bedroom.
The bed is wide and flat,
holding up almost no weight.
The apparition on it
is hard to find in the flat covers
until one sees the head
so much the color of the sheet
it seems transparent. It is Elsie
who has multiple sclerosis.
She moves her head back and forth
as if in a little track.
She has difficulty talking.
When Ralph says hello,
she answers with a faint bubble of voice.
She tries again to speak, her voice
an almost indecipherable whisper,
but Lillian understands it and translates:
"What became of your brother?" Elsie
once had had a dressmaking shop
over Mary Bechtel's store in Bally,
and Dr. Berky's office was next door.
What should Ralph say? All know
Oswin is dead. He says, "My brother's dead."
Another question now,

194

asked with an intentness Ralph catches,
a signal to him
that this is a more important question:
"How are the two cherry trees in the meadow?"
He had been truthful about Oswin, but now?
He knows what she means.
Before she lived in Bally,
she lived with another sister,
Mrs. David Diehl,
across the road from him in Clayton,
and had always loved
two cherry trees in the meadow there
that have since been cut down.
He glances at Lillian.
He sees a slight shake of her head. He says:
"They're fine.
They had beautiful blossoms this spring.
The fruit is going to be heavy—yes."

THE MAN THE COWS REMEMBERED

Just before the Pennsburg borough line,
on the way from Perkiomen Heights,
lives Ambrose Kulp. One passes the woods,
then the gas station,
then a house, then comes a second house
and this is his. The Zauner family
like many others have found their way here.
As Kulp invites them into his living room,
his voice
is a rasp that floods far out.
"So you need an auctioneer."
Zauner says, "Yes, yes, we do,
but we do not know much about it.
Do you want to come over and see?"
"Yes, I'll be over. I'll take care—
I'll take care of everything.
When are you home?" "I'm always home."
"Well, it may be I'll come tomorrow

or maybe not, maybe the day after,
but I'll come, I'll come—"
"What is the charge then, please?"
"We generally go by commission—
I must pay two clerks, advertising—
but it is not high.
Just you don't worry,
I'll take care of everything."
The Zauners start to leave,
but Kulp says, "No hurry, no hurry.
Sit awhile.
How did you hear about me?"
Mrs. Zauner tells him,
"You called sale at Berman's
across the way from us—" "Oh yes,
yeah yeah yeah, I called sale there.
That was in forty-seven." Zauner says,
"They tell me
you have long been an auctioneer."
"Fifty-two years—that's long, isn't it?
Yes, 'What am I bid, what am I bid?' I've called, in all,
thirteen or fourteen thousand sales,
most at the cattle auctions.
At Fischer's in Quakertown I called
thirty-seven long years over there
and fourteen years at Perkiomen Heights.
The cows remembered me when I passed.
Yes, for John P. Hill—Hill—Hillegas,
for Harvey Haring many years—
every week pretty near I called for him—
for Dan Graber thirty years,
for G. W. Wiend, Samuel Freed,
Quintus Kline, all those cattle dealers."
"However did you get started on that?"
Mrs. Zauner asks.
"I will tell you," Kulp says.
"When I was twenty-two,
I was working at the brickyards
and had to stand up eight thousand bricks
before I got to my other work.
That is hard, so, on the knees.
I began to walk like an old man.

196

I said, 'I must find other work.'
Well, one day—I remember it well—
when I finished at the brickyard,
I was helping William Keck
cut corn, on his farm,
and Keck's hired man, John Gehris,
said he had to make sale. He said,
'I don't know who to get—Schoenley
charges too much and Zern is too old.'
'Get Ambrose here!' Keck cried.
'He has an awful voice.'
It happened I had watched auctioneers
and thought that might be some work.
I said, 'Yes, I'll do it.'
I hardly thought what I said.
The sale was October twenty-eighth,
and this thing come closer, this thing come closer.
Just about a week before the sale
I was to home, upstairs,
and down in the yard I heard talking
Frank Hallman and William Keck.
Hallman says to Keck,
'That horse of Gehris's,
Ambrose won't get fifty dollars for him.'
I went to Johnny Gehris and said
I wouldn't call sale for him.
'Why not?' he said.
'I don't know nothing.
Everybody says I don't.'
'Let them say what they want.
You got to call it,' he said.
'The sale is advertised.'
So at last the day of the sale come
and I was there and surely knew nothing.
George Ziegler, he was the clerk,
he read the conditions of the sale,
what one reads at all sales:
'The highest and best bidder
shall be the purchaser
if the article is struck down to him.
If any dispute shall arise
between two or more bidders, the article

197

shall immediately be put up
and sold over again.
Two percent off for cash.
So says John Gehris, vendor.'
I stood there like a little boy.
'Did you understand it?' George said.
'No,' I said. 'Give it again.'
He read the whole thing through again.
'So says John Gehris, vendor.
Have you got it?' he said.
'No, once again,' I said.
Then I had it. I was slow,
but when I got a thing, I got it.
So I begun to call.
There was many come to that sale
that had come just to hear me—
yes, they had come for the fun,
but, so, it made a good sale.
Well, I had to sell some hay.
I stood up in an old sleigh,
and one said, 'How much does that make a ton?'
He thought he had me there.
George whispers, 'Say twelve dollars.'
I said, 'Twelve dollars—so,
you think I don't know what to say!'
I sold a pig with five young ones
for thirteen dollars and thirty-five cents—
a good price yet in those days.
Then come the horse. I called it—
yes, I got it up
to one hundred and one dollars,
then I couldn't get my tongue around it.
'One—one—one,' I said.
'Sold for a hundred and one dollars!'
But I'd got a good price.
Yes, my voice that day
was better even than it is now.
One come to me and said,
'If this is the first auction you called,
keep it up.' Yes, neighbors was there—
Isaac Shaner, old Danny Moyer,
old John Taggert, Samuel Headman,

and John Kehl—later they all had me.
Yes, one neighbor was there
and said if he ever made sale,
he would have me—and do you know
how long it was to his sale?"
"No, I don't," Zauner says.
"Thirty-eight years, but so
he kept his word—Johnny Mack.
He had me as he said he would.
There was not much that first winter,
but in spring I called another sale—
'What am I bid? What am I bid?'
but I still worked at the brickyard.
The fall of that year I called eight sales.
The next year I called cow sales,
and from nineteen eight to now
I haven't done much but auctioneer.
Positively I haven't." Zauner's wife says,
"Do they use signals much?"
"Do they use signals, ai ai ai.
So! One puts his hand in his pocket,
one closes his fist, so,
one puts his hand to his vest.
One came to me before a sale
and said, 'I don't want it known I'm bidding.
What can I give for a signal?'
I said, 'Touch your coat collar.'
At the sale, then, I watched him,
and I'd call, 'Eighteen thousand I got—
who'll give nineteen, who'll give nineteen?'
One said, 'I don't see your bid!'
'Still I have it!' I said,
'and you'll have to go still higher
if you want to get this property.'
Yes, my man held his coat collar,
so at last I sold to him."
"A tricky business, net?" Zauner says.
"No, it's only that it has rules
like anything else, so.
You have to know. But it's all honest."
He smiles. His voice, rasping as it is,
has tolerance in it

for things large and small—
milk cows (horned and unhorned), churns,
half-used boxes of nutmegs, bureaus,
pails of odds and ends, life's sloughings,
family pictures and letter packets—
he values them, his voice
has named and called them all. His call, hip hip,
makes everything clear,
solid as a dough tray,
perfect as a darning egg.
"I will come," he assures the Zauners. "Don't worry.
I will take care of everything,"
and his voice says that he will.

INCIDENT AT THE AUCTION

The auction is well advanced.
The parlor is crowded
with many in open coats.
The linen shades are up, all up,
and through streaked old window glass can be seen
row after row of cars, a few trees,
and in the yard the corner-ball players
flinging the ball from side to side.
"Now we come to the organ." Ambrose Kulp
pumps it and presses a key. It is well
to show its tone. "A good tone. Yes, a good organ,
none as good made at the present time.
So—what am I bid?" "Two dollars."
"Two dollars I'm bid, two dollars.
Who'll give three? Who'll give three?
Three I'm bid. I have four.
Four four four I'm bid—"
The crowd is not offering much.
"Five five five. Who'll make it six?
There—there's a gentleman will help.
Six he bids for this fine organ!
Who'll bid seven? Six I'm bid"—
Kulp looks slowly all around—

200

"six six six I'm bid."
He turns to a man beside him
and says, "Ed, shall I sell it?
It's a low price yet."
"Yes, everything's to be sold."
"Six I'm bid, going going going—
sold to—" "Joseph Requa."
Requa coming up front
is overtaken by a woman
who has just come into the room.
She reaches Ed and says,
"I thought you weren't going to sell the organ,
I thought it was understood.
I was only gone a few minutes
and now it's sold."
"I know. But everything has to be sold, Julia."
"I'd have *bid* on it.
Father got me that organ, you know it.
It was mine, I practiced on it—"
"I sold my old bicycle. Even the Edison.
The will says everything."
"I don't care, Ed. Please.
Can't you just cancel the sale of the organ?"
"That organ's been *sold,*" Requa says.
"Either I get it
or I must go to the squire."
The clerk, marking the clipboard, says,
"According to the law, it is sold."
Julia turns to Requa:
"But you must have heard what I was saying,"
and she explains it all to him again.
He listens without expression.
"Still I want it." "No!" She bursts into tears. She leaves the room.
Kulp hurriedly directs his great voice
to a cupboard. "All right,
here we have a fine corner cupboard.
What am I bid? Ten I'm bid.
Ten ten ten—"

WILLIE GEHRIS REMEMBERS
WHERE HE WORKED

Young Willie Gehris worked three years
at Wanner's farm, a good enough place:
"Yeah, I liked the place.
But cows, don't say nothing about them. No.
Some days I had to milk them when they ate,
and me they did int like yet.
Some days it rained.
Breakfast was maybe slower then.

"I slept in the barn.
I used to go to a neighbor's, talk some at night and go home.
One night I did int go. I talked on the porch at Wanner's
and fell asleep. The family went up.
About one o'clock I woke up.
I tried to find the cornfield where I went home.
I climbed a fence, I walked up and down in the dark.
Then I remembered, I was home.
I come back across to the barn.
The dog barked. 'Shut up,' I said.
I climbed to the loft, I went to sleep.
Two o'clock, pip ip, the truck horn.
Hired hand with a load of cows.

"Once I had a half hour for breakfast.
Mrs. Wanner cooked the pancakes one at a time.
I did int mind."

THE FIRST TRADE OF THE
HORSE TRADER, MILTON LONGACRE

"When I was fourteen,
I had a friend, Joe, another like me,
and he had gone to the auction"—
to the pen with the heavy fence
where the western horses were brought in
herded like steers, to be sold—
"and he bought this horse, an outlaw.
He paid only forty dollars for him,
and with difficulty brought him home,
and planned so to break him.
Him and his father tried to do it,
but this horse was too wild.
This horse kicked and bit
and tried to paw them down with his front legs.
You know a horse like that is frightened,
and my friend's father was such a one
to make any fear him. Was mean.
When the horse would not be broken,
he threatened to kill that horse
unless Joe sold him by nightfall.
'And don't go in that box stall.
If you do and get laid out,
I'll let you lay there like a dog.
Won't help you.' What made Joe's father so mad,
the horse had broke every pane
in the box stall's fourteen pane window.
But that was the man's own fault.
He hadn't watered the horse,
and the horse in his thirst licked the windows
where some steam was, and broke them.

"Joe came to me and said,
'Do you buy the horse from me, else
my father is just such a one
he will kill the horse because he said so.'
He asked for it what he had paid.

I said, 'I have thirty dollars.
I'll see if I can get ten more.'
Thirty whole dollars was a lot then
for a boy to have. I got it
trapping and hunting. A muskrat skin
brought then from four to twelve cents.
I hadn't spent a few cents even—
no, not a penny.
I'd had to save it all.
But so I had saved and I had it.
I took the thirty dollars to my father
and tried to get ten more.
'If I can't get ten,' I said,
'Joe will let me owe him five.'
'I'll give you five dollars and so
you buy for thirty-five dollars outright,'
and that was how we settled it.
That was what I bought the horse for.
It was a pretty hard bargain,
but it was the best Joe could do.
'Joe, you must help me bring him home.'
We lassoed him, wild as he was,
and pulled him on the floor and choked him,
and that way got the bridle on.
Then I took a rope and went ahead
and Joe come behind with another rope,
and a whip also in his hand,
and so we brought him to my place.
I knew how to break horses
and had got it agreed with my father
that I was to break this one.
I would have had no trouble
had nobody else tried first.
But so I had to abuse him,
do something I didn't like to do.
I waited till my father was away,
then I went to the woods for hickory.
Hickory, that is the hardest wood.
I cut three pieces of it;
one was like a fishing pole,
one like a baseball bat, but not thick,
and one short like a policeman's club.

204

With those three sticks I went.
When I came up to the horse,
he lashed out with his front feet
and tried to bite. I hit him.
Each time he fought, I hit him.
I kept on hitting till I wore him out,
till he was too tired to do anything.
Then I gentled him and talked to him.
Gave him sugar—a horse is wild for sugar.
So with the hitting and gentling,
he gave in and I trained him. In six months
he was a perfect trained horse.
At that time my uncle from Jersey—
that was my father's brother—
needed a horse. He wanted mine.
'He's not for sale,' I said.
'Well, and if he *was* for sale,
what would you ask for him?'
I set a big price. I said,
'A hundred and seventy-five dollars.'
Next Saturday he was back,
carrying a bridle and saddle.
So, it was my first horse:
'I didn't say I would sell.
I only said if he *was* for sale,
that's what I would ask for him.'
But my father then interfered.
He said, 'It's a good price.
You said it and now you must sell.'
Twice he told me and so I sold.
But that night, big as I was, I cried.
I had become fond of that horse,
and truly I didn't want to sell him.
Well, but so I had to sell,
and so from that I began to trade—
yes, I furnished horses where there was need
here and there from then on."

THE LIFE OF THE BLACKSMITH

Out of the deep sky
the sun warms grapes that signal fall,
ripening and pressing their underskin sweetness
against the arbor posts. A window shutter
beats and knocks, warning of wind,
but all is sweet yet with the grape.

Past Ed Kuhns's shoulder, his open smithy
is a room with the front wall taken down.
The anvil, a grub, curls by the furnace.
The nozzle of the bellows waits.
Hammers, tongs, and hooks litter the floor,
and on the rafters rows and rows of shoes
hang like medallions on the nails.
"I was born right here," he says, pointing
across the hollow of Dale that sends him
its muscadine warmth.
"I'm sixty-seven, but what year I was born,
that I can't keep in my head.
How about it? When I was eighteen,
I was apprenticed to a blacksmith.
I worked hard. I got up at four o'clock
and many nights I worked till ten or eleven.
The pay? The first year, twenty-five dollars.
The second year, fifty dollars.
Would any work for that now? How about it?
The old mine now at Boyertown,
we sharpened drills for that mine.
We sharpened two for five cents. Is that cheap?
Three of us worked: one heated,
one hammered, and one hardened. Working so,
we sharpened three hundred a day.
Of course, there I learned to shoe a horse,
but you don't learn so much at that
when you're an apprentice. How about it?
You learn from yourself, later.
Yes, later I learned when I had to.
I'll tell you—how about this?—

206

one came to me once with a racehorse,
he wanted to level the horse.
I put a timber on the ground, put side pieces,
and put a timber on top.
Then I measured the horse's legs.
One leg was five-eights of an inch short,
so by the thickness of the shoe,
I leveled that horse, yes, leveled him,
then that horse won every race.
Then come one with a black mare.
That mare had long hair on the legs.
I pushed back her hair and see
she had one clubfoot and one flat foot,
so I made a short heel and a high heel.
The hair was hanging over the feet,
and they couldn't see what I done,
but the mare wasn't lame no more.
They asked then what I did.
I wouldn't tell. Would you tell?
They won't tell *you* anything. How about it?
Yes, I was a hired smith.
I shoed ten or twelve horses a day.
I could shoe a horse
in twenty-five minutes, so,
if only the horse would stand right.
But, being fast, that don't say
I wasn't careful. I was careful.
I had a feeling for a horse.
Some smiths have no feeling for them.
They do any kind of shoeing job.
I often think, a horse must stand it.
He can't take the shoes off or on,
and that must hurt. How about it?
To shoe a horse right, yes, to shoe right,
you must know the bones in a horse's foot.
One lays just like the foot,
one comes down so and fits in,
loose, and the other goes so.
When I learned myself, I found out.
I took the foot of a dead horse
and I sawed it lengthwise in half,
so I found out." Now he frowns.

He gives a quick look to the Dale creek,
toward the haunting sweet of grape,
and flaps his overall bib.
"But what good was it? How about it?
The cars come. It's all cars now.
Then the tractors. It's all tractors now.
You go from here to Boyertown,
how many horses will you see?
Lucky if you see a dozen.
In summer now there's some work,
but there's no work in winter.
The cars and tractors do it all."
He picks up two nails from the ground
and rubs them together in one hand.
"I had a thought, when I was old,
to get lame horses, fix them up,
then I could sell them again.
Well, I'm getting old now,
but—where are the horses?"
He tosses the nails away.
"Well, so it's better so.
The work give out and I did too."

THE JOHN HORSE
(Ed Kuhns speaking)

"You ever hear of Old Wallach
who dealt in horses in Boyertown?
A Jew, yes, he began
as a *graemer,* so we called it—
the ones who peddle with a bundle.
He tried several different businesses
till he made out with horses.
He shipped thousands of horses to Germany.
There is this story about him.
He had a horse named John.
That John horse was ugly-looking,
not a nice horse at all.
Yes, he had a temper.

208

One day a customer
had words with Wallach
and called him—I guess you know what. Just then
that horse licked out his heels
and knocked the man down.
'That John horse,'
Old Wallach said,
'I'll never sell as long as he lives.'
He never did. How about it?"

TOWARD A PHILOSOPHY OF HORSES
(Dale Graeff)

"Steve was a good workhorse,
none better, but ai ai ai,
on the road! When I drove the buggy,
I put blinders on him,
but if he saw the least bit of paper, especially
if it was to blow,
off he went with heels flying
and it might be miles before I got him reined in
and could drive him back home again.
Railroad engines! Don't mention them!
If one sounded even out of sight,
he was off. Or I had to get out
and hold his head and talk to him.
Once day he got loose from the stall,
and the barn door was open. I had
a half acre of asparagus
just ready to cut. That was what he ran to, of course,
ran all over it and neighed.
Then again,
that Steve, when he worked,
he was altogether different,
couldn't be a better horse.
That was why I kept him. He'd plow all day long,
furrow after furrow, straight,
never tire, never let up.
Quiet. I'd let my small son ride him

209

while he plowed. No, seldom
can you get everything in one horse,
and what he had I needed. Like one says,
it depends. Take this thing
of being scary,
even that might not be so bad. In nineteen eleven
a Civil War veteran said to me,
'I had the best horse in the Union Army.'
'How's that?' I said.
'Well,' he said, 'I'd be riding along a ridge or somewhere.
The enemy mortars would begin firing. My horse
would always turn right around then
and run five miles to the rear,
just couldn't control him.
By the time I'd get that horse under control
and back to the place we'd started from,
the action would be over.' Well,
you can't say that wasn't a good horse."

EMMAUS AND THE CIVIL WAR

On April fifteenth, eighteen sixty-one,
President Lincoln called for volunteers
"for a term of three months."
The Pennsylvania quota was fourteen thousand.
Being a border state, it "loyally"
gave what was asked. Its units,
among then the "Allen Rifles" of Allentown,
were the first to reach the capital
and so were called "The First Defenders."
But, later,
in the years of stalemate,
a draft act had to be passed and this
was received differently. In some places
there were riots.
Emmaus, a town of peace,
had to send seven men.
The Town Council voted
to exercise the option

of buying substitutes as was allowed,
and for this purpose laid "a bounty tax
of $2.65 per hundred . . ." War was bad,
but a civil war, a *Bruderkrieg?*

THE HAND

Val Gehman says: "When I was a boy,
I knew an old man
who had once shaken hands with Lincoln.
As often as I could
I shook his hand, wanting
to touch the hand that had touched Lincoln's."

THE LIFE OF AMELIA ELTZ

Lace. The center mat is strong and plain,
but something more is needed, an edge
running the thread's wave into foam.

"I was born near Forge Dale
July twenty-eight, eighteen sixty-two,
and in December
my pap, Magnus, *gschtarava*—he died, yes, he died—
he went to the Civil War
and never returned, my pap,"

At Forge Dale:
"a stone house my grandpap Anthony built."
From its windows, across the creek,
she had the sight of trees.
In fall, the leaves dropped like curtains parting
and revealed the gray rocks,
threshold of the winter's snow.
The snow fell in cold winds
and laid its waves out from the rocks.

211

"I became a child nurse at thirteen,
at the John L. Bauer family.
They had two children, the Bauers,
Irwin four and Laura two. At fourteen,
I went to the Levi Meschters.
After the Meschters, I went to Monroe Schneider
who owned the big mill below Palm.
Then I went to Frank Melcher on Crow Hill,
then I went back to Bauers'.
So I worked, from place to place,
until I married Jim Melcher."

Somewhere in her working childhood,
she learned to make lace. Fine lace.
Her needles clicked along in the constant patience.
It was something to do for herself. Pads.
Doilies. Blue-white flowers
stiffened with starch. Slow slipcover edges.
The thinnest of transparent handkerchiefs.

"I met Jim Melcher at parties and such.
We talked and laughed. Whether parties now
are like they were then, *Ich denk net*.
I haven't been in a long time.
After we married, we farmed.
We had the farm by Fischer's Mill,
and the first spring, March eleventh and twelfth,
was the blizzard of eighty-eight."
The snow came down for two days
and the house stood so in the gale.
The white surrounded it in buttes,
in circles grooved and heavy,
and the circular drift seemed to be
a doily of the sky.

Agnes, November, 1889.
Joe, October, 1891.
Gus, January, 1893.
Rose, February, 1895.
Marie, September, 1897.
Evelyn, November, 1900.
Anna, September, 1903

212

Instead of lace now, work.
"Grandpap went to Alphinus Eck
and bought fifty pounds of flour,
the following week he bought fifty more,
the following week fifty more."
Ten loaves of bread twice a week.
Handmade underwear, children's dresses.
"We butchered twice a winter.
We butchered four hogs and a beef
before the holidays, and four hogs and a beef
after the holidays"
She made a whole "furnaceful" of scrapple,
made sausage, liverwurst,
tripe, "that was kuddleflek,"
bludwurst and sauerkraut. "One spring
I boiled seven kettles of soap.
You put caustic soda with fat
and boil it down, and after it gets solid,
you cut it so in pieces."
There was sickness:
"Agnes was the first
that had the scarlet fever,
then Joe, Gus, and Rose come down with it.
There was none to help.
When Agnes and Rose had diphtheria,
I myself had it too.
I would get up out of bed,
make the dinner, and go back to bed."
It seemed work would never end,
the needs of the fields, the house,
but year follows year, year follows year,
and at last one year it ended.
And there was a resurrection of lace.
"From memory" or "by directions," the steel needles
clicked again, quick and hard,
whipping along loops that spilled out
the same grooved, foaming waves.
All the years' weight then
dissolved in her hands
and melted into the white, the cool.

LONGING FOR THE PERSIMMON TREE

She comes up the walk toward her back door, Mama Longacre,
     trailing her shyness over the lawn, so well kept,
     so wonderfully green in the cold morning.
She passes the persimmon-tree stump.
There it sits, a dark wedge like a lump of firewood, with
     the memory of its red fruit in the damp of its slanting
     black rings.
Persimmon Pudding—the recipe's in her kitchen drawer:
     "1 cup persimmon pulp, 1 egg,
     2 tablespoons butter, 1 cup sugar,
     1/2 cup cream (or milk), 1 cup sour milk,
     1 teaspoon baking powder,
     1/3 teaspoon soda, 1 cup flour,
     1 teaspoon cinnamon
        Mix as for cake and bake in a greased and floured
     pan 45 minutes.
               From Mrs. Henry Hustand."
Such good pudding, Milton liked it so much, and just about
     now, with the first good hard freeze, the persimmons
     turned so soft, sweet, and juicy.
Funny, something that, before the frost, made your mouth
     pucker like alum.
A funny-leaved tree—with bees buzzing in the leaves,
     and the blossoms dropping to the ground like popcorn.
Then a redbird sitting in it like another fruit.
Yes, the tree was forever messing up the ground with twigs and
     branches, and in the fall there was the stain of its
     fruit on the walk—much raking like currying a horse.
But it had become a friend. It seemed to notice her, it seemed
     to shelter her, it seemed to shade her particularly the
     days Milton was away, to New Holland and such.
And its leaves were so funny, so pretty.
The wind had such a sound in it,
such a shining,
not to have it
          now
            any longer.

Ai ai, Milton must clean the stump down to the ground and I
        must forget it once and for all.
You get old
and friends die.

KATE MANDEL

She strides short
in bleached print and sucked smile,
hair cut to a bowl, flax
padding for a helmet. Suns go by
in her shadow. Down the yard
along the fence, chickens wander,
placing small dusts of claws.

"It iss a bad year."
Her hair rounds
her agate face.
"I don't know what it iss—"
The pullets don't have clean legs.
White runs down. They don't lay.
The young cocks eat the corn, useless.

She walks sometimes seven miles, carrying
cocks to sell
killed, in a pair of buckets.

MULES

Near Kate Mandel's chicken house,
two mules are turned
into a field of burned dust.
Loosed from the gate, they adjust
themselves to liberty—
run with no body roll, their muzzles
burning with the same stale chocolate

as the ground. They kick the dust
and back their rumps together,
falling to the earth as bisons do
on the plains,
scuffing sulfuric clouds
toward the dried-out creek,
then rise,
shaking and quietly
long-eared again,
contained and calm.

MILTON LONGACRE'S DEATH
(Mama Longacre speaking)

"We moved from our place in September.
The water company said,
everything around the reservoir a certain distance back
had to be leveled. Our place had to go down.
I had that three-colored cat.
Once she had had young out in the tree
and brought them in. This time she'd had them
in the silo at the barn bridge.
When they burned the silo,
she went right through the flames after them.
She didn't know, of course,
they'd took them out—so she died.
They burned the silo and barn to put them down.
Milton never would speak about that.
They put the house down.
Two years later, he was driving the truck
and it went off the road
below Perkiomen Heights, toward Ambrose Kulp's.
It went to the side of the road
and threw him into the ditch
where there was some stones. He was hurt so,
I don't know how he got up out of there,
his head bleeding and all, but he did.
He walked, not so far, to the old place.

Nothing there by then,
just a wire across the lane,
but he managed to get over that and walked in
and lay down there and died."

WINKLEMAN'S BABY
(Wilson Graeff speaking)

"Bert Winkleman,
some of us called him Winkie
from what we called him when he was just so,
a boy in school. He was one
never talked much, or answered.
He liked mainly animals.
I don't know that he wasn't right
in that liking. He bought a racehorse,
a strange thing now in this country,
a mare. He kept her to run in circles
as I suppose
generations of her sires and dams did.
He put a bench at the corner of a meadow
where she ran
and he would sit watching her
Then he bred her and she had a foal.
You ever seen a foal born?
I tell you that is something worth seeing.
I was around when she dropped it.
The long, thin legs came first, then the head,
and all encased in a white bag
like a plastic, the caul,
that you could see through, and out of that
it burst shining like a chestnut.
For perhaps an hour it rocked back and forth
on its stomach to get its strength.
The mother cleaned it up,
and at the end of the hour
it stood up and went to the teats.
I'd say the mare then

217

as she swung to nuzzle her babe
was just like a Madonna.
Now Winkleman
had then a child of his own,
born that same year of the foal.
The mare and the foal, you could say,
were the first companions of that baby,
for Winkie took the baby to the field
where he tilted him up in a cradle
so he could gaze out like nothing so much
as a little horse clocker.
He had a solemn look,
watching the mother and foal
as they circled past, together. Dust and earth
would fly in the air sometimes,
but the baby would keep watching and blinking
as if it understood everything.
It must have because
its first word was *wh'h'h'nnnnn.*"

THE LEAKING HEART

Old Mrs. Holtz's voice is thinly stretched.
She remembers more of her young days
than of those that loosed her strings:
"My babies come close together.
I rocked one with the foot
and another one by hand,
and when I fed one, I let it sleep.
Yes, I let it sleep till it woke.
Only George was restless. Yes, he cried.
I couldn't make him easy.
The doctor come and he explained—
George had a leaking heart.
Anyone's heart is only a pump.
If it don't work good and the water slips,
it don't get a hold.
So George's was. He cried,
wanting something—he didn't know what.
He cried, yes, but he could smile.

218

"He was the only one I lost.
I grieved. From the grief I seen
many are like he was,
wanting something they don't know what, maybe
only for the heart to pull."

DELIA LONGACRE FALLING ASLEEP

At the bottom of the scale
the low note,
night's
last-held thought:
put-off fear,
put-on dream,
the brief seam
of a distant scar.

BEETHOVEN, MOZART

Delia Schultz Longacre,
the music teacher on the branch,
has never married. She likes her independence
but takes a lively interest
when a couple whose house is near hers
have a baby.
He's been growing, she thinks,
behind those blowing curtains.
Her keen ear hears him.
He mostly sleeps at first,
but then begins to make himself known.
He cries, like half notes,
but when he gets mad, it's a long nasal
whole note—no half about that.
His crying—she thinks it's like Beethoven's
early quartets where the strings cry
complainingly, unlike
the great wringing sadness of the last quartets.

You can get tired of some of Beethoven
and turn to Mozart who swells with a wholesome
sweetness that seems as if it could never end,
as if nowhere was a weakening sadness let in.
Good. If you're to have courage to live,
you have to forget the minor keys, their grief, lucky
if it leaves you unchanged
and lets you go back to the major's health.
And the baby too,
a baby crying isn't lonely.
Those half notes
are maybe just asking to know
that, in spite of hunger and fear, cadenzas of happiness
can run in the clefs. A baby has to cry.
What would he be,
what would life be
without those sometimes sobbing strings?

THE LIFE OF RUTH LARBAUGH

When Ruth Larbaugh was small,
one day in the heavy August
she pulled a stem of Queen Anne's lace.
It was like one of the tufts of fog
that clung so close to the Lehigh River, mornings.
She held it to her nose to smell,
then to her ear to hear.
No sound. It drooped
its grains in a white circle of quiet.

She was born on a quiet day, Sunday,
May tenth, eighteen seventy-nine, a first child.
She grew up along the edge of the Lehigh
on a farm, a running-around farm girl.
When she was out of high school,
her parents moved from the country
to Boyertown, to one of those brick row houses
off Philadelphia Avenue. Next door,
Philip Spoontz,

a graduate engineer at twenty-two,
liked her, liked
her thin, long-hanging "hank of hair."
They married and went to Niagara Falls.
The Falls' noise frightened and pleased her. After the honeymoon
he took her to that raw foundry, Pittsburgh.
An off year, but from their steep street
she listened to slag slide now and then
until, in a city-wide firing
Philip lost his job. After that,
since he could get no work,
he decided to farm. To her,
it was a way to go home.

On the first farm, near Bechtelsville,
in their first months,
she had a cold in her right ear.
Some yellow liquid came,
and the prescription and the cotton wads
that, at the doctor's orders,
Philip put carefully
into the shell of her ear
did not relieve her. "Let it be," she said.

She had John and Margaret. When John was six,
they moved to a new farm
a mile down the Congo road, and there Elsie was born. And there
the world began to change in her ears.
At first it was only that one sound
stole another. The step of a cow
went silent at the cawing of a crow,
and the crow's slow-motion hammer of the sky
stopped at the creaking of a door.
The baby's voice took the door creak,
then all sounds lowered and went down.

Some fifty feet from the house
was a spring with twelve green steps, in April
all but the top one under water.
As the rains lessened in summer heat,
the water sank step by step

221

to the last clear bubble at the bottom.
So the hearing dried in her ears
until at last
when John killed a large snake at the spring,
from a distance
she did not hear the hitting stick.

The years otherwise were good.
Philip designed a barnyard wall,
the base of it engineered to hold
against the sloping ground. He helped Ruth plant
cannas beside it. He installed
three homemade drains
to reclaim a tract of swamp
that had disfigured the meadow,
and she spread red shoots of raspberries there.
But as she worked with him and the children,
she found herself watching their lips
to guide her to what was said.

When John was fourteen, Margaret ten,
and Elsie eight, she lost all hearing.
She lives now in a zone of silence, having
in her eyes the hurt
of that loss of sound.
The children stamp on the floor
to get her attention. She hears their steps
through her feet. She hears the pressure,
not the creak, of her neck bones,
and her breath tickles her nose. A problem
is when she speaks loudly or too low.
Embarrassed either way, she adjusts
to the level of room sound in which she talks
only as others help her to.

Hearing no sound, at last
she hears everything. So her look
is not always one of uncertainty.
The shoots of the pronged raspberries
rub against one another, whispering.
The back of a black steer, shining in the heat,
speaks like a lowing throat.

A bird, as it flies, whips away
previously unheard utterings from its wings,
and she goes back to earlier things,
to the child
who listened at the cotton tufts of summer,
to Queen Anne's lace, the world now
day by day confronting her there
with a presence she can hear,
though Philip's words are stolen from his mouth.

THE LIFE OF THE HARNESS MAKER

In Pennsburg is a small shop, painted white,
a little clean yard-end place
reached by a walk,
where a retired harness maker, William Johnson,
cousin of the Reverend Elmer Johnson,
sits on a day of winter rain.
He does no paid work now, still he has
the shop. A wood stove, draft on,
warms him, sounding like
the ronronron of a dove.
The rain corrugates his big window,
and in the rain-pale light, his bench
flickers with awls, belts, and riding bridle.
His shoulders are a great arch facing the bench
as he sits knife in hand, recollecting
his life.

He was born in eighteen seventy-eight.
April twenty-ninth. At New Berlinville
just outside of Boyertown on a farm,
a particular nesting of land there
between the town and the creek and its willows.
"I liked farm work, helping Father,
and went to school in wintertime."
Congo was the school, south of Schultzville.
Then, the farm work not enough,
"I answered an ad of Harold Bower

that he needed an apprentice
at his shop in Boyertown."
So that life began—
farm harness, express harness, coach harness.
"Sewed six or eight stitches to the inch."
Learning as he went,
he sat on a "stitching horse,"
the foot pedal a beating stirrup,
riding standing still—
pushed the awl close to his finger,
and like a seamstress for the real horse
hawed the threads through the hole.
A half-moon knife cut them close,
and so his apprentice time wore out.
"Later I worked to East Greenville
in the big shop there.
Every town had a shop:
Macungie, Chapel, Shimersville,
Emmaus, Red Hill, Sumneytown,
Boyertown, Bechtelsville, all
had their own harness shops.
Besides the regular harness making
and repair, I used to make fly net"—
such a net that is put on a horse
to keep the flies off, jointed strings
of leather that rippled on roundnesses
of sweating belly and flank—
"and one day a man came in to buy.
He'd been drinking.
He had a toothache, he said.
To see he got
the same fly net he had bought,
he cut some of the strings to it.
Then he went away and come back
and maybe the pain had sobered him.
He looked at those strings he had cut
and said, 'Well, it's mine, all right.'
Yes, we often laughed at that."
Bridle, body harness, lines, halters.
"Collars in my time we bought,
but older harness makers yet than I
could make collars. But we made

224

all other harness for horses—" workhorses,
riding horses, carriage horses,
road-pacers spotted with brass and gold,
carrying plumes, heads hard-checked-back
to shower manes on the summer sun.
"I never had a horse of my own."
He sat only the stitching horse, his canter
a succession of perfectly cut,
perfectly sewn and fitted harnesses.
"Well, I guess I didn't miss it."

From a box in a corner
an old dog lifts himself up,
stirred by the sound of talk.
"Come here, boy. This fella I hitch up
and he pulls my grandchild.
He has a breast collar. I made it.
Regular bridging like the regular harness.
I do a lot of hand-stitching yet."
Laying his knife down, idly
he scratches his dog's head
as rain scatters grooves on the window.
"I must put some sticks on the fire.
Yes, there's little to do these days
except keep the dog and me warm."

SPRING

With the end of snow, the pheasants hide
into the yawn of the year, the brush, the thorn,
tangles where the watercress
leaks down.

Less often now their washboard rattle
bursting loudly over a tree.

NO ACCIDENT

"Old Stotsfus drowned.
It was no accident.
He walked above the dam
and walked along the log
and jumped in the water there.
It was one of those days, I guess,
one too many."

OUTSIDE MUSIC

Delia Longacre goes to New York occasionally
to concerts—Mozart, Mahler, the moderns.
One Saturday morning she sets off
to hear Olivier Messiaen's wife play his difficult
Vingt regards sur l'enfant Jésus,
a piece she herself has tried.

She takes the train at Allentown, walking
across the brick boarding way. The train slides
out of the station and, passing
piles of sulfur and mounds of white clay,
reaches Bethlehem. At Bethlehem
smokestacks rise to write on the sky
gradations of rust and rose. Furnaces glare.
A thin sound, like catgut burning,
hisses a transposition of metal
to the molds. She vibrates,
even safe on her straw seat. She wants to get by,
get past these atonal flames, hear only
in the great hush of farmland
the train advancing through fields.

226

THE LIFE OF REINERT REINHARDT

Reinert Reinhardt had five children,
three boys and two girls,
and was sharp with them. A good man
with divinations of insight with others
but none with his own children,
and all, as they grew up,
balked him in some deep-going way.
As many knew.

In his age
he let some currant bushes grow up on his place
at a bad turn in the road.
When, twice, neighbors almost ran over
youngsters sleigh riding,
there were complaints. Reinhardt: "No sir,
I'll not cut my bushes back.
Make your *kinner* stay off the road.
Can't you control your kids?"

EDUCATION

Heimbacher says:
"This education, it isn't always good.
There was this friend's boy,
he was brought up a farmer,
then he went away to agricultural school,
to the State School, for a couple years,
and came back and started farming.
He knew all the new things—
removed the stone walls, planned his crop rotation,
set everything up to farm right,
but he had some debt from his schooling,
that weighed him and he just didn't work,
just didn't want to work like a farmer,
and quit."

227

WHAT CAN HAPPEN

For many years Henry Benneman
had had good crops of potatoes.
He cut good seed, and the slope of his fields
prevented undue moisture.
He got more than the average crop.
Then one year no different from the others,
the new potatoes just brought to the barn
gave a strange smell. "The rot."
It meant a potato turning wet
and melting, and where the wetness touched,
the rot spreading. "We'll have to sort."
He and Mary and the older children
sorted. They worked until, late at night,
they had several piles of "good potatoes,"
but overnight wetness started again
and those healthy piles,
clean, with good dry dust,
caved in. The third day
a single decent truckload was left. He knew
he could take this to a distant market
and sell, but it made him uncomfortable.
It would not be honest.
This truckload too might rot.
He waited. It all began again.
He threw what was left on the public dump
and scoured the barn clean. Potatoes,
so necessary, so ordinary,
so common,
to have to buy them now for his own use.
He'd make crop again, of course,
but there was that terrible thought:
what can happen. Then—

One hot day Lila,
little more than a baby,
started a fever. Dr. Hottenstein was called and came
and said it was a chest infection,
but he wasn't sure. He listened and again listened.

228

After he left, it worsened;
the child moaned and cried. Mary called Doc back,
and Doc ordered Lila to the hospital
where her temperature went steadily up.
Nothing, it seemed, did any good.
The next day she was dead. The autopsy
showed that something in her brain had ruptured,
something that regulated the temperature, and from then on
her death was inevitable. Doc said
he had heard of very few such cases.
"Such a thing almost never happens."

A MEMORY OF SWEDEN

Mama: There Pa sits, so large,
with the bare panels of his chest
like nailed planks, naked to his belt.
So easy to make laugh. Braun
telling him that when one asks,
pointing south, "Is that land yours (Uhr's)?"
he says, "Yes." And Pa coming
especially through the noon heat
to tell the joke to me. Yes,
I married him,
big, unvarying, good.
He misses Sweden, the wave of spruce
that rolls toward unseen Lapland
and the reindeer north, the trees
sheered off by the latitudes.
On the slope behind Braun's back field,
he planted a whole acre of spruce
and likes to go under them and breathe
in the dark there. "Little Sweden."
One hears him mention his "Little Sweden,"
and questions him. "There,
the trees," he says. Mama:
Where is my Sweden then, my consolation?

229

Småland. That's my comfort.
The short summers of that small land. No wonder
I would throw myself on the grass
and hug it like a ghostly breast
that would soon go, that would soon leave me.
Everything was always leaving me.
The green of the grass, the light.
I was a girl of fears.
We had a large house of nine rooms
near a small grove of birch.
In winter, the dark came early.
The light that was so low all day
hurried off on scary feet,
and the dark of foxes
with their running shadows and tongues,
the dark, the growling dark,
came down on the unlighted house.
Sometimes I was brought home by an aunt,
and already all had gone to bed.
Then I felt alone in the house.
I put on the light by the door.
I walked in the silence
to a second light in the living room,
and put that on and walked back
and put the first one off. Then all the way
to turn the light on in the hall,
and back again to the still-lit globe
in the living room. Spiral stairs
led to the long upper hallway
and I climbed up them and down them,
forward to a light and backward
to put the other light behind me out
until I reached my bedroom. In the bedroom
I felt panic in my knees
trembling under my dress. A child
has thin legs, nothing but sticks
in the wide circle of her skirt.
I sat down on the edge of the bed
and thrust my hands into my lap
and stared at the something waiting
outside the window. I suppose

230

that board of naked chest was waiting,
that giant with his jokes.
I suppose it had to be
I would marry laughter.

BURNING OVER THE MEADOW

I hate fire
and when Pa insists in spring
on burning over the meadow—
"It burns the seeds of the weeds, Mama"—
I stand at the meadow edge
and shake my apron at him
as if I could kill him. And later,
maybe only an hour later,
he'll put me on his knee
and caress my face
and say, "You will never grow old,"
and smile that sneaky smile of his.
And I,
what do I do then?
I kiss him.

MAMA'S SWEDEN

Mama pulls her yellow jacket tight,
and such a frown—so she broods, frowning. Old,
the lost is lost. *Adjö.* Good-by.
I was raised on *Fattigmans Kaka,* Poor man's cake,
then came to Pennsylvania with Pa.
I brought, in my bright blue tote-box,
sheets, clothes, and my few years. The midwife
told me how I was born:
Mother worked till ten at night
and I was born at midnight.

The midwife arrived just in time
to wash me. She told my mother
I was a shapely thing
and my mother went to sleep,
tired from the cooking. Shameful—
I was an angry child.
I used to scratch and clutch the midwife
and used to kick my mother.
The midwife was a general nurse
so I knew her from time to time.
She wormed me when I was six.
I frightened easily and felt neglected.
I played with a kitten. I'd shake my head,
dangling my pigtails for the cute thing,
then I'd pick it up and kiss it.
I loved my sister, Dagny. Father fished.
He bicycled to the lake
five kilometers from the house
and caught *gädda* (pike) and eels.
We cried all of us in turn
to try to make him take us with him.
He was usually disgusted.
I picked lingonberries
and wild strawberries behind the barn.
I would go into the woods.
I went only a short distance
and ran back home. For more courage,
I took Dagny with me
and we hunted for the *spökslått*,
the house where the old woman
lived deep in the woods.
It was said she had had a sweetheart,
a young man who had been killed.
Sometimes now she had dreams
and ran outside and screamed.
We never found the *spökslått*,
but we found the *prestkrager*,
the little white priests' collars,
and the delicate *vitsippor*.
I sang about the butterflies—
"Fjariln vingad syns på Haga."
But one must grow up, no? In my teens

232

I began to go to barn dances.
A farmer would let his barn,
and sweep it out and rosin it
so that it was smooth and slippery.
Birch trees were put along the walls,
green and white in the night sunlight.
As I danced the schottische
or hopped along in the faster polka,
I felt the heat of the night.
I deliberately got the broom
in the *Kvastdansen*. Yes, the broom
became the one I would love—
and never did it look like Pa.
As I danced, the sun
went partly under the hill
and a half-light came as in the woods.
At dawn, tired,
I walked home, carrying my shoes. Later
came Midsummer Night's Eve
and once we took a trip to the ferry
and ferried between Hälsingborg
and Helsingör.
Many were drinking then.
I leaned on the ferry rail
and watched my hair swing above the water.
Lost, gone, that ferry, that Småland.
Adjö, good-by, thin smoke
and beloved hasty summer.
Good-by, dear grove of birch
and all the priests' collars of the woods.

THE LOST SPRING

It was a poor farm to begin with, that's sure, poor land,
sixteen acres lying on a slope,
and when the buildings burned without insurance,
the farm was gone. None bought. None wanted it.
It grew over in first-growth woods and weeds typical
of the infectious ruin of the hills.

When it was auctioned for taxes, the next neighbor, Frank Althouse,
bought it, remembering there had been a spring. Yes,
there would be water for his cows:
they could walk in and drink.

The spring was near the bottom of the slope
and the day he went to look for it, he pushed in
through briers, shoots live and dead, early green showing
like shadows off the winter coldness.
All the ground was "springy," sodden and wet,
but to his surprise, he could not find the spring itself.
Where could it be? He went back for his wife,
thinking she might remember where it was. He noticed
she was getting old, a little heavy now
and planted her feet one by one, shifting her weight,
but he could still see the young girl she had been.
For her, he cleared a path to the marsh patch
and guided her and asked her what she thought.
"It was by a rock, I remember that," she said. "Yes,
it was such a rock, and water come out beneath."
"For years the ground has come down here in the rains,"
he said, "and so it has covered, it has forced it underground."
"Once it went away in a little stream
over along the stone wall there where the rains drain now,
but then it ran, yes, it ran
all the late summer and into the fall."
"We must dig," he said. "That's all there is to it. Wait."
He went for shovel and ax and, choosing a place,
began to dig, tearing at the brier roots.
He pushed aside sod and gritty dirt, and as he trenched along,
a trickle began to come in here and there,
but somehow it was not to be traced back.
Each vein led away to nothing.
"It is by a rock," she said. "There must be a rock."
He went along the pliant sod
sheathing itself with the muck of spring,
and shoved the shovel in here and there
till he struck a stone. When he dug there,
no water came. "It is not the right stone,"
she said. "It was a wider one than that,
and yes, it had one side that was completely flat."
Another one, but it was still not the right one yet.

234

Then his searching shovel scraped against a rock
with brier roots clinging all over it.
He used the ax to cut the roots so that he could lift them away
and she helped. The lip of the rock widened.
"This looks like, this looks like," she told him.
So he began to dig. At the third stroke,
he was thrown off balance by the muck giving in.
As he straightened up, with a rush
like something alive pressing at the weakened earth,
water broke through and, in rhythmic pulses, gushed out.
"Ah, that's it!" she cried. Bubbles rose
and ran swiftly from under the rock. To him
her face seemed flushed and fair from exertion.
A look went between them that was not
all for the found water, and the water in its pouring jet
wet the side of her foot and the side of his foot.

AN OLD WOMAN LOOKS AT HER PICTURE

Friends had taken several snaps of her,
one very clear.

She began to laugh at it. "I like it.
It makes me laugh."

Then in a different tone: "Look at the wrinkles."
Then: "It's me, *ja?*"

Once in a house in Oley
she had pressed that same face, smooth then,
to a man's cheek—from that to his lips,
and so a sultry flame
spread in the scaffold of her skin.
And left
this photograph.

THE WOMAN AT THE SPRING DRIP

Always running, always there,
the pipe end brought from the hill
drips into the green lair
of the trough, the center a dull
eye, an eye.

And I, day in, day out,
hear the water run to the rim,
I hear the sound louden
like the voice of him
I loved, I loved.

He bathed his head in the drip,
he drank at the cold tap
when the summer was hot.
Now he is gone
and I am not, I am not.

THE WEAKENING

Emma Louellen Gery grew up in one of those New Berlinville
    houses where the knives and forks glimmered under a gauze
    cover between meals and where the meals were meat and
    potatoes.
Always meat and potatoes.
Emma Lou ate meat and potatoes.
After the table was cleared and reset, she put the gauze
    back and kept everything as clean as could be, as her
    parents wished.
Then she married and had a husband with peculiar tastes. He
    liked, for one thing, Brussels sprouts.
She humored him.
He was particularly fond of strawberries. To give him what
    he wanted, she opened a new large patch of ground.

236

She bought plants, things with brittlelike leaves and runners
   with leaping roots. She let the roots spread the patch out.
Every year after that for twenty years she served dozens of
   quarts of fresh strawberries and preserved forty quarts,
   which he alone ate.
One summer day, as she was hulling a large bowl of berries
   like diamond wedges, she noticed one. It was a beauty.
   All over the fleshy red, it sparkled with fine points
   of seed dust.
She held it hesitantly, hardly aware of it, hardly conscious,
   that sparkling wedge of red, and
bit into it, crushed it in her teeth.
She looked at her stained hand, at the empty hull, looked at
   a brilliant leaf fallen beside the pile of hulls and at
   the wide, well-tended berry patch below the window.
And again at her stained hand.
It was delicious!

HARVEY LARBAUGH

Harvey Larbaugh drives all,
boys, wife, himself. Sometimes people say
so he can't hear, "He has the devil in him." As the fall
mounts toward frost and closing ground,
he works without sleep. Then sleep
comes as he moves: "I started toward the house.
Then, yes, my eyes shut.
I opened them at the edge of the spring.
I was a hundred feet past the house."

One noon, in the barn, darkness dropped
so distinct the goats felt it
and huddled on an inward ledge.
Harvey, currying a horse,
worked through the noon twilight. Out the door,
a first rain drove by. Mist
passed under low-hanging clouds
as if pieces of cloud dragged on the meadow.

The rain came harder.
The meadow became a surface of water.
At its end, a maple
in a burst of wind dropped its leaves
in a golden replica of itself. Apple trees
wet and shaking, reached their ankles
into the temporary lake of rain.

Harvey yawned and thought,
The rain's slowing the work,
and in spite of him, his eyes shut.

DAVID AND
MARY HOTTENSTEIN LOOK BACK

David and Mary step with son Davy
over the clover, the bee-humming field.
The East Penn Valley
stretches before them
to the ridge of mountains to the east
beyond which lies their own Butter Valley,
Bally and its outstemming roads—
the doctor's roads. Above them,
a few scattered thunderheaded clouds
shadow the level land.
The graveyard is a square of farmland,
death sequestered by a wall.
As they approach the wall,
"Look at the Canadian thistles," Mary says.
Thorn and brier and half the stones flat:
In this fastness of the field
weeds push up life
where five generations lie dead.

The original David Hottenstein
bought some five hundred acres
and built a small house nearby, now gone.
The main house, built later, was called

"the plantation house." David goes
to the stone of the elder David.
The inscription on it:
"wurde geboren in Europa—"
("was born in Europe—")
Seven generations
are the line from him to this David:
four doctors—before that, planters.
To the left of the first planter, close
along the wall, he can see stones without names
that tradition says are those
of two Negro slaves. It could be.
A few did have slaves.
He and Mary and Davy
pick their way through thistles
to two graves
where a later Hottenstein and his wife
had coats of arms carved on marble to give
a snowy memento of their lineage.
In front of the upright stones
two marble slabs, crumbling,
make for each a mattress on the ground.
"I like these graves," Mary says.

They go now
to the final stone of Edward, David's grandfather.
When David was a boy, from a window,
being too young to attend the funeral,
he saw the winding line of mourners
and saw the doctor's body being lowered
into the ground, and cried.
He had loved his grandfather,
smooth-shaven, gaunt, with a mind
burning and venturing.
His grandfather wrote in the margin
of a textbook on obstetrics:
"Have noticed if I dip my hands in quicklime
after attending a case of childbirth fever,
I don't carry the fever to another."
He was a knowledgeable herbalist.
In a time of scarce drugs,
he got his own drugs from the earth.

Seeing a plant at a certain growth,
its curative virtue at its height,
he would dismount from his horse and cut or dig it
and put it in his box.
David had seen that box
about which his father had told him.
I ought to have it, he thinks.

He and Mary leave the stone
and carry Davy to the graveyard wall
and stand him on it. There the three-year child
smiles down the vale of Maxatawney
as they hold his hard young legs.

THE LIFE OF DR. BENJAMIN SCHULTZ

Benjamin Schultz was born July twentieth,
seventeen seventy-two,
in Upper Hanover Township,
Montgomery County, Pennsylvania,
first of seven children.
Abraham, his father,
was learned, and though a farmer,
was a one-time Representative
in the General Assembly of the Commonwealth.
At first
he himself taught Benjamin at home
in German. Then the boy went to the excellent
Schwenkfelder School System
under George Kriebel. Though no school year
ran more than four months,
he "got" an English that, unsure at first,
eventually enabled him
to write and speak as well
as the leading men of his time
in that new country, the United States.
In seventeen ninety-two
he was accepted as a student
at the Pennsylvania Hospital.

240

This pleased his father, who wrote:
"Next to a teacher of the Gospel
I think there is not a Class of men
that should be more circumspect and careful
to promote the Happiness of Mankind
than a Physician," but, he said,
such a one should not go after money,
"the most delusive Phantom
of our depraved Nature," but should give himself
to the aforesaid "Happiness of Mankind."
Benjamin did just that.
He studied medicine and science
under Caspar Wistar and Benjamin Rush
and became their friend,
but even more important,
he learned from Benjamin Smith Barton
how botany applied to medicine
and for his graduation "dissertation,"
wrote a paper on his research
on the "Phytolacca Decandra."
Phytolacca Decandra
was nothing more than pokeweed,
that roadside commonplace, in spring
succulent and peelable, faintly tart
in its first shoots, then opening to a high
fretwork of branches tipped with red berries.
In the introduction to his paper
he said, "There is, in this country,
an immense variety of native plants,
as yet but little known, which may,
at some future day,
furnish valuable matter . . . we might
extend the natural history of our country
beyond its present bounds,
and bring to public view an important object,
hitherto unexamined except by savages . . . plants,
which may perhaps deserve a preference
to remedies now employed
in obstinate and acute diseases. . . ."
The paper described his investigations
of pokeweed. First, he said,
he had tried to find a binder or fixative

that would make pokeweed juice an unfading dye,
especially for cloth. He used alum
and nitrous and vitriolic acid,
but none worked. Failing in this
(but a useful failure with negative value),
he tried the effect of poke on living bodies.
For his experiments,
he used two "middle-sized" dogs,
and the results were startling: poke juice
acted as emetic, cathartic, diuretic,
and soporific, all at once.
Now he extended his investigations
to a human. An adventurous druggist,
Samuel Cooper, offered to help him,
unintimidated by the threatening qualities
already demonstrated. He reported:
"I took two scruples of finely powdered leaves
of the Phytolacca. A slight nausea
ensued, which soon went off;
it returned and about an hour
after I took the medicine,
vomiting was produced. I vomited
three times; the intervals were short,
with less straining and disagreeable sensations
than I ever experienced from taking
tartar emetic or ipecacuanha.
I felt somewhat drowsy afterwards."
A good result. Benjamin had evidently
worked out a new emetic better
than any other then-known formula.
On the basis of this work
as soon as he was graduated,
he was made a member
of the Philadelphia Medical Society.
Two months later he gave a speech.
His subject was the "perfections"
of "Simplicity and Equality . . .
Under their regulations everything prospers
and rises splendidly, yet unrestrained.
Moral and natural life, sciences,
civil constitutions . . ." He even spoke of
"infallible tests" on unexplored nature

242

that, once followed through,
would prove these two great qualities
"the brilliant spectacle" of a new people. Later:
"I am induced to make a few observations
on cancers . . . and . . . I shall take the liberty
of thinking for myself; and though the ideas
which I offer may appear strange,
they may, I think,
excite reflections which may lead us
to a more successful investigation
of this hidden and obscure
part of pathology.
    "Cancers
have certainly too often
been considered as incurable;
and this idea alone is enough
to render them so. I believe this idea
of cancers has arisen, not so much
from our want of proper remedies,
as our ignorance of
the real nature of the disorder."

Meantime he had gone home
to undertake a medical practice, but,
more than that, he had in mind making
some of his "infallible tests"
to explore the "as yet but little known . . .
native plants." To do this,
he bought a small landholding
in Hereford Township (having as neighbors
John Bechtel and Jacob Latshaw),
and started a "balsam farm," balsam
the producer of oleoresin,
expectorant and tonic. At once trouble:
The boys he hired to plant it got fighting
and trampled down almost everything.
It was a hint of the way things were to go.
There were more hints. He used dogs
again to experiment on,
but at a critical stage
in one of his series of treatments,
a dog slipped into a tub of soft soap

243

and drowned. His general practice fell off
since he was giving his time to "science." Worse,
he bought expensive equipment.
He set up a still house
and three distilleries: alcohol
is the base of many medicines.
He began to borrow money. He borrowed
in all from seventy "creditors"
and found himself in
"a very critical situation,"
as he wrote to a friend. He was afraid
"they would rush upon me
and crush me all to pieces."
He believed his outlook, in spite of all,
was "very flattering"—he had skills,
insights, transcendent starts of knowledge
that seemed only a moment from success—
another experiment, another test,
and those glories as yet cloudlike
would materialize, would make him
(as he hoped) an American Linnaeus. Then
the dream collapsed. His more demanding creditors
went to court and the court
ordered his land and research projects
sold at forced sale. In eighteen six,
his bankruptcy revealed he owed in all
2519 pounds, or better
than ten thousand dollars.
He was jailed. How long is not known.

When he came out,
he was housed probably
by his brother Adam, but,
feeling dishonored,
unable now to face his neighbors
of Hereford Township,
he wrote to a Mr. Pearson,
a Philadelphia harness maker:
"Sir,
        "You will furnish the bearer with a compleat
Saddle at about $14.00,
including a pair of Saddle baggs in good order

at about $3 or $3.50. Whatever
you have not in your possession
you will procure for me and dispatch
the bearer as quick as you can . .
By so doing you will greatly oblige
your humble Servant . . .
                    "Benjm. Shultz"
Shortly after he received the saddle and bags,
he put them on his horse and, taking
no more than he could conveniently carry with him,
he rode away.
A gap of years. Little was known
except that he settled near Middleburg
in what is now Snyder County As
he had to live, it seems likely
that he practiced medicine again.
This is known. In eighteen fourteen
one day in early March, the weather
still wintry, he broke his leg,
it may have been in a fall from his horse. He decided
he needed an amputation.
With no other doctor to do it,
he called in a veterinarian and step by step
told this man what to do,
cut the bone, tie the arteries.
The operation failed. Infection set in
March fifth, in his forty-second year,
he died.

WHAT HEIMBACHER REMEMBERS
OF THE INDIANS

"I never saw them,
but when I was a child, when it was cold,
they would sleep in our kitchen lean-to—
my father let them—
and in the morning,
the ground would be warm where they had been."

COAL, A STORY
(Isaac Stahl)

"Now you go up past Hosensack station,
up the hill past the station there,
and you'll find holes, you'll find where they dug now.
My great-great-grandfather, his name was Johannes,
he was a blacksmith, he had his shop near there,
and one day he was fitting on a wheel rim,
he was heating it by the charcoal, like they did,
and could not get it hot enough.
Some Indians was sitting around watching.
They said, 'Give us a bake basket
and we'll get you what will make it fit.'
He give them the basket, one like you bake bread in,
and they went off to this hill
just past where the station is now,
and pretty soon they come back with some black stuff.
Now this Johannes put that over the charcoal
and he make a real hot fire with it.
He got the rim fitted on.
Then other people they went to that hill
and dug around, looking for more black stuff,
but they couldn't find no more.
Later they find the Indians traded it

246

from some other Indians further west.
Well now of course that was coal,
but that was before coal was known here—
that was when we used only charcoal."

WITHOUT SOLDIERS

In the late seventeenth century, George Fox
sent missionaries to America
"to go and discourse
with some of the heathen kings"
and he even came over himself
in 1672
and preached to them
"God's everlasting truth."
When William Penn was organizing his "country,"
he wrote to the Indians:
". . . God hath been pleased to make me
concerned in your parts of the world;
and the King of the country where I live
hath given me a great province therein:
but I desire to enjoy it
with your love and consent,
that we may always live together
as neighbors and friends; else
what would the great God say to us,
who hath made us
not to devour and destroy one another,
but live soberly and kindly together in the world?"
And in fact
Quakers and plain-sect Germans at first
dealt fairly with the Indians
and the Indians showed them "how to live."
When William Penn himself came
in sixteen eighty-two,
he entered Lenni-Lenape (Delaware) homes easily,
eating food as they served it and liking it,
and running races with the young men. He made

247

his famous "Great Treaty" with the Indians,
which was, Voltaire wrote, "the only treaty
between those nations and the Christians
that was never sworn to and never broken."
Penn wrote to London
about the Indian "Kings":
"It is admirable to consider
how powerful the Kings are,
and yet how they move by the breath
of their people." The Lenni-Lenape
went almost bare in summer,
greased against insects, shining in the sunlight,
heads shaved except for a black tuft.
Penn wrote:
"Their language is lofty, yet narrow;
but, like the Hebrew, in signification, full;
like shorthand, in writing, one word
serveth in the place of three,
and the rest are supplied
by the understanding of the hearer. . . .
I have made it my business to understand it,
that I might not want an interpreter,
on any occasion: and I must say,
that I know not a language spoken in Europe,
that hath words of more sweetness,
or greatness in accent and emphasis,
than theirs." He found
Indians were slow negotiators.
They all wanted to think together, they wanted
the agreement of the tribes. He understood
and allowed them to make up their own minds—
with them as with others
he was natural, willing to defer, and fond.
When he left for England
in sixteen eighty-four, he said,
". . . not one soldier, or arms borne,
or militia man seen,
since I was first in Pennsylvania."

DES IROQUOIS AUX GALERES

Louis XIV wrote a letter
in 1684, four years
before his various letters and directives
to Louvois in the Palatinate
about the devastation there.
This earlier letter
was to the Governor of Canada:
"As it would be of great value to me
to reduce as much as possible
the number of Iroquois, and as moreover
these barbarians, who are strong and healthy,
could serve very usefully in the galleys,
I desire that you do all possible to take
the greatest number of prisoners of war
and that you have them shipped to France."

BEHOLD BELOVED

Not only Count Zinzendorf
proselytized the Pennsylvania Indians:
the Reverend George Michael Weiss, a "Reformed pastor,"
suggested to the classis of Amsterdam
that churches be established
to "win the affections" of the Indians.
In seventeen thirty
the Reverend John Philip Boehm
wrote a letter saying that, at Oley,
Weiss "celebrated the Lord's Supper
without previous preparation"
and "baptized at the same time
a number of children, among whom
(as is reported) were also Indian children
who, as unbelievers,
go about like wild animals,
without a knowledge of God or His word."

The Reverend Weiss persisted
and in seventeen forty-two
painted a picture of the "wild men" and sent it
to Europe, pleading for them.
He also wrote a long account of them.
He said they were "very interesting."
He said he had talked with them
and had baptized many of them
"at their request."
He expressed surprise
that "no sufficient urgency" was felt
"for the conversion of these savages."
The classis next year wrote back
encouraging him
"to bring over that waste of wild heathendom."
But some said
the Reverend Weiss's baptisms
were "unscriptural actions."
In anger against "the principle of conversion,"
Boehm wrote, "Behold beloved . . .
where did our Lord command this?" As usual,
it was impossible to find in Scripture
what one did not want to find.
Indians "are imbued with blood
knuckle deep." They tear and devour
"even as the bear or other wild beasts do."
They are "wrapped up in the fog and misery
of their iniquity." One could obviously
do nothing for them and in that case,
many implied it was best,
since they were in the way, to kill them.

CHIEF PAPANAHOAL

In the middle seventeen hundreds, Noah Pattison,
happening to meet Chief Papanahoal
going from Philadelphia back
to the Indian village of Wekelusing
near Bethlehem, rode along with him.

So much "satisfaction" did he have
from certain conversation with this chief
that he decided to write it down.
He wrote that Papanahoal was "quiet and easy,"
yet had a becoming "Solidity and Gravity."
"Being ask'd what he thought of War,"
the Indian answered, "It has been told to my Heart,
that Man was not made for that End"
and so "I have ceased from War."
When talk turned to religion,
Papanahoal mentioned that believers
in one faith contended with those of another:
"These things should not be," he said,
"but whilst one is speaking,
the other should hold down his head
till the first has done, and then speak
without being in a Heat or angry."
He said that he thought he himself
could have "the flesh whipped off me with horse whips"
and "endure it without beeing angry"
after he had been shown God's goodness.

There is also a letter
the Indian Agent to Shamokin
wrote October 16, 1760:
"The old man," so Papanahoal
is called by this agent in his letter,
"thoght it was unlawful to warr" and
"when they argued very strongly
for a defensive war," saying
"if a man was to come and kill
when it was in their power to prevent it,
they should be accountable for their own deaths,"
the chieftain said to these casuists,
"the White People had a book
which God had order'd to be wrote for them
wherein they were inform'd that God
had made the world and that he had sent
his son Jesus Christ into the world"
to "shew" them how they should live,
"to which they answered that it was true:
well then said he why did not
Jesus Christ fight when the People

251

took him to kill him. To this
I do not understand they made him"
the agent wrote, "any satisfactory answer.
Then he (that is Papanahoal)
told them he believ'd the White People
were wery Wicked as they had
so great an Advantage of that Book
and lived so contrary to it."

FROM A LETTER FROM A MENNONITE MEDICAL VOLUNTEER IN BIAFRA AFTER THE BOMBING OF OZU ABAM

28 February 1969

"The lorry was indeed full—
full of shattered victims and full of blood.
One man with half of his face blown off
was lifted onto a litter,
breathing air and blood
through his open face. He died
about an hour later despite
attempts to restore the airway . . .
Others walked if they could,
clutching exploded hands and arms,
breasts and sides. Some lay gasping and white,
already in irreversible shock
and soon to die. . . . So much wasted blood.
And loss of life. They aren't to blame,
but every time I sawed through bone,
I experienced a feeling of contempt
for bomber pilots. When I saw
a bucket full of amputated limbs
and smelled the stench of decay
that sets in quickly in the tropical heat
I despised the chiefs of staff
who sit at their desks plotting war.
When a little girl greeted me
half fearfully, yet trustingly,

I could hardly see for a half minute.
She calmly took the fluothane mask
and went to sleep for the operation
on her mangled leg . . . in the aftermath
we stopped long enough to realize
that wasteful bombings such as this one
have occurred thousands of times before
in a thousand places. But we hope and pray
that they will not happen
as many times again."

Linford Gehman, M.D.

UNCIVILIZED AND KNOWING NO BETTER

William Penn wrote, about the Indians'
habit with possessions:
"Pay or Presents I made them,
were not hoarded by the particular Owners,
but the neighboring Kings and their Clans
being present when the Goods were brought out,
the Parties chiefly concerned consulted,
what and to whom they should give them?
To every King then . . . is a proportion sent. . . .
Then that King subdivideth it in like manner
among his dependents, they hardly
leaving themselves an Equal share
with one of their Subjects. They care for little,
because they want but little;
and the Reason is, a little contents them:
In this they are sufficiently revenged on us;
if they are ignorant of our Pleasures,
they are also free from our Pains.
They are not disquieted with Bills of Lading and Exchange,
nor perplexed with Chancery-Suits and Exchequer Reckonings.
We sweat and toil to live; their pleasure feeds them . . .
their Seats and Table are the Ground."

BLUE MEMORY

Suppose in this meadow
back from the Unami, in this large, rough, larch-shadowed space
where cows' horns dig holes in heal-all, mud, and nettle,
suppose here
the original Delawares reappeared
and planted
two nine-foot poles, fastened a crossbar, and on it hung
    gourds hollowed out
for purple martins, nests of noise companionable to the
    nearby tents.
The gourds would be tied
with threads of larch root torn from the creek ooze—pull-and-
    reel, pull-in-the-rain, pull-and-peel.
No Delaware knew that those blue immigrants skimmed
from Brazil
to these nests under a hill,
but the moment
for attaching the crossbar and gourds was timed
exactly to their coming in. Once homed,
they swept the air clean, flying faster than dragonflies,
    hunters' bolts.
The young birds' throats
called incessantly to be fed—run-and-catch, run-in-the-sun,
    run-and-snatch—
an aerial wampum of blue hawk heads threaded by the wind.
Under the communal dazzle of those wings
the Indian wars began. White settlers
reminded the Delawares of the treaty
that the settlers could buy from them "as much land
as a man could walk around in a day." In the "Walking
    Purchase,"
three white men ran:
"No sit down to smoke, no shoot squirrel, just lun, lun, lun
    all day long."
Brother Onas changed. Penn's sons changed. No matter that
    the Iroquois had told the Delawares:
"We made Women of you."
The no-longer-women broke the peace.

As fighting started,
Conrad Weiser talked to his Indian friends
with the inveterate hope of his concern for them.
"To fly with my family I can't do. I must stay if they all
    go."
He stayed. The martins
still hunted with their blue strokes, skeins
of harsh song, *zhupe, zhupe,*
but their gourds were gone.

DEVIL

Schwenkfelder David Shultze of Upper Hanover,
whose farm bordered what is now East Greenville's Main Street,
wrote in his diary
January 1, 1756:
"An unhappy action at Gnaddenhutten."
He had heard that the Indians had massacred soldiers at
    Gnaddenhutten, now a fort.
A few months earlier they had burned the "huts" to the ground,
killing unarmed Moravians and converted Indians.
"God knows what will become of the Province,
if no Stopp can be put to the incursions
of these cruel Monsters."
Some settlers, he wrote,
"are or pretend to be principled"
against killing. To encourage killing,
a "Reward" was posted
"for common Scalps . . ." (that is, not of chieftains)
"but however but few can be got,
since they carry off their dead
as fast as they can when they happen
to lose some."

August 4. "Finished mowing oats at noon."
4–6: "Bound oats—
nearly 1500 sheaves."
Twice that year—
it was an interest of his—

255

he made lists of words
learned from the Indians:
"Issimus—Bruder—brother."
"Netap—Freund—friend."
"Wicwam—das Haus—house."
"Eilhanilhab—seyd gegruesst—a greeting."
"Noha Matappi—setzt euch zu uns—sit down with us."
"Gecho ki wenkimem—was belibt euch—what would you like?"
"Poon—Brodt—bread."
"Menitto" he translated "der Teufel—the devil."

A man of many parts,
master of four languages, including Latin,
he was thoughtful, kind, given
to transcribing hymns.

October 17 of that year,
1756: "My mother died.
Death is the king of fear."

FRIENDLY ASSOCIATION

The Quakers still believed in nonviolence
even after Gnaddenhutten and a number
of other border killings (Adam Trump's wife
at Allemangel "escaped, though upon her flying,
she was so closely pursued
by one of the Indians, of which there were seven,
that he threw his tomahawk at her,
and cut her badly in the neck").
Some Philadelphia Quakers formed
"The Friendly Association for Regaining and Preserving
Peace with the Indians by Pacific Measures"
and were given money by many Schwenkfelders
for their fund.
David Shultze contributed several pounds.
His cousin Christopher wrote,
"The Quakers as well as we and others
who have scruples of conscience

256

against taking up arms against an enemy
. . . felt that the Indian war arose
on account of the unjust treatment of the Indians"
and said it would take
"heavy labors and expense"
to "restore peace with the Indians."
At first
the Lieutenant Governor and "Commander in chief"
of the province, William Denny,
was "rather stiff" in his "opposition"
and said he would not "on any Pretence . . .
suffer Presents from such persons to be given
to the Indians," and the Quakers were furthermore
to stay out of treaty making They did not.
They persisted. They gave presents
that were a kind of loving indemnity
and sent a sizable group of "Friends" to Easton
to the seventeen fifty-seven treaty conference
to try to procure
"an honest hearing of grievances."
At the conference
Teedyuscung demanded to see the deeds
that "fraudulently" gave land to the English,
and after much talking and delay,
"the Council" showed him the deeds
and agreed to "make satisfaction."
"The peace belt was then grasped
by Teedyuscung and the Governor,"
and at length there was a real peace,
or so it seemed. David Shultze
wrote in his diary
July 28, 1757:
"Rode to Easton to the Indian Treaty,"
and August 3: "Rode to Easton a second time,"
this time to take part
in the celebration of the treaty.
It was the usual bonfires and drinking, carousing.
He was satisfied to watch
and go home.

SOMEWHAT LATER

The whites, "inflamed" (Dr. Preston A. Barba's
word in his history of Emmaus),
threatened in the mid-sixties
to kill all Indians. "Moravian Indians"
were "removed" to Philadelphia
to save them, and in seventeen sixty-five
the government removed them again
to Wyalusing and then to Ohio.
That ended the Moravian mission on the Lehigh.
By about seventeen seventy-two
all were gone. Heimbacher
heard a friend once say,
"The Pennsylvania Indians were wiped out."
"They weren't wiped out, they were shoved out,"
Heimbacher corrected him.

NAMING

This naming—
the natives called by whites "Indians"
after a wrong continent,
and Lenni-Lenape, "Delawares"
after an English lord.

ERNST FUHRMANN

In the nineteen forties
when he was still alive in exile,
the German scholar, Ernst Fuhrmann,
said to Fred Braun
about the Pennsylvania Germans:
"In terms of world history

they're inconsequential.
What past do they have?
What about the evil in their lives?"
It was his character
to try to provoke people, anger them
to make them think.
During the Holocaust,
the time of the Hitlerite ovens, he had said,
"To be Jewish is a mental matter,
not one of race, so
I am a Jew."
Mennonites and Amish
name their children Israel,
Abraham, Sarah, Ruth, and Naomi.

THE EXTERMINATORS

From an account of what happened
in the Sobibor death camp,
a little-known camp in Poland,
in September 1943:
" '. . . they are taken to a second yard
where everyone, without exception,
must gather. There they are told
to lay down their bundles and undress
before going to the "bath." The women's hair is cut off.
Everything is done quietly and efficiently. . . .
Two buildings are standing there,
one for women and children, the other for men. . . .
At a first glance
everything looks as a bath should look—
faucets for hot and cold water, basins to wash in. . . .' "

From early colonial times
it was believed by many
that the Indians were really Hebrews,
descendants of the Ten Lost Tribes:
So William Penn described their language
as like Hebrew. It was his thought

that this origin enhanced them, placing them
close to the Biblic patriarchs, for he loved them.
Other colonists had other opinions
of the Jews. In Loskiel's
"history of the Indian Missions"
published in seventeen ninety-four:
"The humane behavior of the Governor at Pittsburgh"
in releasing some "believing Indians"
in the spring of seventeen eighty-two
"greatly incensed those people, who,
(according to the account given
in the former part of this history),
represented the Indians as Canaanites, who ought to be
destroyed from the face of the earth without mercy,
and considered America as the land of promise
given to the Christians. Hearing that different
companies of believing Indians
came occasionally from Sandusky
to the settlements on the Muskingum" in Ohio,
"to fetch provisions, a party" of Americans
"about one hundred and sixty in number,
determined first to surprise those Indians,
and destroy the settlements,
and then to march to Sandusky,
where they might easily cut off
the whole Indian congregation."
These Indians were a large number
who had been converted by missionaries,
David Zeisberger and John Heckewelder mainly.
Living in peace, helped by the missionaries,
they had built up three settlements
with "flourishing fields and well cultivated gardens,"
Schonbrunn, Gnadenhutten, and Salem,
but fellow Indians had come in force
and moved them a hundred miles west
"to their own country." From there, hungry,
the believing Indians sent detachments back
for provisions. So the plan to kill them.
A Colonel Gibson in Pittsburgh,
hearing of the plan, sent messengers
"to our Indians on the Muskingum"

to warn them. The warning was received,
"But our Indians, who at other times
behaved with great caution and timidity,
if only the least appearance of danger
existed, showed no signs of fear, but went
to meet real danger with incredible confidence."
Now the Americans arrived. They marched first
to Gnadenhutten (in Ohio,
named for the famed Gnadenhutten
of earlier days near Bethlehem).
"About a mile from the settlement,
they met young Shebosch"—he was the son
of one of the Moravian missionaries
who had married an Indian woman.
They "fired at him, and wounded him so much
that he could not escape."
He begged for his life, explaining
that "he was Shebosch,
the son of a white Christian man.
But they paid no attention to his entreaties,
and cut him to pieces with their hatchets.
They then approached the Indians,
most of whom were in their plantations,
and surrounded them almost imperceptibly;
but feigning a friendly behavior,
told them to go home, promising to do them
no injury. They even pretended to pity them
on account of the mischief done to them
by the English and the savages;
assuring them of the protection
and friendship of the Americans
The poor believing Indians,
knowing nothing of the death of young Shebosch,
believed every word they said, went home with them,
and treated them in the most hospitable manner."
They were now told
"they should not return to Sandusky,
but go to Pittsburgh;
where they would be out of the way of any assault
made by the English or the savages."
They thought this was God's "method" of helping them.

"Prepossessed with this idea,
they cheerfully delivered their guns, hatchets,
and other weapons to the murderers;
who promised to take care of them
and in Pittsburgh to return every article to its rightful owner. Our Indians
even showed them all those things
which they had secreted in the woods,
assisted in packing them up,
and emptied all their bee-hives
for these pretended friends.
In the meantime" a messenger went to Salem
and told the Indians there of this good fortune,
that "God had sent the Americans" to save them,
and some Americans then came
and "pretended the same good will and affection
towards the Indians as at Gnadenhutten;
and easily persuaded them
to return with them. By the way
they entered into much spiritual conversation
with our Indians; some of whom
spoke English well." In the midst of this
"the defenceless Indians at Gnadenhutten
were suddenly attacked and driven together"
and were "without resistance seized and bound.
The Salem Indians now met the same fate."
They were brought bound into Gnadenhutten.
The Americans then "held a council,
and resolved by a majority of votes,
to murder them all the very next day."
As part of this democratic action,
"Some were for burning them alive,
others for taking their scalps;
and the latter was at last agreed upon."
The Indians were told
"they might prepare themselves in a christian manner,
for they must all die tomorrow."
They were "patiently" led into two houses,
"in one of which the Brethren, and in the other
the Sisters and children, were confined
like sheep ready for slaughter."

There they "recollected themselves"
and thought of their promise
"to the Lord Jesus Christ,
that they would live unto him,
and endeavor to please him alone in this world,"
and they were glad to have time
"to pour out their hearts before him in prayer."
In the morning some of the Americans
"went to the Indian brethren,
and showed great impatience
that the execution had not yet begun;
to which the brethren replied
that they were all ready to die."
The men and separately the women and children were now led
bound two and two together
"into the above mentioned slaughter-houses."
What happened now is reported
in a "Narrative" of John Heckewelder:
"One of the party took up a cooper's mallet,
which lay in the house, saying,
'how exactly this will answer for the business!'
He then began with Abraham;"
the name of one of the Indians, a "Hebrew" name,
"and continued knocking down one after the other
until he had counted fourteen
whom he had killed with his own hands.
He now handed the instrument
to one of his fellow-murderers;
saying, 'My arm fails me: go on in the same way:
I think I have done pretty well.' "
Ninety-six persons were killed.
"Sixty-two were grown persons, among whom
were five of the most valuable assistants;
and thirty-four children." Blood
ran in streams into the cellars. The Americans
scalped all they had killed, including children,
and distributed the corpses among the buildings
of Gnaddenhutten and by burning the buildings
disposed of the corpses. They also burned
Schonbrunn and Salem to the ground,

leaving nothing but ashes. Then,
carrying with them the guns and provisions
given them by the Indians,
which they divided among themselves,
they returned in triumph to their homes.

Many wondered, after that,
at the further failure of missions.
It must be something, they decided,
in the nature of "the savages."

PART THREE

LEGEND FOR NOW

Along a single thread
in a single shadow
three dark missiles
cross the Crow Hill sky.

Crossing the Crow Hill sky,
three tubular swifts
flick their sickle wings
in a single shadow.

In a single shadow,
in a dark portent,
tubular and terrible,
three swifts cross the sky.

THE CROW HILL MOON

Moon, mole with shining fur
burrowing in the clouds,
digging how many tunnels
at the same time,
one for each watcher. And Crow Hill
waiting now
for the mole's quick run
into the open
Houses and outbuildings,
Kemps' long lawn,
Giagnocavo's lane
snared in dimness,
the colors gone,
gloom
thickening the poplars.
Gehmans' cedars
lying flat,
Uhr's Little Sweden

throwing no shadow.
Millers' woods
a pool without reflection
until
the mole runs free,
and the hill and all its watchers come back
from the underside of darkness.

THE BALLY BLOCK FACTORY

Through the night the saws whine
powerfully, teeth biting wood
in a dust-scooping vacuum
and, whine
or not, the town

sleeps. The moan
crosses
the darkness
out over the valley flats
to Crow Hill homes.

In the evening of a day
of the summer's last heat,
Ed Kulp, manager,
makes his way
back through the factory.

A workman at a bench
beckons him and shows him,
in a planed maple board,
a burnished ring,
a sheared

slice
out of an embedded metal tap:
signet of sap drip where
a tree bled sugar
on some northern hill.

268

"Dig it out,"
Kulp says,
and the workman digs out
and drops
in Kulp's hand the cross section of tap's

curl. Kulp
thinks of his salesman days
when he traveled north
to Canada
to St. Ignace where his sales,

calling for lumber,
opened woods to the sky·
butcher blocks, blocks backing dies
of shoes,
"dinkers" and "clickers," those

various hard cubes.
For years he sold them, then the call
to come home, to take his place
as manager in the noise,
in the center of the whine—

to walk among the men,
and in the office figure
the minimum gain from a thousand
remodeled trees—evenings
to enjoy Mamie and the children

and the garden of his own.
The plane's rip
starts again and accompanies him
as he strolls off with the fragment
of maple tap.

THE NIGHT LIFE OF THE FACTORIES

Twilight brings the frames of neon up,
the mercury flames.
In the small panes of the hosiery mill,
heads are violet. At the Butcher Block,
uneven windows light
hills of drying lumber. The Display Case factory
floods a nightlong lamp
past the Old Mennonites' graves,
and fields come complaining
that factories steal the men from the sun,
so men sleep the wheat away.

SHIFT END

At the Butcher Block, Nevin Yost
has made all ready
for the morning shift. Now
he starts his car
and under a full moon
turns left by the Bally Hotel
and right by Bechtels' store,
and so goes droning up toward home.
He passes houses
where Bally climbs Crow Hill:
Honey Miller's—he wonders
that this dollhouse
holds ten children;
Luther Koch's, a lift of tulip tree;
a further rise
and Isaac Stahl's with its tiled wall
rimmed with glass.
After a sharp slope,
at the spruce-bordered reservoir
the road bends,

270

the trip ends—
night transit,
town to country,
factory to bed.

THE LIFE OF ISAAC STAHL, THE POTTER

Not far from the Perkiomen, on Hosensack Creek,
the kiln's fire has been going
twenty-five hours and is nearing
its end. Under the full May moon
the smoke meanders against the pines.
Occasional flags of smoke
droop over the boards of the platform
that goes around the top
of the great globe of brickkiln bound
with a strap of iron. Beneath the high platform,
four electric bulbs light four firers
who run with fuel to four openings
at the base of the kiln. There,
what began low as "soaking fire"
they whip now with final thin-split wood,
and—like the hellfire of old plays
lavender-red tongues of flame shoot up
through the center of the kiln,
gathered around a white-hot hub
that indicates the end of the burning.

Isaac Stahl walks on the platform,
quickly crossing paths among the vents,
sorcerer of this globe
where three thousand single objects,
the work of the wheel, lie in the heat.
He is son of a potter,
son of a potter, and so on back.
At six his father built him a small wheel
and as he "kicked" it, his unformed hand
felt the pull of the clay.
In his father's pottery

he worked with his father and two brothers.
If there had been only them,
he would have been "perhaps average," but—
"When I was nine or ten,
there come an Irish potter to work.
This potter's name was George Sorch.
Though Irish, he worked in the German style.
He was good, yes, and was fast.
I'll tell you how fast he was!
Potters then had to do
a hundred eight gallons a day, that is, pots to hold that many gallons.
George finished often at two o'clock,
then he could stop, his day was finished.
That made the other potters mad,
but my father told Sorch, 'You can stop.'
One day Sorch said to me,
'Come, sonny, I'll show you something
none of these Germans can make,'
and he showed me how to make a ring vase,
a vase with a hollow ring and three spouts
such as they have in Ireland
and set on the eaves of the houses there.
That was a hard thing now to make.
I practiced the ring vase on my wheel,
I practiced till I learned to make it good. Yes,
the first vase I ever made
I have yet in my attic."

Childhood was not all work: he assembled
from his father's pots of many sizes
a glockenspiel of two full octaves
and played on it with slender sticks.
One day, challenged by a Prussian potter
to "*spiel der Laudenbach*,"
he summoned the old waltz out of the bells,
and, charmed by the music, the immigrant potter
skipped in the clay dust.

The pile of red clay used and renewed
carried Isaac from child to a man
whose longer leg and heavier foot
kicked the wheel to his shaping fingers.

272

He worked now with his grown brothers,
making plates and bowls, pots and saucers
for "a few cents each."
Besides the traditional patterns,
he would draw on the clay
occasional designs of his own;
a small schoolhouse with a flag,
a train traveling across a plate bottom, the stack
followed by a furl of smoke,
designs worked out in a kind of play
So the pleasant work went on
into the new century
until one day,
against the brothers' will,
machine-made ware closed the pottery.

The brothers found other livelihood,
all in factories,
Isaac in Boyertown as cutter
in the coffin factory—day labor.
He who had dug clay, rounded it,
and burned glazes on it, who had been
master of a total process,
now did one repetitive act.
So it went for thirty years until
one afternoon
he happened to attend a household auction.
Among the items put up for sale
were some full-sized marriage plates
with tulips back to back,
sign of woman's and man's affection,
made by himself and "sold for seven cents"
thirty years before. They brought now
seven dollars for the one plate.
He thought,
But I can still make those plates,
and other pottery even better.
He talked with his brothers about it.
Tired of factory work,
they who had the art of the wheel—
the circle under their skillful fingers
lifting the wet clay—

agreed with him. They built a kiln
by a barn in Powder Valley
where they could put their wheels. Kicking the wheels,
the returning sorcerers
faced the iron-strapped globe of brick,
and the perspective of two hundred, two thousand years,
as if preserved through a small opening,
let down its light again
on snake-bending necks of peacocks
and on doubled doves, birds of Persia,
mated like the tulips on marriage plates,
plates dotted with rain,
bean pots bordered with brown,
aquamarine fluted saucers,
pitchers laid in the gray of the sea,
vases ochered with hill lime.

As the heavy May moon climbs upward,
the hub of flame at the center vent
clears to pure white.
All char is burned away.

RALPH BERKY
AND THE CONCEALED WORLD

"Here's a cross section
of western hemlock, Ralph.
Take a look at this,
if you please."
Harvey Oberholtzer

under the dining room center light
adjusts the microscope for Ralph. "There."
Glowing in the round depths,
itself round,
the wood, so hard and plain before,

274

loses substantiality
and becomes a mere honeycomb
where rows of cells in ordered clouds
drift,
and through their drift

sap pores burst in large holes,
empty, the size of eggs.
Resin ducts, aerially clogged,
deepen the tan
as even as a winter field.

"To get the surface smooth like that,
I froze the wood, then cut it
with a chisel."
He
is one of three

on the wood-purchasing commission
of the casket factory in Boyertown.
Yes,
he
can buy a tree

for the wooden clothing of the dead.
"Here is one of two American elms
from Josephus Gerhard's place."
Under the eye of the lens
he puts a disk

that has a lighter hue.
"They were good.
They were immense trees,
those elms,
and we used the poplars by his porch,

the ones with the limbs raised up close
that he called French poplars."
"Lombardy," Ralph says.
The solid tree
under his eye

dissolves and shines.
"Now look," Oberholtzer says.
"Here is a frost ring I took,
a chisel cut
from a white oak tree we bought

at the new Mennonite Church,
the Reverend Johnson's church in Bally.
It was the thirty-first ring in."
The eye
follows the wood gradually

from light to dark where a line
of early cold on an autumn night
thickened itself around the tree trunk,
frost
staining into the tree like rust.

"You would not know
that that mark would stay so,"
and the tree hold the year
permanently
in its own kind of memory.

"You keep samples
from all the trees," Ralph says.
"Many I have, not all,
but I
have that hobby,

to keep a part of what is gone."
From his pocket Ralph takes
something that is little more than a glint:
"Could we see where a tree comes from?"
It is a filament

a half inch long,
ending in the dark of a pod,
the seed of a red pine tree
near Barto.
Oberholtzer lays it on a slide

276

and sets the mirror
at an angle
to flood light up through the small wing.
"Look," he says.
It is a beveling

of glassy white,
a milk blade of moonlight.
Threaded through it,
following its corrugations,
go a few lines of red

brighter than blood.
The seed that flies
out of the cone
to its own color,
the ground,

here has flames of sun,
enameled warnings of space,
intensities
released from
the universe's original fire.

The light of the room dims
as the eye sees
not seed,
not wingspread,
but inward

planes of birth,
the earth's core, rays
whose heat
here in sight
comes from the furnace of the galaxies.

MARY BELTINGER

The back road is the woods
I've gone to since running loose
in the grass. Gosling to goose,
I wound the hem of my skirt
out of the dew and dirt,

and waded close to the earth,
and wanted its smell—flowers
on my legs, skewers
of greenbrier and, above the brier,
all the leaves.

Now I'm grown. No running now, I'm worn.
Though young, I know my forehead
has the crease of work.
But work or not, the day
wild cherries break

their first cloud
out of the sticky bud,
I'm back in the wood,
in the fire
those petals make in my eyes and hair.

A LIFE OUT OF THE SHOOTS

"Mary," Alvin Albitz calls to his daughter
from his ground-floor room. But her name is Alma.
"I cared for Mother," she says.
"I resemble her, they tell me."
"Mary, help me to stand," and lifting up,
he looks through the front window
at what? The view when he rises from his chair
is two Bally street blocks
ending in the fields. Past North Church Street,

278

a thin line of chicory.
"I like to look out," he says, "stand and look out.
I like to see the fields.
I like to see them now
or just as much in winter.
How many times I walked them,
when the road was closed in the snow,
to Seisholtzville! It was awful deep.
Sometimes you went over a fence
and fell in and almost got stuck.
The winter before I was born,
eighteen seventy-five,
that was a long winter as I know.
My father, Henry, at that time worked
in the old Zionville ore mine
and also burned winter lime.
He burned it late, for I thought
I smelled lime the day I was born,
April twenty-eighth of that year."
He stretches his arms out through his shirt sleeves
and seats himself again. He says,
"My father and George Snyder
dug together in the ore,
paid so much rent for the separate place,
and got so much a ton, and so
Father raised a family. After me,
there were five more children:
Charlie, John, Clem, Robert, and Stella.
When I was about eight yet,
I was put to my uncle's to work.

"When I was twenty and at work,
living at 'Saniel' Bechtel's,
the first farm back of Clayton,
the best place I ever was—
Nathaniel's wife was blind,
she that was Susie Clemmer,
she peeled potatoes, she was the cleanest woman
you ever saw—well, that year
about midsummer I met Mary Grill
lived up on Kroppa Berg
there where Kate Mandel is now.

Mary was my first steady girl.
She was small and thin, nothing—
ninety-eight pounds. Coal-black hair.
But the prettiest girl around here.
It wasn't a long courtship.
We married October twenty-eighth.
She was strong and kept young.
At seventy-four she still had black hair,
most beautiful hair for her age—like they say,
you worked hard, you lasted.
After I married, I still went on
doing farm work and then cutting.
I never thought of mining, then.
John Chelius—I sawed for him at Forge Dale,
fifty acres of oaks and tulips.
At times I went the other side of Pottstown,
took the Colebrookdale Railroad there
and then went in horse and buggy.
I went to Alburtis
to cut for Henry Benfield.
None will ever see such trees again.
The pin oaks, full of fine needly branches,
you had to cut your way in to get them,
closed with such branches from the bottom up.
I cut poplars
that measured over five feet through—
a big chestnut above the Clayton Church
at the boundary of the John Diehl farm,
it took a plowline to span that one,
twenty-three feet around, that was.
While I was cutting, once
there was this tulip tree
three feet in diameter
the lightning hit and split,
also the tree was in a stone fence—
it split that and tore through the field.
It hit near me, but I was safe.
I always liked outdoor work.
Never minded rain.
Did cutting. Farm work.

"But after we had Lizzie, the third child,
the second oldest of the girls,
I needed more money.
In the mine it was eighty cents a day,
thirty cents more than other work,
and the pay was regular.
My father had done it, I could do it,
so I got a job
at Bittenbender's Mine at Seisholtzville.
They told me there, as they told all,
that it was ten hours a day,
starting three quarters of an hour
earlier than the standard time.
One week I was on days,
the following week, nights.
You had to work two months
before you got your first pay.

"The vein
was three hundred and seventy-five feet deep—
that's deep—
and went seven hundred sixty feet
this way and about as far,
seven hundred, on the right-hand side.
The lift took the men down. The rail truck
carried them to the breasts,
but some climbed the slope to the breasts
even if it was slower. None
too much liked the rail truck.
John Geary, John Nuss of Bechtelsville,
Oswin Heimbach, and Jim Wendling
were on the truck one day,
two sitting on the sheer, the crank part,
and the other two inside.
The rope got out of the sheer, broke,
and the truck went down through nine props
straight back down seventy-five feet
to the pump in the cellar.
The four men couldn't get off.
None was killed, but Wendling
was hurt so bad he asked that they should kill him.
Bones stuck out through his flesh,

281

but they carried him out so
and Dr. Rhoads fixed him up.
Yes, he returned to work again.
The water! Even with the pump,
ten minutes down and I was soaked.
Charlie Reese was at the breast
and one day his drill
went through the shaft.
When that happened, I bet that water
flew halfway
over into that field there
before it went down. We pulled out—
golly, we pulled out.
Always that danger of an accident.
Always I was careful,
but even I had an accident.
One day I had a hold of the truck,
I wasn't allowed to leave go,
and between the plank and the rail
I got stuck, I pulled my ankle joint.
The engineer drove me home in horse and buggy
and old Dr. Yeakle cut my boot off
and fixed the torn ligaments.
Then we had a windy rain
and it threw the chestnuts down, plenty,
and I put my bad foot in a felt boot
and went out to get the chestnuts
and got the foot wet. Ai ai ai,
shmardsa—hov ich net shmardsa kot,
how the pain was, oh yeah.
I drove a nail to the rafter
and hung my leg up in a rope
and so I lay till I got better.
It was over a month till I was up.
I got my pay, though, and kept going.

"I was a *drammer.*
I took the ore mine out of the shoots.
It was shot loose. I shoveled it up
onto my cart
and pushed it by hand to the shaft
six hundred and sixty feet from the breast,

and there I dumped my little truckful
into the big truck and sent it out.
Two loads filled up the big truck.
Yes, that ore then was carried
to a railroad siding
and taken to Alburtis
there where Percy Hertzog's father worked.
There it was melted down.
That went on for a time,
but the ore was not so good,
too much manganese in it
so it magnetized the iron.
The mine couldn't make enough money,
so at last it closed down.
All the mines around stopped down.
That was the end of it."

He says, "Mary. Alma?"
His daughter comes.
"Where is that crock I have?"
She brings him a pottery crock
that he holds in his hands
as if about to put it to his lips.
"Isaac Stahl made this crock.
It was such as many of us had
to bring our coffee down to the breast.
It kept the coffee warm.
It was good then at midnight
to have such a drink of warm coffee.

"Mining, I tell you now,
it was all right while it lasted,
yes,
but afterward we made do.
We did, Mary, didn't we?"

ABOUT LIME
(Alvin Albitz speaking)

"Yes, my father burned lime, and two winters
I had to burn it too to keep going,
two ovens at David Clemmer's quarry.
They took a week to fill,
first a cartful of wood, thrown in,
then hard coal,
then a hundred bushels of lime,
the natural stone as quarried.
Every day you added
five or six rings on top
and so many shovelfuls of coal
until you got the kiln filled. Then
you pushed in rails at the bottom
and lit them. When the flame
had burned through up to the top,
it was ready to take out. It was sold
a dollar twenty-five for a hundred bushels.
The farmers put it on the fields in heaps
and poured water on it and as it powdered,
they scattered it. Yes,
it was also used to whitewash;
they sanitized the old houses with it
when there was diphtheria.
It was a clean thing
and it made the ground sweet and green.
All the farmers I knew used it."

HOW THEY WERE IN THOSE DAYS

Alvin Albitz looks down.
"My knee still bothers me."
Rubbing it: "Yes, what happened—
once when I was on my way to the mine,
I jumped over a fence

and this knee went apart for me.
I couldn't walk with it
so I put it over the rail
and with my linked hands I hammered it
and the knee jumped back. I went on.
No, I didn't miss the day."

THE MINES

"In these hills
there's almost every metal you could name.
Rich yet." Even within memory,
every rock promised a fortune. Quartz
offered silver and gold. Hematite
glittered with pyrites and garnets.
But iron was the madness, the money metal
hunted by compasses,
divining rods whose deflections
opened mines at Forge Dale,
Colebrookdale, Seisholtzville,
even on Crow Hill. Above Frank Eline's
a crevice still pushes toward the blackjack.
Larger holes went down,
fending off rain as the sump pumps worked,
and wealth poured up where ponds are now.
"Closed now but rich" is still the word.
Some mines had lifts. At others
a minehead winch would turn
through sun and rain,
winding the pit buckets up.
Some remember those buckets
swaying up, carrying ore and men.

Mines of treasure,
mines of doom,
miners' hope
over soon,
and all the money brought home.

At Codorus Creek,
yellow tons of sulfur and saltpeter
were burned with brushwood, fired
as Revolutionary powder.
"Ohne Schweffel und Saltzpeter
gift's keine Freiheit."
"Without sulfur and saltpeter
there's no freedom."
Down, *"Kaiser König,"* down—
the Eisenmeisters in these hills
forged cannon and the cannon balls
to beat the Kaiser's bully boys.

Mines of treasure,
mines of doom,
miner's hope
over soon,
and all the money brought home.

This is remembered in the area:
Two were mining a shaft, near Farmington,
and quarreled. One swung a pickax on the other.
The other managed to get home
and was told "not to bathe the blood off,
but to go so to the sheriff."
Remembered yet,
the one who went with his blood.

Mines of treasure,
mines of doom,
miner's hope
over soon,
and all the money brought home.

In Washington Township, iron mines
carried the names of local families:
Stauffer, Eline, Spaar, and Gilbert.
All these mines had "primitive ore."
They still have it. At the Ehst Cave
on Crow Hill, visitors can walk

through a vertical cleft of stone
and stand where the miners once stood
at the ore shelf, wall of pastel rust, to some
a magnet yet, "rich yet."

THE "BELGIAN BLOCKS":
LIVES OF THE BLOCK CUTTERS

In Sumneytown, on his back porch
under a three-year trumpet vine,
those red horns pointed across the twilight,
Harvey Long says, "There,
that's hollies down there, all hollies.
You have to have two kinds,
male and female. I took three sets home,
hunted high and low
for burlap bags to bring soil for them,
the soil that they grew in
and also the gravel they like.
They must have that gravel to do well."
He is a big, heavy-set man.
He is one of the few still living
who worked on the "Belgian blocks"—
blocks for street paving—
drilled, cut four and eight block:
"Yes," looking toward the north,
"you can find some wedges of mine
in the rock yet." The blocks and blast powder
still sit sharp in his memory.
He was born in Green Lane
February eighteenth, eighteen seventy-eight,
and "after I was two, I went back
there to where Camp Delmont is now—
then when I was nine,
my parents moved here to this town.
In eighteen ninety-two
they built this house. See those spots
in the plaster there?
On Ascension Day that year

287

come a hail when it was freshly plastered,"
so the house carries this freakish wound.
He meditates on passing time:
"I have four boys, all getting to be old men.
I remember once when I was young,
not much more than a boy,
and I stood on the hotel porch there,
and there was Francis Emert
who ran the hotel in those days.
He looked at me and some other boys with me
and said, 'I guess you all wish
you were twenty-one. Can't wait.'
Yes, but then it begins to go faster
until at last
you can't believe how fast.
After you're fifty, one year
and you just turn around till the next one.
You asked about the stone:
They were big granite boulders, big as a house,
sitting on top of the ground.
They were no good for tombstones.
Too much iron in them and they got rusty.
Yes, you could polish them up,
but in a couple of years they rusted.
So they were cut for paving
the Philadelphia streets," paving blocks
that would take the beat of horses' shoes
indefinitely—as it proved,
longer than the horses lasted.
"You had to break them—the boulders—
to tell if they had seams or were good.
As a rule it ran along good.
There was a grain to them
and the cutters worked along the grain.
They used a wedge and half rounds,
or, if they had to, they blasted
with a black powder made nearby,
on Unami Creek.
From a single boulder
they'd cut twenty-five thousand blocks,
sometimes thirty thousand, sometimes more.
Since almost all the cost was labor,

money came to Sumneytown
with the cutters. They had to get many
from outside. Among others,
Negroes. These came up from the South.
In the South they could only drill;
here they were allowed to cut blocks,
and that they wanted to do.
The driller got a cent a block.
The cutter got two cents.
A real good cutter could cut
thirty blocks an hour. He worked ten hours
and cut three hundred a day.
Sometimes he worked only three or four days,
then he had made enough for a week.
Yes, a cutter's job was good,
but there was the bad weather too
and the winter when he couldn't work."
About the processes:
"If we opened a new stone, that was hard—
we had a drilling party for it,
then after it was opened,
it went easier. We used a peener,
so we called the chisel we used
to make a line across the stone."
A drill, new,
was fourteen to sixteen inches,
some square steel, some six cornered,
drawn out thinner at the bottom,
and "star drills," ones that had a star shape.
Yes, he has them all in his mind. He says,
"Out on the hills it's grown up now,
the old driveways grown over,
but many of us still remember.
Yes, just across the street here
is the Britisher, Joseph Worwood.
He can tell you much. Go to him."

The Britisher is ninety-one
and still erect. "I live a normal life.
Don't hurry.
Don't go too fast, that's the secret."
He was born in Old Furnace

near Ludlow in Shropshire, England,
and, one of a large family,
he learned a trade early—block cutting.
When work was scarce in England,
with Edwin Bytheway, also a cutter,
he sailed to America.
He was twenty-four when he got here,
in eighteen eighty-eight,
and he and Bytheway
worked what they called "the hobo trade"
through New England—Maine, New Hampshire,
Massachusetts—then, tired of the drift,
and hearing they could get steady work,
they came to Sumneytown.
"We got here on the eve of the first day
of eighteen eighty-nine. That day
a couple of boys had the idea
to make a New Year's blast, and stole
dynamite. They were playing cards
and it got heated and went off—
tore all their joints off,
their intestines in the trees.
When that blast sounded,
I was standing by those bushes there,
just to the right, and beside me
Mr. Miller, my boss. I remember
he shook his head, didn't say anything,
just walked off." Day after New Year's,
Worwood and Bytheway went to work.
Plenty of work,
for there were many boulders
and many streets in Philadelphia.
The drills drilled on into summer,
and that was an important summer.
One day Worwood, short
but straight and strong, walked down the street
with Emma Bowman, a "tall and slender"
Sumneytown girl. As they walked,
"the thought of agreeing" began between them.
They became engaged. Emma was the sister
of Jim Bowman who owned a flour mill
along the creek. She liked to wear white.

It is in a white, high-collared dress
she sits in the living room photograph
beside Joseph and their children,
Wallace, Alice, and Ernest.
They gave English names to these children
who spoke the *Deitsch* and whose English
had the local German accent.
Worwood, married,
settled into work seriously.
A fast cutter,
he nicked the blocks with small hammers
and with a big one knocked them apart.
A maul, "that you stood up to."
A reel, "that you sat down to."
The different hammers dressed the stone
and he averaged one in two minutes.
Sometimes he used powder
to "spring it," but watched it always
with unfailing caution.
He had determined to live.
Small wounds were nothing, unavoidable—
if dust seeped under the skin,
a blue mark remained like the miners had,
but none cared about that.
Being experienced,
he was made a teacher of newcomers.
He taught the arriving Negroes
"who lived twelve in a shack,
one on top of another—
some of them boarded with whites."
More and more he liked the place, the blocks
humping on wagons out of the valley,
the morning fog
reminding him of England. He prospered.
He saved enough to build his own house.
In winter when blocks could not be cut,
he cut blocks of ice from the ponds.
It seemed as if it would go right on—
the good pay, the good year's earnings—
but ten years after he came,
"cement knocked the blocks out."
He didn't want to move.

He had had enough of drift.
He found new tools
to keep on making his living.
He strolls now down his front walk.
At its end, at a drop to the road
are five stone steps, granite slabs
he cut himself. The chisel's bite
can still be seen along the sides.
He stands there on the topmost step.

On Water Street in the first house
from the hotel on the corner,
a Negro lives, Al White.
He was born (it is written
in the family Bible he still has)
May tenth, eighteen seventy-two,
in Virginia near Richmond.
He lived along the Six Mile Branch
where a brook ran through,
and he liked the sound of that brook.
"I walked three miles to school
and three miles back. No trouble.
I played along the road and ate berries."
He began to work early with stone,
for he was early full grown,
taller than he is now—that was tall—
his muscles hardening as he worked
along the James, in the granite. Hearing
he could do better in the North,
with the chance to be a cutter,
he came to Sumneytown.
"I come in eighty-eight in the blizzard,"
snow up to his chest,
and before the snow was gone,
he had learned to cut blocks.
"I made second class and first class.
Italian—he was the man inspected—he come along my place
and the boys said, 'Now you gonna see.
He gonna throw them all out.'
He jumped in my blocks,
and he throwed only two back.
We was laughing so

you could hear us here to the store."
Lifting his work-pants cuffs,
he shows the scarred front of his legs:
"All that blasting powder. We used say,
'Man coming round, take my name.'
Meant Death. That's true, ain't it?
But Death didn't take my name.
Naw, I had too much to do."
He used up "plenty of wedges,
plenty of half-rounds, plenty of chisels."
He became the friend of powder.
From his childhood loving God,
he looked around for a church.
The Old Mennonites attracted him.
He listened to Elias Kulp preach
and liked that man of the fields,
liked a preacher who worked for a living
as he did. When the Old Mennonites
built a church in Finland,
he helped. "I broke up stone for that church
to get it out of the way—
looked at the grain, then I knew
what way to hit it." His voice, a tenor,
was heard in the men's pews, singing
along with the Mennonite brethren.
He married a Pennsylvania-German girl,
Emma Hauck, and she,
being of a young and teasing nature,
"put her face in my face
even when I told her not to"
and kissed him in public. Some trouble there.
His fist was quick and "it seemed
I never could hit easy."
The difficulty, after that, stopped.
With the blocks money
he bought a house,
vines and yard like the German houses, not far
from where Unami Creek runs through.
He lives in the same house still.

ALL ONE

She held his head of close hard hair
that knotted in the wet,
and his lips against hers
were large but soft yet.
After she kissed him,
she could not keep her eyes
from casually or not casually
questioning his eyes.
She saw there dark. Past dark, light:
both in his gaze,
and she wondered which the white
and which the darkness was.
So the old tangle
of longing limb and limb
found her forgetting
which was her or which was him.

THE DREAM

Al White tells this story
about the time after "the blocks":
"James had the powder mill—
yes, that old Jim Miller
used to own everything around here.
So I was working in the powder mill
and then a dream come to me
the powder mill goin' blow up,
kill three, wound one,
and one go in the water.
And one morning not long after,
nobody expecting anything,
whole mill running hunkadunk hunkadunk,
one o'clock it blew up.
I was standing across on the head gate,
and when I saw the fire coming,

I jumped in the creek and swam to the mill.
When I come out, three were dead,
and one was afire—
Frank Schafer. I grabbed him up
and tore the burning clothes off him
and carried him to his father
who had charge of the engine,
so I put him down in the door.
Frank was the one that was wounded."

CHICKENS
(Joe Heimbacher)

"I'm against all this factory work with chickens.
Like Requa's, you've seen his—
thousands of them in those rows of cages,
dropping eggs down the incline
to this rack. So all you do is go by
and pick them up. And the chickens,
no room to move. There they just stand
or sit, looking miserable.
I let my chickens run. Late July
when wheat, oats, and barley are in,
I take them out to the fields. They glean,
they have a feast. You can't tell me
they don't give me better eggs."

HAWK MOUNTAIN

Harry Ecke, out early with his dogs
the fourth day of hunting,
a cold, raw, clearing day,
follows Swamp Creek and breaks through gaps
and so up into the lower hills,
but finds nothing. Two hawks plummet
out of some trees. Before he gets a shot,

295

they've slipped sideways out of sight. Predators.
Damn them, that's why there's no game.
That's why he walks with his bags empty.
And to think that at *Sparbenbarich,* Hawk Mountain,
he used to kill them fifty in a day!
To make that a bird sanctuary,
the best shooting he ever had!
He hasn't been there since it's changed over.
It's early in the fall yet to go.
Even so, there'll be hawks,
and is there more than just a signpost?
Are there guards?
It might be worth looking into.

After his noon meal, leaving his dog to home,
he takes the car and drives beyond Kutztown
toward the heavier hills. Out of Kempton
he takes a winding gravel road
past the "Pinnacle." On the further road
up to Hawk Mountain, partway up,
is a closed entrance and yes, there are guards. You might know.
They look at him. He wears hunting clothes
with the license's small printed block
on his back. They ask him why he came.
"Oh, to see the place."
"All right, leave your gun." He leaves his gun
and heads for the familiar "lookout" trail
and plods straight up it,
up the old wagon track where fine sand
from white sandstone—
beaches on some inland sea—
was carted down.
The road ends in it, its remnants thick
between sliding slabs. Climbing further,
he reaches the flat top where the stone
is bald, exposed to light and bleached,
marked towards the sides with lichen's
leathery petals and buds.
In the cracks of the boulders
empty shell cases still lie.
For years it was a business
for scavengers to scoop the cases up

for the paying metal.
He crosses a plateau of stone,
wedge pointing north
over a growth of oak, chestnut, and black birch.
The woods seem thicker, but he can still see
the strip-farmed fields of Schuylkill,
the river a horseshoe on the red earth.
He recognizes to the south
the hills he passed coming: Berks's "kettle,"
Thunderhead's lonely crown toward Kutztown,
and the push of the gray Pinnacle
To the north a spine of wooded hills
is the course the hawks took
in their southward flight. Air currents,
thrown up by the hills,
helped them under their wings.
How often he saw them,
an almost unbroken line at certain hours,
morning and afternoon,
skimming down over the long ridge
to this outlook, this perfect shooting platform!
It was their nature, they had to come,
and it was a feast for the guns,
the hawks falling
there and there on the bare stone
where they lay with their mottled wings spread out.

He goes to the East Lookout,
as they called the other side,
walking through a screen of black gum trees.
To his surprise
in some rocks below, a boy
sits in a crevice, knees spread,
holding a pair of binoculars to his eyes.
"Don't mind me," he says to Ecke.
"I guess you come to see the hawks,"
and he waves his glass toward the north: "Of course
it's early for them, but a few'll come.
The storm is driving them down.
There's something there, over number one—
that's to say, the number-one knob. For observing,
we've numbered them one to five.

It's a vulture." He wipes the binoculars' lenses.
"It's an army kit I bought and assembled.
It was a hundred dollars more
to buy it assembled." A cloud
passes overhead,
its shadow moving on the trees below
with an edge shivering like flame. It goes
up the slope of the nearest knob
and outlines it clearly, and slides off.
The boy wheels his binoculars straight up:
"Sometimes you can't see them come, high up,
till they're overhead against the clouds."
Ecke recognizes that trick
that had formerly helped him kill.
"What's your interest in hawks?" he asks.
"I'm a watcher," the boys says. "I count them.
Not many now, but later
they'll fill the sky. Some days
it's hard to count. You've got to block-count.
It takes two or three watchers to count,
at least one to a side. Look! Look there!
Two sharpshins." He points where they come,
dark-headed with banded tails,
out of the empty sky. Ecke thinks,
Counting hawks. This is what they call
getting civilized,
coddling birds of prey. He says,
"I'm sure you see my jacket and license.
I suppose you think it's wrong to hunt."
"Did I say that? No,
you have a right to hunt,
but I'd say, Don't shoot hawks.
Do you want to hunt weak game?
That's what hawks get. You get the best.
Best keep the hawks alive,
try to keep the balance of nature
if it's any longer possible."
You can't argue with kids.
Two more sharpshins appear.
The boy points them out:
"I almost missed them."
While the boy puts his glasses on them,

Ecke notices something appear
over what he heard called "number three,"
and mentions it. It's coming fast.
"An eagle!" The boy jumps up
and climbs to a higher rock.
"It's a bald-headed American eagle!"
He glances at his wristwatch, to get the time.
"Ten minutes to two. Just look at it!"
As it nears,
in plain view now to the naked eye,
it rides the wind in a long glide,
showing no interest in the watching pair.
"That's a full-grown one. It takes four years
to get white. The young ones fool you
They look like turkey vultures." The eagle,
its angular, regal head
edged with snow, slow,
banks and circles in the wind
but always keeping south along the ridge.
"Look at the wingspread on it!" Seven feet.
It floats to the side
at about their height,
passes the boughs of a dead hemlock,
and, widening its tail to the following draft,
tilts behind the gum trees,
and in that instant is gone.

"I've been watching here for two years,"
the boy says, "and that's only my fourth eagle.
I just had an idea that after the storm
there'd be something. Well,
you picked a day to be here!
You saw something few ever see,
you saw the best. And say—
you saw it first!
Wait till I report this at headquarters!
What's your name? I've got to write it
on the report for today." Ecke thinks,
What have they done to this sky?
Tamed it to a notebook, made it bloodless.
The repeated blast of shells
that echoed down to the Schuylkill

two by two sounds only in the tattoo
smoking in his brain. "Sir,
what do you say your name is?"
"I didn't say. Never mind my name."
Keep my name out of it. He turns,
and crosses the lookout back, and goes.

THE GUN-LOVER

Will Rotenburger's house—such a spire
like a church or chapel,
built that way by himself—not inappropriate,
for this is a temple of guns.
Long-barreled guns hang on racks. Pistols
lie about
with snug caterpillar grips
for the handhold under the rod.
In a side room are workbench and vise.
He can make and remake guns,
even do the same for bullets,
for there is an art to that too.
He is getting old,
his neck cords standing out,
but he has strength yet,
he can keep on with his passion:
"Since I was a boy, I loved guns."

Look then at such a boyhood.
His father left his mother, or the other way around,
and his mother burned to death
in a house where she worked.
He is not sure even where he was born.
"Ich bin eens fon denne des
der eesel aus der wand g'schlage hut."
("I'm one of those kids
a mule kicked out of the wall.")
His mother's parents brought him up
on a farm on the Niantic road, and there
he learned guns. He's still fondest of those

300

that fitted his hands as a boy.
Such he still makes and remakes.

The sun shines at about the day's half turn,
burning from the south in the window
as he lifts down a heavy rifle.
"Here's an old Springfield fifty
I had as a boy.
I cut the barrel off
and put a three-o-six army barrel on it,
and reamed it up for thirty-thirty."
He takes down another gun.
"Now here's my sparrow gun,
a combination Winchester barrel,
Steven action, and a Mossberg's scope."
He pushes the sparrow gun through the window,
and the cross hairs of the telescopic sight
probe at the leaves of some walnuts. He says:
"The sparrows have been getting bad,
eating the chicken feed.
I fixed this gun up for them—
I just open the kitchen door a crack
and lean the gun so, on the latch.
If I get the cross hair on them,
that does for them! One was even
hid behind a piece of wood,
just the head and tail feathers showing.
I got it, right through the middle of the board.
Yes, they'll soon stop coming around."
He puts the sparrow gun back.

"Look at this old muzzle-loader
with a wooden guard over the trigger.
That you don't see so often.
If I go hunting for rabbits,
I'd just as soon use a muzzle-loader.

And look at this one,
a forty-five seventy.
We used that at Manila.
There was Krag repeaters there,
but they was never issued.

The government didn't care, officers neither—
those West Pointers. I was there a year.
There's the picture of me, there's the pistol
we wore behind the hip."
He gets the pistol and its holster
and shows it against his hip,
demonstrating how he "pulled it out." Then
he takes a blunt kind of gun:
"Now here's my favor-ite invention.
It's something, isn't it?
A pup gun with a short barrel."
He pushes it, too, out the window.
"I made this all myself.
I made the stock and mountings,
all the parts inside the wood.
Some persuader, ain't it?"
He puts the blunt gun down
and stares out the shining window.
"Walnut trees . . . the squirrels plant them.
Yes, I killed two squirrels
when I was a boy. Afterwards
I never killed one again.
I feed them now, winters,
when the snow gets deep, too deep.
Last winter I fed a cock pheasant.
He looked starved, that one.
He'd come to the window and holler,
you know how they holler, no?—
then I'd feed him out the front door.
What neck feathers he had!
I could never shoot a pheasant.
Could you shoot such a thing?"

THE OLD BICYCLES

In Will Rotenburger's gun room
over a thermometer on a deer's foot
hang several pictures of the old bicycles,
those with the large front wheel. "Ever see

any like that? That was living—
fifty-six-inch front wheel,
near five foot, solid tires,
you knew you was on something then.
Fall? Oh yes, we used to fall.
Downhill, hit a rut,
and off through the air like a bird.
I fell one day at the Catholic Church,
was starting out from the shed there
and give one shove and landed on my back.
Near knocked myself out that time.
We got the safer bikes later,
but I never took to them. No,
give me the big wheel,
fourteen feet at a single turn
and the saddle in the sky."

RAIN

It has rained a long time.
Five days. The clouds sweep low
and rinse the heavy trees. Heavily
a few early yellow cherry leaves
fall in the August wet.
A little girl stands alone
holding an umbrella over her
where the Bally yard stops at the field.
Her face seems to be saying:
"I'm tired of this rain
and I'm going to play outdoors so!
even if I have to stand so!
under this umbrella
on the grass."

LUTHER'S HYMN

H. M. Muhlenberg in his *Journal*
says that when his party of emigrants
left Dover, after the usual provisioning stop,
"a two-masted vessel sailed directly toward them."
The captain had heard that Spanish privateers
sometimes posed as fishing vessels
so he displayed "both courage and strength,"
and ordered a drummer to beat a drum
and the guns to be loaded and made ready.
Through a speaking trumpet,
he asked the two-master what they wanted.
Actually it proved to be only
some French fishermen, harmless.
But before learning this,
Muhlenberg had hunted up
"a certain Salzberger family on board"
to see how they were doing, and was pleased
to find the mother with her child singing
in great spirit
"Ein feste Burg ist unser Gott."

JIM BOWMAN'S BIRTHDAY PARTY

It is his seventy-third birthday.
He came to Bally from Sumneytown
where he was known by most as "the miller," only that.
Wife dead, yes, long dead.
His daughter Emma that married "the Britisher,"
she's dead now too.
And he had "one only son"
who died at twenty-eight.
"He talked clear. He talked like this.
An hour later he died.
Gott im himmel, to die in an hour."

304

Like many well-to-do retired,
he has a housekeeper,
and likes friends in, likes crowds.
He can hardly wait now
for his "surprise" birthday party.
His eyes seize the guests, his voice
whirls them around as they enter:
"Yes—yes—glad you come.
Hello, Russell. Hello, Kate—come in.
Yeh, I'm still young. Come in. Come in.
Ain't music yet. Come in."

Thirty friends, come to the surprise party,
talk and tip their assorted chairs
back against the kitchen walls.
One overhead center bulb
sheds yellowish light along the wallpaper
and at the windows
colors some intruding lilac leaves.
Jim is waiting for the quartet,
referred to as "the boys,"
whose voices, under talk,
tune up in the back room.
Some muffled chordings and runs of song,
and they appear in the door.

Russell Bechtel, Ed Kulp, Ralph Berky,
and John Simmons catch half shadow,
half door-light, facing
more toward one another than toward the guests,
as they begin to sing,
and Jim Bowman's birthday smile aches
with wanting
everybody now to listen.

"The boys" start
with a hymn of Francis Daniel Pastorius,
the first German hymn writer
on American soil. Retrospect,
listening back: Behind Pastorius,
plainsong.
The *Ausbund,* the sects' hymnal,

repository of the hush
of unmeasured Gregorian chant,
and men of the Ausbund, martyrs who wrote in prison,
knowing they were going to die.
O Gott Vater wir loben dich
Und deine Gute preisen . . .
"O God our Father we praise Thee
and extol Thy goodness . . ."
Hymns often written to secular airs:
"A Flower in the Meadow," "By the Waters of Babylon"
and, as the tempo slowed,
improvisations flying among the notes
and changing them again. Beissel
and the Sisters of Saron at Ephrata
in white robes, and the ascetic
four- and six-part breathings
of Beissel's hermetic harmonies.
In the open kitchen door
Russell, Ed, Ralph, and John
call the martyrs and the *Magus* back,
and Jim Bowman's smile is like a child's
anxious and glad. What all hear
may be just "the boys,"
but it's music at last, his smile says.

THE BOROUGH BEST

Luther Koch sits out in the evening, talking.
A giant tulip tree near him
holds up its alabaster cups
dripping light. "I always like music.
I heard a trombone once at Willow Grove—"
Italian trumpet lengthened and augmented,
tube all one size, a conduit
going in and out in its smooth slide
until it was a sluice for the soul,
calling and drawing, the call
seeming just for him. Young,
he rode a freight to Philadelphia,

and bought his "first one," now
on the shed rafters, stem and bell
like a flower on its side.
"It corroded, yes, at the joints,
and I bought a better one later,
but I always kept that one—"
green, with the bell pointed out.
"They say the trombone cannot be played perfect
because of the temperament. It has no stops
like the trumpet or the fife has,
But the one I heard at Willow Grove,
that played perfect. Yes, that was perfect.
There was no mistakes when that one played,
and I decided I'd play perfect too.
I did." From *Tropic to Tropic,* flawless,
after long self-training,
his control of the sliding bell. One night
in the quiet
he wrote a "solo" piece, a voice
running liquidly among his thoughts.
It was part the ringing of the moon,
part the throbbing of the insect hum
outside, and yet a nearer pulsing,
and when he had his own band later,
"The Borough Best,"
he made his piece into a march,
and played it at that same Willow Grove
where he had first heard the trombone play.
It sounded as he had meant—
overlaps of the heart's pounding   .
when the breath comes like a night secret
out of the very base of the body,
mouth against mouthpiece pressed,
getting a correspondence of notes
flowing and slowing
to their absolute end. It was right,
and with a young man's confidence
in what he had done, he thought
to find a publisher. He tried.
None would take it. None knew
how the bell became the horns and drums
repeating in the day the night's ascendance.

His "success" was real,
but local as the thousands are,
and never went beyond Willow Grove.
Under the tulips' tumult,
those multiple rigid blooms,
he wonders why it was.
What had held him to a single bandstand?
Why did the solo die upon the horns?
It sings yet in his mind and in the bell
as the tulips' tallow petals fall.
What's local? What's not? Where is the voice
of that moonlit night and its thought
whose unchanged truth slides out,
obsessively possessing him yet,
a voice he cannot let
just go as if it had not been.

ALL THEM NOTES
(Koch's daughter speaking)

"Yes, for many years he led the band,"
Mamie Koch says, "so for them
he wrote the music out. I remember
once when I was a little girl
I sat under the table, he wrote,
and all them sheets come down to me there
as he dropped them on the floor.
I never moved,
I was so proud. I thought
it was me that he was dropping
all them notes down to."

THE DAUGHTER

Clay and Laureen Fegley,
some years after their four boys,
had a girl, Laurie. Clay thought, she resembles Laureen.
That bump of behind of hers as she stoops down,
those soft black eyes, that never-ending
interest in the world. At three and a half
she'd take Clay's hand on a Sunday morning
to "go for a walk" and would walk
down the arbor slope from the house
to the first field fence. Here
there was an abandoned wagon
still with the bleached side rails
and she'd ask to be put in it
and trot around in it, enjoying
the feel of height, of possession,
and touch the rails and a few hay wisps
left like jackstraws on the bottom.
Then a change: Am I to be abandoned here
like the wagon? "Don't leave me, Daddy!" And Clay
lowering her in a reassuring arc
to the ground.
She liked to work. He'd see her
following her mother in the yard,
picking up raked grass or the dead leaves of winter.
Or she'd set table, lugging
all the silver. Intent, not tiring.
One Sunday morning,
noticing the hens peck at ears of corn
that lay on the ground in the barn lean-to,
she tried to pull the kernels off for them.
It was hard. She got Clay to help her.
He ruffled the kernels off sideways.
She saw the sideways leverage
and began to shell that way too.
The hens clucked their chicks around the tractor
to offer them the kernels. "They're eating!"
Clay tired of shelling corn, but Laurie
kept him at it

309

till they had stripped six ears.
Now he put on his gray formal coat
with the plain vertical collar, legacy
of older Mennonite days,
and drove his family to church.
Laureen and Laurie sat in the pew with him.
A wife could now sit with her husband,
her small white cap no longer seeming
the sign of woman's subjection. The sermon
was about the insoluble problem
of an all-powerful God who allowed
suffering and wrongdoing in the world.
Clay, listening, was thinking
of suffering he knew. Without his noticing,
Laurie slipped to the floor. When he turned,
there she was lying on her back,
her short skirt over her thighs.
He lost the direction of the sermon
and whispered, "Get up." But she wanted to lie there,
perhaps feeling the child's privilege
of mischief. He whispered again, "Get up."
A smile suffused her face.
He saw that others were looking and nudged her sharply
with his foot. Her smiling stopped.
She climbed up to the pew
and seated herself again beside him.
"At times we may not understand Him,
but He brings all to His purpose.
He has told us through Christ
we must moderate all our hope
with trust in His eternal justice."

LOCAL LIGHT

Lightning is local.
First from its pool of cloud
coiled like a serpent,
it flicks its tongue here and there
toward the ground.

First that round
of coiled cloud overhead
and then one or a few
hot fangs following the tongue.
At Pat Giagnocavo's, up the lane,
is a tree notched with the heat
that passed its heart and burned
out along a chain to a goat
and notched her heart too.
At Pennsburg,
two baseball players shared
a single blazing strike. Summer flies
north and in Vermont the writhing folds
bite down a tree
in a small cemetery where
the thunder dies into the grass.
In Minnesota, a lake of darkening sky
floats over a reflecting lake
and lets down a shine of yellow hair
toward the Mississippi, the father.
Now the clouds coil
high above Sangre de Cristo
in New Mexico, above Chimayo,
glowing red in the evening
with the blood of Christ. The Jemez Canyon
in shadow catches the flashes
against the cliffs. At this altitude,
the fang of heat
touches the moisture in a tree,
turning it to steam, and simply
blows the tree up.
A fire may start in the duff
of long-needled ponderosa pine,
smoldering two days, damped down by the rain,
then break out its living flag.
In California, the infrequent storms
signal like shaken sheets
gleaming along the seams of noon.
A hiss of light covers the jacaranda
and stops where the banana tree wavers
in its earthen socket. Uphill
in Laurel Canyon,

311

the decomposed granite
mimicks gold, and rolls with boats
of live-oak leaves.
Two miles from Pat Giagnocavo's tree,
one bolt startles a barn,
and the flames roar into the rain,
eating all the wood, leaving
perfectly straight stone walls
as clean as ideas of walls.
Hard to believe, in sunlight,
that pools of suspended death
wait in the sky, an igneous dream
man makes deliberate
with his own fangs.

TO A CHILD
(Bo-Cau)

At your window, lightning
flickering and frightening,
the rain:

you are safe, but out there
through the trees a glare
looking in.

It makes you wonder
at unknown anger,
danger

that the familiar sky
is the maybe blinking eye
of a stranger.

Now closer and closer
and louder and louder
the thunder!

But anger is short
and love, near or not,
is longer.

THE SAWMILL

Otto Harburgh's sawmill,
in the partly cleared woods,
was an old structure loosely roofed
and sided with unpainted boards.
It leaned toward the millpond
as if built of playing cards
somehow managing not to fall. Harburgh
lived alone not far from the mill
near Forge Dale. No wife.
It was not good not having a wife,
but he had the mill—
that was something—
and from that he had the woods,
acres of steadily self-improving lumber.
One morning
he worked the saw till the water failed.
It was warm. He was wiping his forehead
with his handkerchief when he heard a call.
Downhill, past a pile of four-rail posts,
a man was coming, Ed Brunner,
who owned a tract of well-grown trees.
The tract was in a useless hollow
with rocks, creepers, and dead leaves,
a perfect bed for snakes. Three years ago,
binding on leather puttees,
Harburgh had gone, at Brunner's request,
to make an estimate on the trees there,
and had marked the ones to be cut,
this one and this one, selecting them
carefully, figuring even
the angle at which they should fall
to leave the new growth undamaged.
Though the cost would be somewhat high here

to haul logs,
he made Brunner an offer.
But there was hesitation:
The price was all right, Brunner said,
and true, he had some expenses to meet,
but he would rather wait.
Let him wait, Harburgh thought.
There was no hurry to a growing tree.
How many tracts there still were
to feed his saw!
Now Brunner was coming again.
He passed the slab pile,
skirting a small mountain of sawdust,
and climbed up to the platform rail
where, after a greeting, he stood
saying nothing about his trees
but watching the millpond fill. The pond's
feeding springs had shrunk over the years.
It was hard to note its gradual swelling.
"How's your corn this year?" Harburgh asked.
Brunner said, "Better than knee high.
Doing well." Silence. After an interval,
since that must be why he had come,
Harburgh asked him, "Those trees of yours,
you want to sell them now?"
"Well—" Brunner's glance
slid down the smooth
wooden water chute to the saw. The saw glittered,
the teeth a band of hornets
ready to whine a log apart,
and a log lay bound on the carriage.
Brunner imagined one of his own trees there, trees
he had become accustomed to in their file
with their lustrous litter and lift
over the rocks. "I did think—
No, not yet this year. Maybe next year."
"All right." Good. No need to urge him further.
A decision sometimes takes time.

314

A BLACK LIFE NEAR CLAYTON

From Tony Henry's farm, Ralph Berky
climbs the unused woodcutter's road
moist with springs and sewn
with stubs of "self-heal" or "heal-all,"
cones glinting blue.
Leaving the world below,
he passes a charged wire
hemming cows from the woods where
voice after voice departs—
human voice, cattle murmur,
even the wind in the wire.
Trees become
a likeness of former time.
The road back in
narrows to a track,
the track to a trace,
and yet along this trace
he goes expectantly,
parting larch branches
until he sees
a cabin like a corrugated box.
Years ago
a Negro,
Grant Middleton,
working on Masemore's farm near Clayton,
tried to buy a patch of land.
None let him buy.
None let him "build by."
At last he received
permission of solitude—
allowed to put up a log cabin far
into the woods. Berky used to come,
drawn
to this lodestar home, this room
he should have made himself,
this woods-sequestered square. Now,
walking his recollections here, he crosses
a brier-grown clearing

lit with an eyelid-drooping stare
of blackberries
and a gleam of jewelweed leaves.
The cabin
has overhanging eaves. Its log cracks
are filled with a dried pink clay
the eaves protect. Low,
it has no view
but through the old garden. It is
part of what it was built with,
woods, earth—a cabin with overhang
where the phoebe sang,
cabin that hears yet,
toward night,
the whippoorwill
drill from the trees its throbbing taboret.

Middleton
was already middle-aged
when he hired out on the Masemores' farm.
He carried Lloyd's first daughter on his arm,
she
being quiet as he held her and talked
with his soft a's just for her.
He could not read or write,
but had them print his name in cement
on Masemore's barn floor
he helped pour.
The reason for his coming here
or having left elsewhere, none knew.
An accident of choice had made
Clayton his home,
its woods a dome
of loneliness like that
the early Germans lived with,
their eyes
blocked with the same overlook
he had, of the wild.
Rain fell.
In summer his log cabin
was airy, cool.
In winter, in the worst storm

he turned on
his stove's howling double draft
and kept warm.
He welcomed Berky,
itinerant of himself,
informed self-wanderer
who helped to keep
the woods track open. The larch
were thin then. Time
thickened them out and gave him
its usual hints. He slowed.
He worked for Masemores and "on the road"
and when he could no longer do,
Dr. Hottenstein, seeing him old and ill,
got him into the poor home where he died.

The brier still scrapes Berky's side,
wildness running
back after one who understood
its mood—Joe-Pye weed
staggering its five broad leaves around its stem,
spreading its purple to the woods' brim,
and a few lockets of nightshade
hanging with such brilliant blood
near the spring. Here
Middleton raised a dipper of silence, here
he drank alone.
His garden has its shape still;
the wood, its opening.

THE TREES OF WASHINGTON TOWNSHIP

A shagbark hickory, the trunk
like a barrel covered with bats.
An American elm yellow in its cloak
of Fox's bees. At Forgedale
a willow that leans and listens
to the sassafras treading down
its endless root. In this life,

who thinks of saws,
of buyers of wood? Who thinks of twilight
with sunlight
on the day's green temples?

And yet
the long seethe sighs and stops.
Sawyers
in the first-growth woods
hunt the straight trunks.
Behind pulled-out logs,
stumps
bleach, weakening
with thin worm lines
where the bark slips.

Trees, away from man,
die like birds, unseen.
With age,
in Fred Braun's ravine,
an oak falls. The roots
pull up a wedge of earth
holding a wall
orange as a sun in cloud,
then the flayed clay
drops back again
in rain.
Little Sweden's branches,
an uncontrolled harp,
sing, "*Vår-vindar friska
leka och viska.*"
("Fresh spring winds
play and whisper.")
Storm
peals at the door
of the black ironwood.
The shagbark hickory
whispers "Now"
to its clinging progeny.

NOVEMBER FLOWERS

This ground before the snow,
echoing its flow
at flood, though reined in
and thin,
feints
a fullness in its last renewing.

A clover head,
red,
along its green stem lets down
its small shadow,
the meadow
still clinging to the waning sun.

And bees come
from the unfinished comb
to find the spare sweetness of a dust
hung on
spindles of tone
heard where the yarrow whitens to the east.

Below the hill, a brief
lattice of leaf,
periwinkle, numbed green at the end,
throws
a few sprays
of its pale stamens to the wind

And honeysuckle's silk,
a hint of saffron on milk
unseasonably flowering,
falls
against the hill
where banks of thyme still sing

their two-lipped song.
Wild snapdragon,
a yellow that the spreading spruce conceal,
and small eyes
of chicory
fringed with blue as bright as it is frail

wait, call
even to the final syllable
of the summer in the grass—
then go,
slow,
into the silence of the winter's glass.

BROWN

The earth, wood, all that grows up
darkened or pearled over by rain,
all is the one background,
brown. So, with cold,
the cutover fields of wheat,
corn stubble, and the blowing skeletons
of soybean plants adjust to a scale
of color between gray and yellow. In that dun,
in irregular swamps of mahogany,
the honeysuckle at last really dies.
Brown goes exposed as the core
in switches of brier
that run like flame one way
through the curve of poverty grass.
But what seems flame is not,
is only a brittleness,
allied to ice, that continually
wears the months away, conversation
of daisies thinned to straw
around the surface rocks of the fields,
and basil severed from its year-long scent.
As the year turns,
snow climbs the brown. Flowers

whiter than any known to the petaled world
open in the yarrow's stiffened palms,
and cups of fallen cloud shine
over the inverted blooms of thistle
that hang like tan strawberries in the air.
Fences of flax separate the snow
or the snow rises over them,
and in the indeterminate light,
eyes of twilight dilate
or close on the plane of white.
Yet the brown remains:
ungleaned corn
occasional like a spoor,
weed burs and hulls
for birds' beaks ticking
across the fields,
tiger lilies
with flat, crossed knees,
and rows of milkweed
blowing corrugated horns
down the long funnel of winter.
Through snow, the brown lasts
until, under it, green
waiting in quills of beech,
in the minute knots of crepe myrtle,
thousand-pointed,
cracks outward and cries spring.

ONE OF THE SCHULTZ BOYS FISHING

Consider how strong a person's hand is, sometimes,
at ninety, and the memory too.
Both may be slow
but a moment of backward-going thought
takes the willing mind by the hand
and leads it to childhood:
"There were locks above the sawmill
and the water ran out to the 'swamps'

321

below the hill, but on the swamp we cut hay.
In the creek
my brothers and I and Father
often went fishing with a coal-oil light
with a fish spear and a large net.
We stood so, and in the stagnant water
it was plentiful with eels and catfish.
We had to have our hands full of sand
to hold them and kill them.
We had a spear with four prongs.
The lamp had a large hood to it
that threw the light on the water.
The light, I think, blinded them.
The catfish are good eating.
By moonshine
we went sometimes without a light,
set the net in
and went way up the creek
and splashed, splashed and drove the fish down
into the net—whitefish, catfish, carp, silverfish.
Sometimes
the net was heavy with fish."
He draws yet on the net
of his Douglas Township childhood.
"Yes, the West Branch Creek
of the Perkiomen we fished.
The *hecht*—pike—he was a still sitter,
and we had a red wire loop,
and we moved it slooooowly
so he didn't see it
till it was over his head,
then we pulled and caught him.
In the fall there was eels especially.
They had a notion and were made that way
to go down a stream and I know
that we put—made—a catch for the eels.
We put a lock across the stream
that's below the sawmill,
say about ten feet long—
little slats, little laths.
When the eels dropped in there,
they couldn't get out anymore,

322

weren't like a copperhead
that could crawl up—"
A boy with boots to his thighs
walking with his brothers and father
as water cools and dimples and descends
in the creek, his eyes
on the mirror at his feet.
"We were many to eat,
and the fish helped. Yes,
It was an addition to the fields."

ANNA ROSINA

The Reverend Elmer Johnson
is reading the just-published two-volume
Journals and Papers of David Shultze
edited by Darius Berky's son Andrew.
He comes to the entries
in the year 1750 telling this story:
The diarist David had then
a young male "servant," not much more than a boy,
Hans Seiler, continually "disgusted or spiteful"
because he had a seven-year indenture
and other boys like himself had only four years.
Once, when David was away surveying,
David's wife who had twice boxed the boy's ears
told him he should work faster.
A servant girl heard him say,
"Wait, I'll show you!"
He "sharpened a knife," then early in the morning
came and climbed in a house window on the ground floor
where "Anna Rosina" slept.
He found her sleeping lightly.
She stirred.
He stepped back, but when she was still again,
he again went forward and stabbed her
and the third blow cut her throat. So she died.
David wrote, quoting Job:
" 'Oh that I were as in the months of old,

As in the days when God watched over me.' "
Seiler, the sullen boy,
was tried, sentenced, and hanged.
So, even in our valley,
even in my collateral line,
Johnson thinks,
murder. And now he thinks
of a time when Darius Berky, home
from one of his earth-girdling expeditions,
walked with him up the slope behind his house
and with him looked out over this valley—
its roads mostly surveyed by David Schultze—
and said, "In all my travels
I have never found
a more beautiful place than this."

ERNA HOLTZ

Erna Holtz has never married.
She has run a farm in the maiden way,
living alone.
"There was a tramp come by sometimes.
I always fed him, though I know I shouldn't,
and I see him yet, coming across the fields.
He had a thin face. He'd worked in iron,
in a foundry, he said,
but he hurt his back in some fight,
so he couldn't work. I asked him once
if he'd do a chore for me,
but he said, 'I don't like to.'
Huh!
Once he looked at me as he ate,
and said, 'How old are you?' right out.
I told him how old I was
and he said he was the same.

"I got to expect him from time to time.
Him and talk.
Then, one day, one come

324

and told me a tramp was found dead
only a turn of the road away.
At first I didn't want to go
and look, then when I wanted to,
they had already lifted him.
I asked several.
From what they said, I guess it was him.
He never come again."

LISA

Lisa Bauer as a child
was a big-boned, awkward girl,
"a little willful," resenting
no fun and much work,
her clothes all hand-me-downs,
her father one of those—there are many—
who thought bankruptcy always just ahead:
When a neighbor put in running water,
he said, "My pa carried the bucket,
why should we be lazy?" Yes,
the children worked hard
and slept two and three in a bed. Lisa
finished school, the small grade schoolhouse,
and at sixteen,
she got a job in the hosiery mill. There
the first week she spent all her money
on a new dress. No one admired it
at the long Bauer kitchen table.
All knew
she was "to bring the money home."

The next year she was in love.
The boy was indifferent
so she took the one means she had,
at first no more than a thought, an imagining,
but then made real
in the bed of the woods. Then
what happens happened.

325

Now "another mouth to feed,"
and the boy "paid her no mind."
What with ugliness at home,
worse now, and who knows
with how much need and dislike,
she began to go from work
to Leo Reppert's tavern. There
she just sat still, but in a barroom
the cloud of alcohol and the light
break down silence. The person speaks.

The second of Lisa's children
she had with a married man
who paid her four hundred dollars.
She gave the money to her parents, hoping
it would pacify them. When it did not,
she rented a rundown farmhouse
off by itself,
to which she took her children
and where she lived.
A man moved in with her,
one of those that stays a while, smiles,
makes a baby, and is gone.
She had several such.

Her place was used for parties. Many now
came to drink. One night
she thought a man said something slighting.
Her breasts were full.
She got one out and with her big hand
rounded and squeezed it and shot milk
into the man's face.
He wiped his eyes.
No one laughed.

IN LEO REPPERT'S TAVERN
(November)

"Ain't bad." In Leo Reppert's wide barroom,
filled with farmers and Bally factory workers
who eat there at long tables at noon,
night has fallen. "We can plow yet.
Winter don't come s'easy."

In the thickening smoke,
a Turkish pistol with silver scrollwork
aims savage salvoes above the bar. "Leo,
let's hear you sing."
Gathering his apron back

and warning his dogs to be quiet
(they lie on the floor at his feet),
Leo in his clear tenor
begins to sing. And sadness
sings out in his high voice. His listeners

listen compelled.
They think of loss—
first love lost,
plans scaled down, halved, or abandoned,
all life's random ransoms slowly paid.

A neon moon burns red in each glass,
calling back
all they once were, the blood's first gladness
whipping the skin before
the dying down of that reckless rage.

Leo sings on,
his sex hardly understood, yet his companion
is here. He sits at a near table,
but only one or two notice
the voice is singing just for him.

As the song continues,
its tenor diminishes,
at the end dropping
to a minor note. Now night gets cold,
and, scolded or not, the dogs howl.

THE WINTER JASMINE

On the road it was safe,
but he asked to turn aside,
perhaps with no thought
he would be denied.
Her hesitation brief—
the lane was lonely
and past the Kriebels' gate
she knew it led only
to a birchbarkers' track.
He understood
and was willing to go by.
She said, "No, we'll take it,"
and turned with him and walked,
elbows in, watching
for switches of growing brush.

Some distance in the wood,
a house. At least,
once it had stood,
heimlich, for the use
of those who, with hope,
had struggled with the hills
until eroding rows,
slopes of grain and green
had leaned down with rain
to sumac and to weed
and a glittering of grief.
To this abandoned house
they came. She saw the thin
shoots of ivy closing
the now frameless windows

328

with panes of leaves shaking
where the glass had been.
The glass was on the ground.
In the cellarway, boughs
of winter jasmine bloomed,
sprays of its stars exposing
a memory of home,
how many worked and stayed
in spite of heartbreak years!

Two years before, she had loved
a man who kissed and left,
and she had not believed
what he had said, that he
never would come back;
but time's unstopping drift
that puts all at a distance
no matter what the grief,
no matter who the grieved,
made true what he had said.
Alone and still alone,
though a man at her side,
and love still unknown
other than love betrayed,
she faced the ruined house,
like her, windowless.
Land agents, she had heard,
to trusting Germans sold
hills of impossible slope
like this, misused their hope,
and, heartless, disappeared.

The man beside her moved
to take her in his arms,
when angrily she shoved
and in anger watched
him slipping on the steps
and falling in the flowers,
into the jasmine sprays,
all too timely sign
of all that betrays,
for now she sees

how there impossibly stayed
in her as in this earth,
stems that had not said
that life had left the gate,
that, stupidly bent down
and warmed with cellar heat,
even in winter let
some yellow stars come out,
paler than those of spring,
but still saying home.
He's gone, he's gone,
and there never was home
on the hill slope of his heart,
in the rubble of his breast.

The man righted himself
and, cool against the wall,
brushed himself off,
said, "Thanks," and that was all.

THE SITTER

Harvey Dietz for forty years
had been ailing, with a poor heart.
At Saunders' Tavern he had a beer,
it tasted good, he had another,
it also tasted good, so he bought
three bottles and took them home.
At home he drank one bottle
and went to bed and died.
Mrs. Dietz called William Brumbach
to "sit" while she went for the coroner.
Sitting there alone, Will noticed
the two remaining bottles of beer.
He drank one, it tasted good,
he drank the other. He also smoked
one of Harvey's cigars.
Harvey'd want me to be comfortable.

330

THE DIFFERENCE

A married woman has one youngster
dark-haired, unlike her other children.
One mentions he looks different. She says,
"Yeah, him I got singlewise."

COCK
(William Brumbach speaking)

"One night I couldn't sleep. Happened
I seen a line of light at the chicken-coop door.
It was just enough so I seen.
I come out and swung open the door
and put the flash in. A man I knew
was standing there—I don't tell his name.
'What you doing in here?' I said.
'Well,' he said, getting red,
'my wife seen that white cock of yours
and got to thinking she'd like to have it.'
'If she wants it that bad, take it.'
I found the cock and gave it to him.
'But, you believe me now,
keep out of chicken coops.
In some man's coop you could get killed.'
He took the cock and went away. From that day
I never heard he done anything
in the way of stealing again."

AND COCK

Ed Diehl's cousin, Ella, says: "Ed
had a cock once I swear he liked
better than his wife.
It was blind. He fed it by hand, yeah.
It roosted on a table behind the house,
and any time he said to it,
'Crow, Cocky,' it crowed, even at night.
Being blind, I guess it didn't know
night from day.
His wife once was sick and complained
the cock's night crowing woke her up.
She knew how her husband made it crow.
She complained to her son and said,
'Maybe you ought to cut the cock's head off.'
Just as she said, he cut it off.
I thought Ed was gonna kill his son."

BROTHER SAM AND BELLE

"I'm not sure I expect you to believe this,"
Delia Longacre says.
"You know I have a brother, Sam,
who teaches at Lehigh: physics.
He's married. Happily married. Marietta
is as fine a woman as you'd want to know.
But Sam for many years
had this collie bitch, Belle.
You'd see him looking at her.
There's something about a collie's eyes. Always
when he drove his car,
Belle sat in the back seat
and laid her head on his shoulder.
Always begged to go with him.
He let her do anything she wanted,
like he pretended not to notice

332

when she'd plow through the strawberry patch
under the leaves, gobbling berries—I've seen it myself—and come up looking
the soul of innocence.
He fed her carrots 'for her sight,'
and vitamins 'for her fur,' in a dropper,
and she practically thanked him.
A schoolboy once asked him
if she spoke English. The boy explained,
'The French speak English.' Anyway, one summer
Belle began swelling up, obviously pregnant.
Sam said to her, 'As soon as my back's turned—'
and 'Faithless,' but of course
he took care of her, took her temperature,
felt her nose constantly,
and catered to her every whim.
He gave her Swiss chocolates and English sour balls, saying
she'd developed a taste for them,
and as for the expectant mother,
you should have seen her proudly mope around.
This went on for nine weeks or so,
the whole bit, until Sam discovered
it was a pseudocyesis—
a false pregnancy.
Both of them were embarrassed.
Of course, I didn't say a word. Marietta,
she never said a word, either."

THE CHARACTER OF A PRUDENT MAN
(Rillie Schuler speaking)

"Yeah, I skate. But before I skate,
I take out a pocketknife
and cut a hole. If it's two inches,
that's dangerous. You daresn't go on.
Some go on at three.
Six inches is safe.
Eight inches is better. Yeah,
eight inches is what I want."

THE MEANEST MAN

He carried thistle seeds in his pocket,
and now and then dropped some on favorable ground—
favorable, that is, to his personal dislikes—
and pushed them in with his heel.

THE POWERS OF EVIL:
SETTLING THE ACCOUNT
(Jed Gehris speaking)

"Joe Miller now he was a smart one,
he was a good one at tricks.
You know the grocery store at the crossroads here
used to be kept by Tom Sauerman.
Joe once run up
a thirty-five-dollar back bill there,
and Tom got after him hard to pay.
Joe went to a friend and said,
'Lend me thirty-five dollars.
I'll only need it till tonight.'
He went again to the store and said,
'All right,
I come to pay my back bill now,
but we must go out in the barn.'
'Why is that?' Tom said, suspicious.
'Oh, I get my money from the devil.
You wouldn't want no customers in the store
to see me getting money that way.'
Tom agreed to go to the barn.
On the barn floor Joe kneeled down.
'Satan,' he called. 'Powerful Satan,
you know how I been serving you.
Yes, you are in debt to me, so'—
he now raised his voice—'give me money.
I need money, lots of money,

to pay my bill to Tom Sauerman.'
A dollar bill floated down from the rafters.
'More, more, I need more.
A dollar is not nearly enough—'
A five dollar bill come floating down.
Joe still called out, 'More, more,
I need thirty-five whole dollars to pay
my bill to Tom Sauerman.'
A shower of bills come down.
Joe picked them up and counted them:
'Thirty-five dollars,' he said,
handing the money to Tom.
Tom flung it to the floor:
'I don't want nothing to do with devil's money,'
he said and ran out of the barn.

"Later Joe met his friend
and gave him back the money he had borrowed."

KLINE'S STORY ABOUT GEORGE LUTZ

"Yes, George Lutz, I remember him," Raym Kline says.
"He was a preacher yet
when I was a boy at Long Swamp.
He had a good tongue.
There is many stories about him.
Once he was making a call
and it come to dinnertime.
There was four in the family, so the woman
put four plates on the table.
When they sat down, Lutz said,
'Did you hear a cow at Eschbach had five calfs?'
'Five calfs!' the woman said.
'How did the fifth one eat?'
'He didn't eat,' Lutz said. 'Like me.'
The husband said, 'Woman,
put another plate on the table.' "

COMPARATIVE VALUES

This story is told in Butter Valley:
A minister's son was hired
by the bride's father
to care for the horses at a wedding. Afterward
the son said, "Daadi, look what a tip I got,"
and he showed his father a bright half dollar.
His father said, "Look at mine,"
and from his pocket took
a not-too-bright twenty-five-cent piece.

OCCURRENCE ON A FENCE
(Jed Gehris speaking)

"This happened when I was younger.
Jake Muhler used to drink. Yes, he was a drunkard
and spent near all his money on drink.
He heard that his neighbor Gary Schultz
the stonemason lives near Emmaus,
had some hard cider. He went to Gary—
Gary was cutting down some weeds,
yes, scything along one of his fences,
and Jake said to him, 'Gary,
go get me a gallon of cider.'
'Well, now, I guess I don't get it for you,'
Gary said. 'If I give you the cider,
you'll just go home and beat your wife.'
Jake he sat on the fence,
yes, he sat maybe five or ten minutes,
then he said, 'Friend Gary,
go get me a gallon of cider.'
Gary, he looked up surprised,
but he saw Jake still looked agreeable,
and he answered as he had before,
'No, I guess I don't get it for you—'
and give him the same excuse.

336

Jake, he still sat quiet.
After some time he said, 'Yes,
there might be a fire.' Gary said,
'What do you mean now, a fire?'
'Oh, maybe a barn could burn.'
'Whose barn?' 'Oh, just a barn,'
Jake said, looking at Gary's barn.
Gary got him the cider."

THE PROVIDENT ANSWER
(Ed Miller Speaking)

"There was a farmer in the valley here—
his name, yes, it was Heop Biederly—
Heop is Job in the English,
and like the first one he was unfortunate.
With only a small farm,
he had a family of ten.
One spring just about this time,
he went to an uncle of mine
named Linton Miller and asked if he could borrow
a bushel of buckwheat to plant a field.
My uncle had many acres,
yes, he was a well-to-do farmer.
'When do you plan to return the buckwheat?'
'In the fall, when I get crop in,'
Heop said. Well, that's not long.
So my uncle gave him the seed.
Summer passed. Come fall, my uncle
was out harvesting one day and thought,
Heop must be getting in his buckwheat,
and the next time he met him,
he said, 'Well, Heop,
how did you do with my buckwheat?'
'Ai ai ai,' Heop said,
'with that seed I had no luck.
From the bushel I raised only a peck.' "

THE JUSTICE OF THE PEACE
(Howie Lutz speaking)

"My grandfather, Howard, that I was named for,
was Justice of the Peace for ten years.
He had to see to small cases,
help settle estates, and so on.
He settled one estate
where there was many debts.
There was three daughters to inherit
and when the final settlement was made,
they all came to his office.
They were hardworking farm girls,
and to cover their calloused hands
they all had bought new white gloves.
There they sat in their new gloves
to hear what their inheritance would be.
So he told them,
each one to get two dollars."

BUTTER JOHN'S STORY OF HIS ESCAPE
(Squire Benfield talking)

"Butter John escaped once from jail
and then was caught again. He had this story
about what happened:
'I found the warden
with his head on the table, asleep.
The keys lay on the table near him. I took them
and let myself out. Later
I had second thoughts and came back,
I wanted to give myself up.
I pulled the bell rope,
trying to call somebody,
but nobody came. So again I went away.'

338

'Well,' one told him,
'if we're to believe your story,
it's easier to get out of our jail
than to get in.' "

HEAD FIRST
(Hoagie Lutz speaking)

"You know at a funeral
the right way to carry the body out the church
is feet first,
but at my grandfather's funeral,
why I don't know,
they carried him out head first.
I never heard he complained."

OUT OF THE PATCH

Lee Bausher's dog,
prostrate in the playpen in the backyard,
muffles a bark under his paw, bored.
Lee glances
at the Reading valley below
flashing its ridgepoles in the morning sun
and says, "Llewellyn was a 'patch'
near Pottsville in the coal region.
There Sparky Adams grew up
and played baseball on those rocky hillsides
where the ball bounced on the rocks.
He got so he could figure any ricochet.
He got so he could field anything.
To field on a sod diamond, after that,
was child's play for him. 'Pop' Kelchner
scouted him for the St. Louis Cardinals,
and Sparky made it there to shortstop.

But Sparky
had a girl friend back home,
Bertha Frew, that he still would come to see.
Just then we needed a cook
and Father had some business up in the coal region
and he met and hired Bertha
and she came with us and lived in.
Bertha had said nothing about Sparky
either to my father or to us.
Imagine how we kids felt then
when Sparky Adams came to call,
a big-league ballplayer in the kitchen."

A STORY

Laurie Fegley, at six,
writes a story a day, sometimes two:
"A boy was playing baseball and a dog came a log
and a pisher throu the ball and the ball
mist the boy and the dog cot it
and the hole game was rouwind and the hole game
had to run after the dog and even the ones watchin
had to run after the dog just becus that.
The end"

KATIE, THE SMALL CHILD

When Katherine Harburgh was born
in the spring of eighteen ninety-eight,
she was the usual baby, wrinkled and red,
but soon enough smooth.
All admired her, the first child,
but all noticed that she grew slowly. At four
she was no larger than a child of two,
no, not much larger than that.

340

Herman, her father, who farmed
just west of Clayton Crossroad,
had then a covered wicker basket.
It had been used to carry eggs,
or a few young chicks.
One day he and his wife
arrived at a friend's house to visit.
"Well," Herman said, "I brought my daughter."
He raised the basket lid
and Katie uncurled and stood up laughing

With a father's love, he told her:
She knew, *ja*, about *der Belsnickle*
who could go down chimneys, even the narrowest,
and Hop O' My Thumb—ai ai, listen
about the little Hop O' My Thumb,
how this thumb child,
hidden in the horse's saddle,
brought his *Fodder* his lunch
and, placed in a hole in the plow handle,
he even did the plowing yet. Katie
brought her father's lunch to the field,
and would dream, gazing up
at the slow clouds smoking overhead,
of how she would one day help her father
as a farm daughter should. She loved him,
and all seemed possible in the world
of the white sleights of the sky,
and of the comfort her father gave her,
easy, *ja,*
but in the real world where a rusted nail
could cause septicemia,
when she was ten, her father died.

Forever:
Unser Fodder, der im Himmel bisht. . . .
Faa dein iss Kannichreich, un die gewalt,
un all di eer faa immer, Aamen.
Chords,
calls and softness,
nightfall,
leaf fall in wind,

and over leaves,
grief.
Slowness,
stalls of silence,
loneliness's
kingdom,
and getting
that wreath of last
Aamen.

She went into the woods
to a three-trunked tulip tree.
In early spring, its blossoms' petals
lit up. Its flares spoke.
So she grew taller, but not tall.
Still small.

At seventeen, she met Arthur Hamtramck.
He had come to a "harvest home" at Huff's Church
in the warm October
and said, "Are you a bird?
You don't eat like hardly a bird."
He laughed. She liked
that sound.

When they were married, the altar shone,
but the processional was not to it
but to the *heem* in his eyes.

"I baptize you
Benjamin" and James and Joseph. Eyes alike
and pleated chins. All
tall, then a girl,
running and not small.

One day an itinerant photographer
came to the gate and set his heavy pack
on the well flagstone and showed his display.
"What now if I should photograph you all?"
Arthur agreed, so they gathered by the porch.
"I'm too small." Kate found herself
smaller than her daughter. They placed her

up a step from the others, concealing her feet,
but when the picture came,
the concealment did no good.
There it was,
that smallness embarrassing her so.
Arthur noticed.
"You mind that you're small."
He lifted her up to the barnyard wall.
"Don't you know I love you small?
I like you just like you are,
I don't want nothing else." His voice was near,
his arms around her. In the hot noon of summer, above,
clouds floated like speaking heads:
Unser Fodder, der im Himmel bisht.
Anger ebbed away
and in the pocket of her heart she laughed.

KRUM'S GHOSTS

In the larger parlor
the piano keyboard stays open, a year-round ivory shelf.
Mrs. Krum says:
"Ghosts sometimes play it, they tell me.
All I've seen,
once a rooster was on it, walking, once a cat.
But there've been times
none saw anything when it played."

POWWOW, EXAMPLES

"Some can powwow and some can't.
When I wasn't much more than a boy,
I scratched my leg and got an inflation,
got all red, it was a bad inflation,
Johnny Miller, farmed the next farm,
asked my mother if he could powwow it.

343

My mother said he could try.
So Johnny put his hand on the leg—
'Lady went over the land,' stroked down.
'Carried a burning brand,' stroked down.
'Cured the inflation and gangrene,' stroked down.
Then he said it would be cured.
But it didn't do no good.
I was helped with powwow once, though.
I was clearing brush along a fence
and the hatchet slipped and cut my knee,
it was a deep cut, blood jumped out.
I hollered and Abe Gehring across the road,
he called, 'What's the matter?'
I said I cut my knee with the hatchet
and the blood was coming out fast.
Just as I said it, the blood altogether stopped.
Well, I found later,
Abe had powwowed it.
He never said nothing at the time,
but later he told me he had."

FEAR

Hugh Landis beats his hand on the house side
where nothing answers but the afterdrip
of rain. He calls, he wants to get
any of his own from the house.
None answer. None come out.
So there is a silence of fear.
He notices a nighthawk's cry. There is a tone
of hostility and dread everywhere,
especially in the darkness under trees
where at the pasture end they are evened
by the cattle eating the leaves
and so form a door to the woods.
Rugii—woods dwellers—
whispers of blood, delays
while the moon's horns go up or down,
Segensformen, rites over wounds,

344

breathing the breath of a fish,
making oneself *"kugelsfest"*—
proof against bullets—or making
the sign of the cross three times,
pronouncing the onomatope *tsing*.
He feels such an uneasiness
just where all was safe
there in the woods by the pasture.
He enters the barn,
pulls the milk pail from its peg,
and, putting his stool by the freshened cow,
exorcises the silence and fear
with two beating streams of milk.

THE PRESENCE

In the morning, out of orchard grass,
what is it as the wild poppy opens
where the hairy hands reach for the orange cup?
And over the wrinkling crepe of the cup,
what is it as the sumac calls,
lifting its antlers? What is it in the boughs
of the unkept orchard as the day mounts
and the leaves shrink to blue,
and the tunnel of a barn frames
blue shade? What is it
over Hugh Landis's abandoned shed
when the butternut tree soundlessly drops
its oily pods? Just before twilight
when the screen of the familiar sky
turns green, what is it
in the bell call of the swifts
circling down to chimney vents
one by one till all are gone?

THE LIFE OF DARLING

Hugo Zeissner took his gun.
Best to get her out of her pain
and stop the crying, the scream of apology.
It was that he could not bear.

Seven years ago he bought her,
a four-year-old mare, a modest black,
hair a blanket of shaggy knots,
short ears like a dog's, and patient eyes.
A neighbor with him urged him to buy her.
"She looks like a good young mare to me."
Hugo agreed and took her home
and Minna approved. She worked well—
just a touch and she'd pull.
They gave her the name of Darling.

A year after the purchase, one morning
he noticed her halt, turning her head to the left.
Yes, in the left eye, the start of a film.
He showed it to his neighbor, the one who'd liked her,
and said, "How's that look to you?"
"Well now, I told you you should buy her,
but it looks to me like she'll go blind.
Yes, it seems she has the moon blindness."
"It is the moon blindness so."
"If I was you, I'd sell her now
before it gets that a buyer will notice."
"I don't just like to do that."
And in spite of her eye, he kept her.
The pale film spread
and the one eye became a blind ball
as if white silken threads
filled it up. All the life went out.
Before the first eye was gone,
the second began. It filled up too
and became just like the first.
He asked himself what to do.
Was there nothing he could do?

Darling flicked her ears. He thought,
"She can hear yet." Why not try?
He took her to the field and fitted her
into the long straps of the plow.
His voice helped, yes,
and it took some good use of the reins,
but her willingness was clear.
She kept straight as she could go.
There was at first some stumbling over stones,
but he would call, "Hupp hupp," and she would feel
with her foot, and find her way along.
Where another horse shied at the stones,
she went straight. And more,
she learned to locate field boulders,
count her steps, and reach for them with her foot.
It got so that he could use her, guiding her,
on the worst roads, to haul wood.
Her only fault there was that sometimes
she was too eager, and would fail to listen
if there was some hole or unevenness.

So she continued earning her keep,
so she was accepted and kept,
so it went until,
seven years after he bought her,
one late fall morning, ice
had formed in the barnyard. Not noticing,
he turned her out without harness.
She was in a mood to frisk.
She frisked three steps and slipped. The scream
when she turned her head to him
and lifted up the broken foreleg
was an apology, an asking
to be forgiven for her mistake.
It was that that he could not stand,
that she was so sorry for what she had done.
He ran after the gun
to get it over, to stop that scream.

DER GRAABSCHTEEHACKER
(The Gravestone-Hacker)

J.B. Bis do hie. John Birmelin
born in Langschwamm Township
on the last day of October,
eighteen seventy-three,
heard at birth the *Haerbschtwind* (autumn wind)
that, as he wrote later, "murmured
on the hill and roared in the valley,"
rauscht and *braust,* storm
of contradictory lullaby.
He knew no English till he went to school
except the borrowings in his own speech—
English not the first contributor
to that German that, at its pure start,
scholars with Caesar had heard
beyond their traveling tents, and described it as
*"propiam et sinceram et tantum
sui similem gentem,"* a speech
of unmixed qualities, only like itself.
The Romans were cautious with the Alemanni,
a people with no heroes
but also without submissions,
and fenced them off with a wall of swords.
Behind the swords their speech developed
and passed on to the *Deitsch*
something of tribal intimacies,
closeness—violence and battle, yes,
but the roundness of the breast,
the curve of a laugh, so that Goethe,
reading the dialect-poet Hebel,
called himself "charmed"—and more than that—
transported by the old speech,
earth speech, *Windschproch,* the whisper,
the little kiss at a child's ear,
ai, yes, *Die Mudderschproch.*

Birmelin was to take this mother tongue,
the dialect, and reaffirm it,
making it sing for him
in a new, natural way. Before him,
Pennsylvaanisch-Deitsch verse had run
to sentiment and, too often,
to the nonspecific. Harbaugh with his *Harfe*
covered the real schoolhouse
with a distraction of strings, the German
heart harp: "My muse has struck a tender vein!
And asks a soothing flow,"
and
"little fish still sport and glide,"
little fish
but not a *hecht,* a pike, God forbid,
not a sunfish. Lawyers and ministers,
some out of Harvard,
translated Tennyson into the *Deitsch* or wrote
sonnets, rondeaux,
where through a window of generalizing words
not too much could be seen.
All this time the dialect itself
waited like a farmer
full of work words
like "*heksel,*" "Fine-cut straw,"
"*norecha,*" "rake and bind," "*forschuss,*" "forebay,"
and "*mischtschlidde,*"
"drag for carrying manure."
Dialect as healthy as a horse.

Birmelin's father, George Birmelin,
was an emigrant from Baden. In Baden
he had "lived on the cold side of the mountain,"
as the saying was—not much money
and no schooling. When, at eighteen
six feet tall, he came to Pennsylvania, to Topton,
he squeezed himself into a schoolroom desk
to learn his letters. Later,
farming and shoemaking,
he managed to pick up "schoolman's logic"
and its parallel, "theoretical music."
He married a Pennsylvania-German girl,

Mary Schubert, by collateral descent
a reputed second cousin
of Franz Schubert. Her father
played the Long Swamp church organ,
and Birmelin trained as a chorister.
Music became the clef of the furrows,
the quarter notes of the awl,
the choir of the summer night. Then
the millennial *Haerbschtwind,*
a child swung in the cradle
of sound. J.B. (John Birmelin)
under that autumn wind heard his mother's
breathing and humming, her singing, her words,
and early discovered a pleasant
side effect of his baby voice,
the power of command. Outgrowing that
(or perhaps not), he grew
into another, unencumbered
happiness. At eleven,
guided by Grandfather Schubert,
he played the church organ, evenings
rolling chords out on the waiting air,
levering up the notes
that steadied against the coming
voices of the choir. Words, syllables.
From that, from meters of hymns
and from childhood songs
he sensed syllables' patterns,
and with some distaff of the ear
and the dirty wool of life,
in the dialect—*his* syllables—
he began to spin verses.
His mother said, amused,
"Ich denk mer sodde den Buh
fartschicke far's Reime laerne."
("I think we should send the boy away
to learn the art of rhyming.")
One of his first verses was so vehement
he "feared to show it to anyone,"
and hid it. It damned a man
who refused to let J.B. and his friends
fish in his fishpond. He did other verses,

350

but kept most of them to himself,
afraid of possible mockery. In school
he went only through the sixth grade,
but his learning did not stop there.
His father passed on to him his interest
in musical composition and logic,
making him repeat:
"All men are sinners,
a Frenchman is a man,
therefore a Frenchman is a sinner."
J.B. learned while helping make shoes,
learned on the "stitching horse,"
and learned actual horses too—plowing, cultivating—
the year's round of farm work, fields and meadows
sharing him with the shop. He listened.
The dialect spoke to him. He heard
the saying a *Pennsylvaanisch* mother
sometimes used with a child
waiting for a promised thing:
"*En Silwrich Waard-e-Weilche un en goldich Nixli,*"
"A silvery wait-a-while and a golden nothingness."
From this, years later, came a poem
of a child who falls asleep
toward the teasing of a dream.

But, ai, whatever Mother's promise,
still *Aerwet*—work—all his life
chased him like a *Dopplegänger*. He had a view
of the benefits of farming, but:
"*Im Summer waar's mer schier zu hees,
im Winter hot's mich gfrore.*"
"In summer it was clearly too hot,
in winter I froze," so he left farm work
and went to Allentown
where he made his way
as a weaver in a silk mill, evenings
playing the cello he had taught himself
for the Lyric shows. His bow
also jigged at dances.
Sundays he went to Mass.
At a farm where he had worked
he had read *The Lives of the Saints,* and now,

351

himself his own conversion,
at eighteen
he was baptized into "the Church"
and remained a devout Catholic all his life.

In the silk mill
he met a Catholic girl,
Elizabeth Tecla Epp—
"Father died when I was six,
Mother when I was thirteen"—and she,
like so many girls of that time,
went from school desk to the mill.
"I was warping. You get that big thing
ready and it goes to the weaver."
And there was J.B., that
lugger and hugger of the cello
throwing back the shuttle—if possible,
a harder worker than herself.
The first time she saw him,
something responsive and sweet
came to her face. It lasted—
"He liked me and I liked him"—
and they were married,
August, eighteen ninety-eight,
in the Sacred Heart Church.

Now, still hounded by *Aerwet,*
he moonlighted in a second silk mill
to pay for organ lessons
with Dr. Fred Wolle of Bethlehem. The result:
In nineteen one an organist was needed
in Birmelin's own church, and Father Nerz,
knowing of Birmelin's training,
asked him if he would try out,
play a set of hymns. He did.
On the organ's three levels of keys
his reach was large. The stacks
answered him. His chords,
well modulated to the melody,
shook the light clerestory,
and he brought each hymn at last

352

to an unemphasized, calm Amen.
Father Nerz said that it would do.
At a starting salary,
twenty-five dollars a month.

Was it the right street, say,
here where *Gesang,* song, flirted in the notes?
J.B. had followed Mother, Father, and *Grosfot'r.*
Especially *Grosfot'r* Schubert.
It was the street he wanted

From the first years, two sons,
Cyril and Martin, and a daughter,
Elizabeth, named for her mother,
and now to support his growing family
J.B. turned the home on North Fourth Street
into a shop of notes and scales,
palace of a horizontal harp:
piano lessons. He taught schoolchildren.
They piled their hats on the hallway hat rack
and submitted themselves to his patience,
or impatience:
"Work, work, practice, practice,"
and the fingers tracked beside him
across the keys. All (his rule)
would be given their chance.
Some were aware of their notes,
many more learned by rote. But
the hat rack stayed open to them all.
He hurried himself through dinner at three thirty—
before public school let his pupils out—
and "worked straight through."

Part of his teaching:
by the time they were eleven, his own children
had all learned to play the organ.

A church organist
has as a spiritual hazard
the conducting of a choir. J.B.'s first choir
was "mixed," but women's "warbling voices"
troubled both him and the Pope. Rome,

in a nice correspondence of thought,
decreed that only male voices
should be allowed in church singing,
and for the upper register now
boys had to be used. Now
to his daily schedule was added—
from eleven fifteen to twelve each morning—
the rehearsal of a boy choir
through which he was to learn,
like Bach at St. Thomas's, that music
could be a "laying-on of chains." Seldom
is a child a perfect instrument for singing.
There is awkwardness, inattention.
Birmelin complained
about "the modern choirboy," yet at funerals
he won through in the *Dies Irae*
to such an onrush of passion—
iterative, clear, the peer
of death—that in the dark,
in the twilight of the stalls,
the Mass, under his hand, became
the speaking of the grief itself.

From conducting the church choir
he went to outside choruses:
Maennerchor, Frauenchor,
Gemischterchor, and even *Kinderchor—*
the singing cross-stitch of the rivers—
the Workmen's Chorus of Bethlehem,
the Lehigh Saengerbund,
the St. Francis Chorus, the Nurses' Chorus
of the Sacred Heart Hospital,
the Northampton Liederkranz—
"Choral Conductor," he flew
"skipping as fast as he could"
to the compelling work.

His children helped him. Betty
accompanied the Saengerbund,
and said later, "Mother or somebody
came along and took me home
when my part was done."

Or one of his children, at need,
played the Sacred Heart church organ,
and all three helped him tune it. To tune it,
he got up in the stacks where each stop
had its set of pipes, and all day
they played note by note
up the three manuals.
This work in the stacks
stirred up the dust
"and to keep the dust from his throat,
it was Father's custom then
to chew tobacco.
He'd also chew it in the spring
when he cleaned out the furnace."
The children might at times ask themselves
if music was their father, or Father, still
sometimes the music stopped. Son Martin
says J.B. taught him swimming,
pulling him through Jordan Creek
"with a washline tied to my stomach."
And Sunday afternoons were outings, "usually
going to Easton or to Catasauqua,"
trolleying with Father and Mother,
careening in the wind
through the streets and greenery.

In nineteen twenty these outings
were interrupted for a year.
J.B. had started writing music,
had composed a large choral work:
Deutsche Mondnacht, German Moon Night, and now
Sunday afternoons
he went to Philadelphia faithfully
to study with Niccolo Montani. After
this intensive preparation
he did "an almost radical work,"
Der Jaeger Abschied,
The Going Away of the Hunter. In this
he transgressed normal rules
and used
consecutive fourths, fifths, and sixths
to bring out the hunting horns, hallucinatory

355

vocal flourishes that were to shake—
in the places where it was sung—
concert-hall flats and backdrops.
Few conductors had choruses
capable of it, but New York
tried it and some groups in Germany.
No chorus in Allentown was equal to it.

Hard to sustain an interest when
he could not hear his own compositions,
and he was held to Allentown
by family, by speech, simply
by being *heemlich* there.
Gradually the composing stopped.
The years went by in minutiae,
working out good fingering for students,
selecting and preparing Sunday hymns,
watching the choirboys munch their pre-Mass buns,
invariably
stickying up the music.
His children grew and one day were grown.
With Cyril a priest, Martin and Betty working,
he needed fewer piano students.
The adequacies or inadequacies
of the hymns and choruses
only partly occupied his time.

Around the house now
he wore a favorite housecoat,
in the pockets candy
that he nibbled on at odd hours.

Martin, to pass the time,
began to compile
a *Deitsch* rhyming dictionary.
In J.B.'s own mind, as he watched,
words jostled and came back. When Martin
failed to get on with his project,
J.B.
let himself move it along
and ended with a dictionary
of a full eight thousand rhymes,

of which he made two copies.
Now that all that work was done, he thought,
there ought to be a use for it.
But useless to think of publishing.
In all the dialect
perhaps six poets were working:
Louise Weitzel who wrote
"Wu sin die Deitsche Dichter?
Sie sin vershwunne all!"
("Where are the dialect poets?
They've all disappeared!")
She herself kept rhyming; also
Lloyd Moll; C.C.Z.
(Charles Calvin Zeigler), one of the earliest
admirers of Harbaugh, still following
that tradition of verse;
Ralph Berky writing
a poem each day in his diary.
A few others. No hope
of publishing a dictionary
for half a dozen or a dozen *Dichter.*
All right, all that was left
was to use it himself.

What to write about then?
Quendel Tee is a sweet-smelling plant
that grows in the garden and is used
for tea. A servant girl, he had heard,
a little on the hefty side was one day
perspiring just as she was expecting
a visit from her boyfriend. Desperate
to make herself smell nice for him,
she rolled in a bed of *Quendel Tee.*
The boy friend no sooner came than he left.
What was it? Ach now, she remembered—
Yesterday
she saw the cat digging in the garden.
The poem he wrote,
for he wrote about it,
was no love lyric.
It was in the mode of the Chinese,
of the Sung dynasty poet

357

who wrote about war and equally well
about snot in his small son's nose.
J.B.
with this *Quendel Tee* poem
and its commonness
renewed acquaintance with an old skill.
It nagged at him and he continued.

He wrote a poem
about *The Twittering of the Birds.*
The birds through their generations
give their twittering to man
to take away his grief. Should they stop,
"we'll take up their twitter."
The *Volksdichter* was back again,
just some common chirping birds
making their common quick sounds.
"Mir hen vun de Alde
En Haerrlichi Schproch;
Die welle mer halde,
Mer Switschere nooch."
("We have from our elders
A glorious speech.
We want to keep it.
We'll continue to chirp.")

The chirper had a thought now—
go and see Dr. Preston A. Barba
who lived in Emmaus,
just a few miles along the "ridge."
A Muhlenberg College professor,
an authority on the dialect,
he ran a weekly column,
the *Pennsylfawnisch Deitsch Eck*
the Pennsylvania German Corner,
in the *Allentown Morning Call.*
He would be the one to see.
J.B. took his rhyming dictionary.
It would be an introduction.
He was welcomed into the Emmaus home,
a place of pleasant vistas
opposite the church,

358

and found an agreeable man with farmer's shoulders,
smiling,
full-faced like himself. They sat down.
When he offered his dictionary,
Dr. Barba looked at it. As he handled it,
a sheet of paper fell from the leaves:
a poem. Naturally
he asked to read it.
He read it the right way, knowing
the "good lines," effects
of surprises of perception
and tonal freshness, casualness
curling around like a dog
about to lie down as sound
made itself known. He said a few things
relevant to his knowledge and J.B.'s,
and the *Dichter*
had an audience of one,
the necessary minimum.

Mornings, undisturbed
in a comfortable chair
in the room where he taught music,
hour by hour he dipped down
into those wells
of the deepest waking man knows, the *Wind*
calling again at the wellhead—
autumn wind, spring wind. Storm.
His technical skills grew. Dr. Barba
had said to try various forms—one
the four-line ballad stanza. J.B.
tried it and ordered or disordered it
into a flick and ripple of *Kleindichtung*,
consonances, within-the-line echoes,
speed, absorptions, bursts
unknown till then in the *Deitsch*.
After the "old homestead," after
Harbaugh's heart-harp, *Das Alt Schulhaus,*
back to the folk.
"Sie quackse un sie quickse
Un sie schiele un sie blicke,"
and a whole poem entitled

"Buchschtaaweschpielerei."
a torrent of alphabet stuttering
for which there was folk precedent.
(The chicken calls to the guinea hen,
"Iss der Parre noch do?"
"Is the preacher still here?"
and the guinea hen replies,
"Bleib zerick, bleib zerick, bleib zerick."
"Stay back, stay back, stay back.")
He translated the folk poets
of Germany to get practice—
"Der Streik in Himmel," ("The Strike in Heaven"),
about the rebellious angels, and one of Hebel's,
a farmer begging his wife
for enough from his weekly paycheck
to get himself some pipe tobacco.
He did not just translate,
he doubled and tripled the lines
and "adapted" the poems to himself.

For children, *Mammi Gans (Mother Goose)*:
"Bussi Bussi Bussi, wo waarschte du dann geschter?
Ich waar in Magunschi bei deinere Schweschter.
Well, Bussi, was duschte bei dere dart draus?
Ich hock unnerm Schtuhl un ich fang re die Maus."
("Pussy pussy pussy, where were you yesterday?
I was in Macungie at your sister's.
Well, pussy, what did you do at her place out there?
I sat under a chair and caught her a mouse.")
Over two hundred *Mammi Gans* rhymes
he translated for the children,
then a poem of his own, *Die Fimf Meis,*
about the five different kinds of mice:
about *Die Maus,* the usual mouse,
about *Die Fensemaus,* the chipmunk,
about *Die Fleddermaus,* the butterfly,
about *Die Schpeckmaus,* the bat,
and about *Die Kaerchemaus,* the church mouse.
His first collection of poems
he gave the title of the early one,
The Twittering of the Birds.
The ballads he was writing

were about people: a universal
story of the disaster of love,
how Cecilia von Bernville
went walking with a Colonel Bouquet,
and her father's hired man who loved her
lay in ambush to shoot the colonel
and shot her instead (on her tombstone,
her birth and death dates
and under them, two words—"*Ach Gott*").
A ballad about *Regina Hartman*, a ballad
about *The Walking Purchase*, and one
perhaps closer to his heart,
Es Gschpuck vum Lange Schwamm,
The Spook of Long Swamp. This spook
was that of a *Plantagen* farmer
who worked his hired men like slaves
as long as he lived; now, dead,
he haunts the scene of his misdeeds,
still making men uneasy.
Powwow and hex doctors
are summoned to exorcise him.
All fail. At last
"the priest from the mountain," robed and caped,
rides around on a black stallion
and prays. He has six men with him
carrying *Wenuring*, logging hooks.
With the hooks they grab the ghost
and carry it to *Diehle Kopp,*
Diehl's Head Mountain,
a barren place used for charcoal burning,
rising like a wall above Long Swamp,
and there they bury it.

So Birmelin in his armchair. Sundays
he still played the organ. He still
had choruses and students,
but only the best now, the ones he wanted.
He summoned the choirboys
to repeated, still-hopeful
attempts at linear tightness.
He walked the floor and nibbled candy. He also
nibbled at the agony of words.

His son Martin said,
"He'd spend an entire day
just to kick one word out of a line."
Poems
in the *Pennsylfawnisch Deitsch Eck.* A few
like *The Outhouse*
let go unsigned, anonymous.
Copied and recopied and recited
throughout the eastern counties,
they invaded the annual *Versammlinge.*

Ach, where did verse belong?
Did it not start as song
and had he not lived with song
all his life? So the pen
that had scrawled notes and rests
for the singing voice now wrote
the metric of words alone.
"And all for love," Martin said.
Birmelin was never
paid a cent for his poetry,
for his county-limits tune.
Poetry was a fellowship,
a singing with others. Martin
remembers at a *Saengerfest*
when one of J.B's choruses
had won a loving cup, they filled the cup
with sparkling wine, passing it
from hand to hand,
filling it again and again
till J.B.'s face got "rosy."
It was another rosiness
brought the line out right. Shuttle-thrower,
he brought the threads together.
His hand gathered
stories, legends, old hurts—
meadow songs, songs of the seasons, verses
for children, the singing
at last easing,
dropping off to the *Haerbschtwind,* the autumn wind.
In such a wind of impulsive sadness

362

he wrote *Der Graabschteehacker,*
the hacker of his own epitaph:
"*J.B.*
Bis do hie . . ."
"J.B.
Up to here.
Further surely none has come yet.
Seeing the long time it took him,
Many years and many months—
Don't mind if he rests
And if we also add the days on
And count the hours too?
But all this means nothing
Once they haul his bones away.
One might better save the effort;
For him it is R.I.P."

THE FOREGROUND, SINGING

Long before John Birmelin were the firstcomers,
the colonials, who wrote poetry
in High German. Francis Daniel Pastorius
wrote excellent German verse
and wrote English verse for practice.
Nicholas Ludwig von Zinzendorf, that egalitarian
count, while still a boy
composed a *Passions-Lied* and a satire,
but his singing majority
came in Pennsylvania where, charged
with the changing new world around him, he wrote
forty thousand lines of German poetry.
He wrote everywhere, wherever
he might be, at sea,
at the dedication of a graveyard,
"On the Kittidane Hills in Oct. 1742"
(he was looking for his lost Hebrew Testament).
He recorded himself as against
"making poets out of prophets," saying,
"We got a decided taste

for the simplicity of expression
of Luther and the Bohemian Brothers.
We considered their neglect of versification
a real glory. . . ." He wanted poems
"sung from the heart."
On Christmas night, seventeen forty-two,
in church in Bethlehem (Germans, Britons,
Swedes, Danes,
Delawares, and Mohicans attending),
he extemporized a hymn. First
the musicians played the melody,
then the count composed a line
and the congregation sang it back.
This poetic spontaneity
was common among the Moravians,
who developed more than sixty poets.
The anthologist John Joseph Stoudt says
they sought
"fluency before pattern, spirit before form."
One of them, Gottlob Büttner, a missionary
to the Indians at Shekomeko
brought into his poetry "the musical sounds
of Delaware and Mohican words." At Ephrata
ex-baker Conrad Beissel, preceding modernism,
"fixed the meter, not according to custom,
but as the nature of the thing demanded it."
He started with Alexandrines,
but advanced past such meter
into an idiosyncrasy of such passion
that song and so-called prose became one. He wanted
to put the whole Bible into song. Stoudt says:
"From the bitterness of his earlier years
when he was still licking the wounds
of his trial and banishment from Germany,
to the later experiences
of the in-breaking Spirit"—
from penitent grief to exultation—
"Conrad Beissel's poetry
is without doubt
the most profound creation in colonial literature,
English or German." He was "learned in
the labyrinth of the human soul,"

exposing "the self," knowing
the Unconscious, the inward motion
of symbols, myth, and dream. In one year
in seventeen fifty-four
in Ephrata's own *Paradiesisches Wunderspiel*
he published four hundred forty-one poems.
He was not alone.
Sixty Cloister brothers and sisters
wrote with him—songs and poems. Up near Pennsburg,
David Shultze wrote poems. So did
his ship companion Johannes Naas.
Conrad Weiser between translations
of the speeches of the princes of the woods
wrote a memorable poem, *Jehovah, Herr und Majestät.*
Susanna Hubner
wrote an acrostic and a meditation.
Caspar Kriebel wrote a lullaby. Everywhere
there was verse-writing,
in letters, in notebooks, on gravestones, on slips of paper
put away, often lost. But if much is lost,
much has lasted,
an unforced "fluency" of singing, syllables
like a brook, meter
like a moccasin
at ease in the *Mahikandern* woods.

SOME TROUBLE OVER A BULL

Jake, at fifteen, nearly six feet tall,
has knurled hair across his forehead like the bull
he is so hotly arguing about.
The bull, so, is his own bull—
his own. Who bought the calf?
He earned the money for it
building a *steimauer,* a wall
with heavy stones to be handed up all day.
Winter, he earned it cutting wood
stick by stick, cord by cord.
His father: "Ya ya, what you wanta do now?

365

Sell, huh? Then who gets the money?"
"It's my money, so! I earned it."
"We shall see whose the money is,"
his father says and as Jake runs:
"Where you goin'?" Jake
slams the door, and in the lean-to
takes his gun.

He passes the dappled shade
of the cherry trees under which the young pigs
are nudging constantly, spying up
over their own plowing suspiciously.
At the orchard end, he enters the woods
and makes his way to the hilltop where a rock
hides in the last mist of morning. On the rock
he seats himself cross-legged. The mist dissolves
along bracken fern green now
with sallow, unfolding fronds.
The light on the ferns dips. In the silence
a "preacher" calls like a ventriloquist.

A hundred feet from the rock, among boulders
a hole open with no dug-out gravel . The recesses
must be a natural cavity,
for it is a woodchuck hole.
He has seen a woodchuck go into it.
A half hour passes, an hour,
and he sits waiting, his rifle on his knees,
gazing at the hole, then
from the dark the thick fur rustles up
and a woodchuck emerges. It stands up.
It holds its forelegs in, manlike,
in the clear woods light, facing away.
Slowly
Jakes rides his rifle up on his left hand,
the rear sight meeting the forward bracket
so that like an eye
it sees what it will kill
and becomes still. Now
he holds his breath . . . the bullet whines

in the silence and the woodchuck
falls over sideways, dead.
I never seen one fall like that
without no running at all.

He climbs down from the rock
and goes to the carcass. It is lax.
He lifts it by its small stiff tail.
He searches for the wound but cannot find it.
Back home, he ties the carcass
to the clothes wire and as he peels the fur off,
he comes to a red spot on the spinal column—
that was why it died at once,
that was why he couldn't find the wound.
He'll show it to his father.
He'll get the bull money, too, he thinks.
Ma will see that I do.

THE THEFT
(Aaron Reissig)

Ten years ago he bought the farm on mortgage,
and little cash to start,
the meager part
saved from his wage.

The first month his tools were stolen,
it may have been by some
vagrant mean one come
unknown in, for none

hereabouts was ever known to steal—
all honest, those
who owned and those
hired—proud as well.

He brooded. The theft worked in him.
To a neighbor cutting through,
he called, "You,
what you doing,

coming round my barn without permission?"
The tone new,
though
it was in his own nature, imbuing

his lip and unblinking eyes
with stubbornness. Perhaps
he knew the lapse
bad, but had no wish to apologize.

So a neighbor accused of stealing tools,
for so it was understood. Friend told friend.
Some took offense,
some kept the pulse cool.

Years went by with the error unrepaired,
and what so ill began
he let continue on
till at last he stared

over his farm line, that
measure of more or less
success—
the mortgage paid.

THE MARK

Ed Linbach's mother, on her arm,
had a dark birthmark, walnut-size,
that she kept hidden in her sleeve.

One summer a porch eave of Ed's came off
and left a spot on the house front
where the whitewash didn't reach:
"Son," she told him, "fix that eave
and cover that spot up there.
I hate to see a blemish anywhere."

HOW TO TREAT PEONIES

When I came to live on Crow Hill
early in spring, early in spring,
the peonies were pushing up
their heads of green.

A woman, come to a new house,
one told me, one told me,
must say a word to the peonies
and whisper to them kindly.

For they need a word of kindness,
to be wanted, to be wanted,
or soon or late, those green heads,
they'll die as if abandoned.

True or not, to greet them
I hurried out, I hurried out,
and dug my love around them,
speaking to every shoot.

THE LIFE OF THE HOUSE

John Moyer turns down the sound
so that the TV circus tumblers
somersault in silence. "Yes,
it is strange now, I tell you,
the temperature in winter. It is the ice.

It is the ice that does it.
Six degrees warmer here
than in Pennsburg." His son, Harold,
is not sure it is the ice.
"It may be a pocket of air
caught by the woods. It is something."
Pennsburg, that long-street town,
fades across the fields
into the white of the wind.
"I wish we could take you to the old house,"
John says against the increasing snow.
Harold: "When I was a boy,
I knew an old man in his seventies
or eighties, and he said
his grandfather came to that house courting,
and even at that time
they called it an old house yet.
Think how far back that goes." John says,
"It must be two hundred fifty years old."
"If it was not closed, you could see it.
Those that live there now are gone
so you must not go in.
But I wish you could."
"Yes, if you only could!"
"The floors. The floors are oak boards
handfitted by an overlap.
That must have been done with a knife.
The walls are oak boards and I will tell you
how they plastered them.
They took splinters, so, broke them
and nailed them to the boards,
small pieces here and there,
and plastered with straw and clay.
No lath. I broke some off,
and that straw was bright and glistening
as if just taken from the fields.
The woodwork throughout is walnut.
None would go that expense now.
Around the base of the walls
they used 'lock beams,' big
hand-hewn timbers,
and through the center of the house

370

runs a beam like a singletree
that sticks out a foot on either side.
Yes, they built it then to stay."
"Such a house is stronger," John says,
"now than when it was built."
"It is," Harold says. "All that timber
gets harder the older it gets.
You remember when we cut the windows.
We wanted to widen two windows,
and cut down one side of each. It took
the whole day to cut the two sides."
"Saw saw saw. Such a fine powder came.
And the saws were sharp too." "Ach."
"In the cellar is a spring Such water
is a gift to the house—it keeps the house
warm in winter, cool in summer.
It was good in Indian days
not to have to leave the house for water."
"Yes," Harold says, "that house goes back.
How many generations
were born in that house,
for all were born to home in those days!"
John says:
"That house is like a visit to the old days.
Yes, from such a house one can learn much.
Too bad you cannot go there
If it was not closed, you could see it."

THE RIDER TO THE ROCKS

"You have heard of the outlaw,
Bill Wade?" Harold Moyer says. "He always stole
from the rich and gave to the poor. Not money.
He'd come to a rich farmer's smokehouse,
where hams were being smoked,
and clean him out. Next morning
on a poor farmer's porch
there a ham would be hanging."
"But I guess he kept some for himself too,"

371

his father, John, says. Harold says,
"It was said, and all believed,
he could not be hit by a bullet.
One would shoot after him
as he was riding away,
but never hit him. Some tried with shotguns.
Nothing worked. He would always
head for Turkey Buzzard
and disappear among the rocks there.
There they could never find him.
He kept for such times
two or three months' supply of food
and there he would stay hid. He could even
have a fire. The smoke was spread out
that it could not be seen among the rocks."
John says, "Yes, but he had a house—"
"Yes, he had a house,
not so large a one. There
they said he made counterfeit money."
"Maybe that was said
because he always had plenty of money.
Of course it may be he could not
always avoid cash loot."
"Yes," Harold says, "that may be so."

THE PERKIOMEN RACCOON

The tree-slit moon shines on the Perkiomen, on low grass,
the damp padding of the creek bank. Down the grass
a raccoon runs, fumbling the ball of an apple.
He turns on his back and plays with it
and leaps, his mask winking in the moonlight, toward the water,
toward old winder Pakihmomink, crawler of the cranberry flats,
whisperer from stone ravines to stone barns.
At the creek margin,
he throws in the apple, which floats in the shallows,
and follows it in himself, washing what he will eat.

He gets out of the water with a backward leap,
juggling and hugging the apple, his mask laughing,
and the creek crawls onward. Powerful survivors,
water and the water's humorist.

ISAAC STAHL HUNTS THE OLD COON

"Yes, now, when I was a boy,
there's nothing I liked better than hunting coons.
There was an old one at Powder Valley
we hunted near four years and couldn't get.
Once we think sure we get him.
There was a place where two rocks make a hollow—
this raccoon run in there
and the dogs was at both ends.
Well, then, we thought we just get something
to work through and drive him out.
But he watch—yes, he watch good,
and just in a second he get out
and get past the dogs. He climbed up
a big sycamore tree by the dam.
Then we put the bull's-eye lamp on him
and tried to shoot him down.
But he knew about shooting,
yes, he knew about guns,
and he threw himself out of the tree
and run down to the dam and into the water
and he swim across the dam pond.
Some of the dogs went in after him,
but he was too fast. Yes, that and other times
he got away.

"It was winter when we get him.
We was going down to the ice pond,
and we had the dogs along.
It had come warm with fog
and snow was heavy, yes, and soft.
The dogs scent this coon—it was the old one—
and they was coming fast after him

when he throw himself in the millrace.
One dog went in after him
and that coon get on his head
and he was drowning him.
'Jump in and save him,' they yelled to me.
'It ain't my dog,' I said. I said
the one whose dog it was should go in.
So that one went and watched his chance,
freed his dog,
and he managed to throw the coon out,
yes, he threw him out on the bank
and the rest of the dogs get him then.
It was only so, at last, we catch him."

TWO PORTRAITS

In Isaac Bauman's back attic,
over the kitchen, what they call a crawl attic,
a painting rests against the roof slant.
It is of a forbear of Isaac's,
painted by one who traveled the back roads
and did portraits for a modest fee:
a week's board, including cigars.
He painted this Bauman's face
weathered and fixed but alive,
and got into the hands the gnarled look
of their gripping grain sacks.
For a Sunday mood,
he painted on those working shoulders
a suit gray and stiff as slate.
Itinerant artists of those days often
had suits already painted on,
or dresses,
and just put the hands and head in.
What does it matter now?
The head is there.
It says what a head has to say, truth,
Wahrheit,
even with less than masterly brushwork.

In nineteen forty, one afternoon
Ralph Berky came with Stephen Pillsbury
to show him the Perkiomen Seminary
and particularly
a new-hung portrait of the deceased
Dr. Oscar Schultz Kriebel
who, before he took charge of the seminary,
had swept the Hereford Literary Society
with rhetoric—that was in Ralph's father's time.
Ralph himself wanted to see the portrait.
He had been told it was by a famous artist
who "got five hundred dollars
for painting such a single portrait,"
so he and Stephen went in,
and just inside the main door hung the picture.
Ralph took a second look.
"What!" he said. "The eyes are brown
and they were blue." Turning to Stephen:
"Why, those blue eyes,
they were the whole soul of him.
So bright. They had a shine.
The man lived in those eyes
and everybody noticed them."
The treasurer, who had just come from his office
and had overheard him, said, "Yes, it's true
the eyes should be blue.
The artist worked from photographs and forgot
to ask what color the eyes were."

BACH ON THE BRANCH

Elda Maria has the come and go
of Delia Longacre's house on the branch.
She runs there
of a Sunday afternoon, familiar,
able to lounge on the pillowed sofa
and listen while "the ladies" play. Outside,
the house-width front porch, new-painted white,
is extended by peonies

dripping the heavy perfume of June
down to the barn, and in the barnyard,
a white donkey stands listening.
He flips his ears. His slanty eyes say,
"I'm lonely and funny. I can skip
lightly over the ground
on my small hoofs that crisscross
sometimes as if I'm dancing,
but here I stand kind of lonesome."
Four swallows perch
in their well-cut blue-and-pearl capes
on the barn eaves, then flap off
like souls of bats, wavering
up and down above daisies.

Inside,
violins play as the ladies practice,
Delia ruling them supportively
from the keyboard: *Concerto*
for Two Violins in D Minor.
"Try matching those triplets like single notes."
Mrs. Brumbauer asks
what is *calando,* please,
pointing her bow to the fine print,
then momentarily to her neck
where a fly is walking.
"It means slowing,
something we don't want to do right here.
Those triplets again, please." Fingers race
and the notes race after them, racketing.
A tower of digitalis on the table
drops thimbles, *fingerhut,*
finger hats that "help the heart."
Sweet William glows
with a stain like a strawberry squashed
on white china. Delia asks
if they can't go still faster.
"Not me," Mrs. Gruber says.
"I'm fading now like a tired harp."
But they do quicken the tempo anyway.
"Bach is cold, cold in his demands,"
Delia tells them,

"but if you do exactly what he says—"
As Mrs. Brumbauer waves her bow, sighing,
"Fifty times, Annabel!
Fifty times without a mistake!
Then we can play at the PTA."

Elda Maria lounges
full-length, her long legs over the sofa top,
Annabel Brumauer whizzes the notes along,
and the donkey skips
out of the barnyard and, hoofs twinkling,
skips through the window and tinkles
across the yellow ivory keys,
pianissimo vivace.

A WALK TO LOU GENTZ'S

About once a month Joe Reifsnyder
went to his neighbor's, Lou Gentz's.
He was going now.
It was his habit to wear overalls
till their blue faded to a rainy white
at the knees. His shirt
shone with a special intensity of bleached white.
He always had a straw in his mouth.
When he came to Gentz's place,
he sauntered back to the apple warehouse
where the McIntoshes thumped in the sorter
like balls thrown around in baseball practice.
Under that commotion,
the cloths of the apple polisher whirred:
"Machinery! No good comes of it, none!" This
was an old complaint of Reifsnyder's.
Gentz eyed the sorter and said,
"What machinery is this yet?
Down they come—*net?*—by gravity
and fall through the holes of themselves."
Reifsnyder: "Rollers—and a lift yet.
The polisher's a machine, I guess!"

"I guess you'd have those men of yours
do it by hand." "I'd leave the polishing go.
God made the apples so. Leave them so.
But I hear something else, Lou Gentz—
you're planning to get a tractor."
"Yeah, I can get a good one secondhand."
"I tell you, don't get it, Lou.
What you do ain't my business.
But we manage well yet in the old way.
I still use horses.
I got over four hundred acres—
every farm butted on mine
come on the market I bought it—and all that
my men and I done with horses.
No machinery.
The land feels a difference, it feels it,
the extra care the horse-plowing gives,
plow guided so, low in the heavy
and up some where the soil gets light."
Gentz leaned on a horse-stall door:
"A tractor works day and night
with the searchlight beside the seat.
The difference of this extra horse care
don't matter to a late field.
I got to get the work done, and done quick.
And don't tell me horses feed the land.
Cows can feed mine all it needs."
Talking against a vehement squeal of pigs,
Reifsnyder said, "Henry Lotz—
a second cousin of mine on my mother's side—
he got a tractor, had it two years,
then there was quite a steep downslope
from his barn to the road, yes, a ramp
of thick grass, and in that ramp
a rock stuck up some way like a tooth.
You know them little front wheels of a tractor,
well, the ones on Henry's hit that rock
and turned the tractor over on him.
The whole thing come down on his neck.
He was laid out flat for weeks,
and he's still got a backache from it,
and will have for a long time yet." Gentz

378

unhitched his belt
and pulled his shirt up off his chest.
On the left side above his heart
a pale line of scar
made a livid U by the breastbone's V.
"You got a good look of this here?
Here a horse I raised myself
kicked me and near killed me
and had no reason for it.
That is what a horse will do.
Your cousin could of pulled that rock out.
I got no warning the horse would kick.
No, I'm glad of the machine. No temper.
Eats no hay in winter. No care.
And with it I'll keep up with the fields.
'Stick to horses,' you say.
There's some other advice you gave me.
'Don't grow apples,' you said. 'It's a risk.'
Well, I grew apples and I'm making out.
I'm doing better than I was before.
You'd still like to make the old offer,
wanting to buy my farm—
I see by your face that it's so—
but this farm isn't for sale,
no, and it won't be, either."
Reifsnyder winked and said,
"You're a damn fine farmer,
and as long as you want to go on working the place,
I don't want it.
But as between horses and tractors,
don't be sure the tractor will win."
"Win or not, I'm getting it."

ANGER

Joe Reifsnyder at seventy-three
still likes to cut up a slaughtered pig.
He has the knife sharp, and on a slope
where the land opens below the barn, using the *heesehols,*

379

he hangs up the carcass
fresh from the boiling water, and on the belly
he cuts a thin red line. The dogs, though hungry,
back away, knowing he will kick them
if they come close. And they can wait.
They'll get some of the entrails later.
The men sit near, on the ground, watching
as he chews his straw, winks,
and revolves the knife in his hand.

He had an only child, a son.
Such a son, growing up alone,
means much to you. You get to think,
with no other child, how this one
will inherit. Your hunger for land
is to make a holding for him.
You plan for him.
Now he's dead, and life,
that *schwowa,* that cockroach, goes on.

His son grew up,
he had an interest in the place,
he worked along well.
Then he married a woman
a little older than he,
but that was all right.
She had looks, yes. Brought money, too.
Everything seemed as it should be.
They were to live in the house with us
as it had long been planned,
but the woman, from the first night on,
kept to her side of the bed, was silent,
then went home to her folks.

The knife works down.
The inward parts begin to be exposed,
liver, heart, kidneys, lungs.
Inside where all is protected,
where all floats in liquid,
are colors unknown to the air—

secret
reds, *veiolich,*
hot lamps of tans and yellows.
He tears at them with the knife.

Maybe what it was she wanted
was a house of her own.
We arranged for the other house.
We divided the beds, the bedclothes
between the new house and ours,
so they'd go and then come back
later when Mother and I died,
later when the house was theirs.
We put our pride down.
But no, she didn't want it—and wouldn't talk.
Then my son going to his room,
staying by himself.

To hang himself. To hang himself
for a woman! What's a woman
to die for? Oh, fool, fool,
what is it, what is it?
The next one's just as good.
He has the pig's bladder now in his hand,
the leathery sac like a balloon,
hot with living urine. He squeezes,
he pisses the urine out over the ground
in the full steaming stream
out of its swollen organ,
then throws the sac and its attachments
to the dogs. To die,
to die like that. Why?
What was that stubborn *sehnsucht*
I could not unstick from your eyes?

THE CAT

The cat, after the sudden rain,
walks in the clearing air
slowly, her soaked paws
shrunk to the essential claw.
So death, as sudden, leaves us bare.

"NERVOUS"

"Nervous," a common expression around,
heard against the winter stoves.

To Ed Kline, clockmaker, old,
comes one to visit him
after some time of absence.
It is almost impossible
not to notice a difference in him,
and the admission, as if forced, "I'm nervous.
I haven't worked now all winter.
Nervous. You understand?
My wife died. You heard? Well now,
that is quite a shock, isn't it?
It was just such a day,
I got up at six, was to work at seven,
and then at ten come my son.
I knew right away from the look
something was not right.
'I just found Mother dead,' he said.
Yes,
at first it didn't hit me so hard,
but later, yes, later—"

382

"WHO CAN SAY A LIFE IS FINISHED?"

The Reverend William J. Rupp—
Der Busch Knibbel—
sitting in his small house-front study
near the Zwingli Church in Souderton:
"Death is very final,
but also one does not die.
Who can say a life is finished?"
Saying this, he is thinking
of his father. "Two years ago
my father died. He was always strong,
and then we had word
that he was in serious trouble.
He was. He was gone when we came.
It was late at night, about one thirty,
and my wife Polly and the children
had accompanied me. My sister
was already there with my mother
and the family pastor was there too,
so we all talked about my father.
It was as if he was with us.
We began to recollect
everything about him, even funny things.
How he sang and whistled as he worked,
plowing or milking, always walked fast.
Oh, this—he had a number of ponds
in the meadow he raised fish in,
and he talked to the fish.
He liked to think they understood him,
for they would come when he talked,
but that was because he fed them.
I should tell you,
he had begun to farm in a log house, the house
in which I myself was born.
Father was a tenant farmer,
but four years later he bought his own place,
which he worked till he died.
How he loved to plant!
We talked about that.

If he had a seed in his pocket,
he would stop somewhere and plant it,
pull up the grass in a circle,
enough to get the seed started,
and put up a stick. There would be
a cornstalk growing by the barn,
or two or three beanstalks,
or a melon. Then he would nurture them,
hurrying to bring them water.
The year I was born
he asked of his brother-in-law
an ear of red corn. That strain
he kept going forty-two years.
The year he died, he had planted
a row of that same red corn.
I have a few ears still in the attic
and before the life leaves them,
I will plant them again. Father
planted rows of chestnut trees from seed
and loved them as long as they lived.
Once he found two baby raccoons
in the woods, too small to leave.
He brought them home and raised them.
He excepted from his love
only herons, bitterns, and kingfishers—
they caught his fish, ugh—
but everything else he cared for.
We talked about all that, we told stories
that kept Father still with us.
And that is how it still is.
Death has no hold on him.
Even now when I'm at the farm,
I feel that Father's still there.
I expect him at any moment
to come as always hurrying and whistling
around the corner of a building.
Yes, I expect to hear him singing."

BURIAL

"The old burials was simple, yes,
the undertaker was a carpenter
and made the coffin well, solid and tight-joined.
He done all that was needed,
and the coffin and all the services
come to three dollars and fifty cents."

THE COFFIN FACTORY:
THE LIFE OF DANIEL DENGLER

"Coffin? That is *dodalawd* in the dialect.
I was born at the century's turn, near here,
entered the factory at sixteen,
couple of times quit but went back,
must work at something, *net?* so might as well
keep at the one thing. At first
I worked out in the yard
handling boards, then when I came back
in twenty-four, I started in the mill.
I been crosscutting ever since.
Yes, shell or covered *lode*,
to make a casket, the commission
buys the wood, gets the rough boards in,
eight or nine kinds—
poplar, oak, walnut, cherry—
no pine or hickory is used.
So the boards must be cut.
Three of us use a 'swing saw'
and so the three of us cut
about eight thousand feet a day.
Also we use a 'Linderman special,'
a machine that rips, tongue-and-grooves, and glues—
that's good to do
all in the one operation, *net?*

From the mill it goes
to the assembly room
where they make them together.
Then to the lining room, then to the paint room.
Isaac Stahl, the potter, you know him,
worked in the assembly room for years.
He used to work on tops.

"It is not easy in a factory. Summers
I'd wish I was still outside.
After the sun comes on the roof,
it's a hundred five to a hundred eight.
That's hot.
When I started, I didn't get much pay.
In nineteen forty-six we had a strike.
We were out on that strike
from the first of May six months
to October twenty-sixth.
That was long, and most had it hard,
no income for six long months.
But me, I was lucky.
Just before we went out on strike,
I had an old-type swing saw
that had a guard, but I reached under it,
I reached for a piece of scrap—
I thought it was scrap, but it was the saw—
so I cut my finger off.
That gave me twenty dollars a week
for thirty weeks, six hundred dollars,
and that took me through the strike.
Yes, that was my good fortune.

"I often think how one works
all his life in one place. I think
what other things I might have done
besides make the *dodalawd*.
At least I make what you can say
all will have need of someday."

DEPOSITION OF THE READING INQUEST

The 7th day of August, 1877.
The members of the inquest,
sworn in,
deposed that trouble came slowly.
The strike was general, trainmen
out in ten states, "At Reading,"
the mayor away, the sheriff "lax,"
a crowd like an ax without a handle
gathered
Saturday night at Seventh and Penn—
no hint of riot
as they watched, quiet.
"Sunday quiet too,"
yet from Pittsburgh
a morgue smell,
and when late that evening
a train came in—a yell.
Fires flared.
The Reading fire trucks backed out
and raced toward the cut.
While they were working there
dousing burning cabooses,
the railroad bridge a mile away
went up in flame. On Monday,
Seventh and Penn's four corners
"milled" again. Strikers' spades,
the inquest said,
"spilled coal across the tracks"
and turned it into barricades.
Small boys came to watch
as trains plowed the grit. The crowd
"threatened" as the trains pulled back:
they had heard from Pittsburgh
the morgue count, twenty dead there.
Again the sheriff "lax."
The crowd and its "menace" grew.
Rocks were thrown. At dark, though
the Coal and Iron Police had sense

and stayed away, a regiment
of Pennsylvania volunteers
marched out to the strikers' jeers.
With the crowd ahead of them,
the "brave boys" heard a shout
and, stumbling and undisciplined,
raised their rifles. "Fire!"
Strikers and onlookers both
took the straight-on shot.
Lewis Eisenhower fell,
lead through his femoral,
Daniel Nachtrieb through his eye
the whistle of eternity.
Ten running from the leveled guns
lay down in the gutter's bed,
the sidewalk's hospital, and died
from their brother Germans' lead.
A small boy with pale hair,
Howard Cramp,
was carried into a drugstore
and bled to death there, victim
of the law that draws
a child after fire gong, bell,
or any noise. As the inquest put it:
"Bullets
like lightning cleared the streets
and dispersed the crowds."

THE SHOE FACTORY

The lever of the time clock presses
sharp click by click, the first
of the many leverages of the day.
Ben Hensager comes from a Boyertown street
to the clock,
shaking snow from his shoulders
and scuffing his feet on the floor.
A track of snow follows him
as he goes to the basement

to his machine near the furnace
and starts work. His work,
which never changes, is to cut soles
and tie them into bundles,
soles of children's shoes, women's, men's—
hour by hour and day by day to cut them
into their large general contour.
The soles are the base of the shoe
as the basement is of the factory,
and on his soles all depends.
He stops the ongoing motion
and, wrapped in a cloud of heat
warmer for the snow outside,
holds a sole that for a moment
becomes an identity,
becomes something he sees,
then losing his sense of it, he puts it
into a bundle
and takes all to the hoist, "the freight."

The hoist's doors open at the first floor
where belts flap against steam. Here
Irv Bauer's arms chop in unison
with those of the other men at the flat dies
that cut the lining and the top leather.
Each man, for this operation,
a skilled one, has a presser
he guides around over and presses down
and makes the cuts with two dies.
Bauer seems to work haphazardly,
yet he gets seventy cuts from one hide.
His is the second step
in the sequence of the shoe,
which is interconnected like the belts.
He shoves the presser with its slide of option,
and the dies cut and cut,
and the cut linings and upper leather
at his side flash together, sewn.
Martha Bentz with a gas torch
sears the excess thread off,
the blaze in her hand such
that she must watch,

keeping away from her eyes
that hypnotic, single eye:
In a sleep of motion
the mind can step aside,
think without thinking,
and let the danger come near.

Alwin Schultz puts on eyelets
with a ratatat from a gun.
He is a shanghaied farmer
like so many factory workers,
and sifts the eyelets like grain in bins—
silver, brass, black, and white.
There in their mounds they gleam:
a gleaming ripple of the fieldside brook
last spring as he plowed,
and out of the shining shallows emerged
a line of little ducklings
climbing the low mud to the bank.
They were a clutch
not of his own ducks, but of mallards
that he had fed and that—
not too much to his surprise—
had stayed. Mallards do that,
stay awhile as if tamed,
walk in cow tracks, and eat grain.

With the linings and upper leather ready,
the hoist again is loaded and rises
and opens its doors on a new floor
of lighter machinery.
At a sewing machine here, "Speed" Schenk,
pressing the curving top leather down,
starting at the toe of the last,
makes the final seam, drilling its path
all around the sole Hensager made.
From him, rhythmically the shoe
passes from hand to hand.
Ed Furst trims the sole roughly
with a gashed edge like scissoring,
and young Jim Kempner
trims it close with a wheel knife.

390

A drip of water follows the wheel
to keep the new leather from sticking. Now
Steve Johnson, the "leveler,"
begins his repeated motion,
running a wooden roller over each sole,
back and forward short over the heel,
a long dip forward, turn,
a long dip back on the other side,
again two short runs on the heel.
Breathe, and back and forth again.
Breathe, and back and forth again,
touching all with the leveling
that smooths the sole toward an unknown foot.
Into this push and pulling back of his hand
comes a face: a girl
who holds her head tipped to the side.
Elaine: that a mother scolded her,
that she had faults, stubbornness,
that for years, a child,
she liked to lie on her stomach, reading,
all this—which he knows, for he has known her
"since he can remember"—
is gone into strangeness.
She is dressed in a light
in which all her ordinariness
has left her.
Looking toward him in her new state,
she waits.
Breathe, and back and forth again.
Breathe, and back and forth again.

AN INTERRUPTED ACCOUNT
OF THE CIGAR FACTORY

"I better get those bundles tied up
else I won't get done till night." Baling,
Roy Kintner remembers one year
he used nine needles:

"Oh, I was so mad.
Then I broke another set.
I made four hundred bales
and it broke again." His small son
comes and reaches an arm through his
and leans against him. Behind him
an older girl comes and stands,
stroking her father's hair. "Yes,
the needles broke so many times
on the eight hundred bales of hay,
yes and eight hundred more of straw,
it would have paid me to get it baled.
But about cigar making"—
his son now runs off,
not interested in cigar making—
"I remember it well,
the factory in Red Hill.
We got our materials from the supervisor
and must make so many cigars.
We were allowed four free cigars a day.
Even so, some would skimp
and make a dozen for themselves.
The beginners had this common fault,
they always made them too wet
and packed the fillers too tight.
You couldn't draw the smoke through them, then.
The old hands packed them loose and spongih.
You could draw through them good.
We were independent now, I tell you.
We worked whenever we felt like it
and stopped when we felt like it too.
Yes, anytime
we'd bring up our material to the supervisor
and leave. The factory was always open. We'd come
five, six o'clock in the morning
if we wanted to." The boy
brings a clicking beetle in his fingers
and puts it on its back on the table.
"Why don't it jump?" he says.
"I'm talking now, Billih boy.
You must leave it alone or you'll fright it.
Leave it alone and it will jump."

Just as Kintner starts speaking again,
his girl pokes the beetle. "Let be now,"
he says. "You must both be quiet.
Only so will it jump."
Having said this, he himself
becomes interested and waits
until the beetle, on its back,
leaps into the air with its click
and, landing on its face, walks away.
"What was I saying? What was I saying just now?"
He can't remember

LONG SONG

This is summer up Crow Hill,
this is the crow runs like a cat,
this is the man hates the crow,
this is Elda Maria's spot,
this is where the winds blow,
this is Uhr's wife holds her hat,
this is the cedar's threadbare sail,
this is the spider's dewy *schnur,*
this is the parlor of the wood,
this is the vireo hidden there,
this is Percy Hertzog's pump,
this is the milkweed's small green lamp,
this is the shrew leaps the sill,
this is the mallard lying still,
this is Linda Yost's dim hair,
this is the Forge Dale tavern bar,
and this is Mars, the rising star,
this is the ma lies down to rest,
this is her daughter on her cot,
this is the moon rows through the mist,
this is the mist the moon forgot,
this is the Old Mennonite meeting,
this is the God-slowed four-part song,

these are the women's voices sweet,
these are the men the voices meet,
this is the hummingbird at dawn,
this is her invisible wing,
this is the early morning rain,
this is the grass it glimmers on,
these are the eyes of young Arlene,
this is the orchard's morning gaze,
this is the sun comes through the trees,
this is the Crow Hill sunlit breeze,
this is the summer of the hill
near and *recht* and still.

PART FOUR

BORDER INCIDENT

Harvey Bauman had a field
ending in a small wedge of woods
owned by his neighbor, Erwin Rauch.
The wedge that was not his own
and made his field crooked at that end,
made him feel *"net recht"*—
he did not like it,
so he offered to buy the woods.
Rauch refused.
Bauman plowed close to the "damn trees,"
tearing the roots, letting the plow turn
at any stone and cross the line.
Rauch nailed up a sign: KEEP OUT.
He nailed it up in the evening
and the next morning, there it was.
It is not neighborly, such a sign—
it is an intended insult,
so in the road
Bauman did not speak to Rauch.
Rauch now made a chicken yard of the woods
in a show of ownership,
though frankly it was inconvenient for him
and he had to put chicken wire
the whole length of the wood edge.
Still he did it. The new wire
leaned in places over Bauman's ground.
Even a few chickens escaped
and scratched here and there in Bauman's field.

Later, coming to himself,
Rauch removed the chickens
and took down the fence and sign,
and the two men spoke again.

Several years later Bauman
decided to sell the field to Joe Reifsnyder,
whose land it bordered to the south. For this
he had to survey. Like others,

397

when he had bought his farm,
he had had the owner take him around
and show him what the boundary lines were.
All did it so at the time,
relying on the owner's word.
But to sell a part was different.
He got out his deeds now
that went back through ten owners
to the original description
of the farm's boundaries.
He read the language: "Following
a line NNW 0.29"
so and so many perches.
"Following a line . . ." This language
was not for him. This was something
for Squire Frank Benfield. The squire,
though eighty-six, still did surveying.

On Tuesday morning came the squire, tall,
a wool shirt hanging from his shoulders,
leggings strapped to his big legs,
and the surveying implements
gathered in his arms like saplings.
"Come," he said, and, earth crumbling
where he walked, they crossed
to the far corner of Bauman's farm.
There the squire established the corner mark
by a boulder and by the side road,
and set up the transit.
He gave the stick to Bauman
and directed him down the wall
that went past Reifsnyder's land toward Rauch's.
He called to have several beech shoots broken
that had come into his line of sight
until he could set the angle.
Then he came measuring with the chain.
When he reached Rauch's slant of woods,
he indicated that the deed boundary
followed the woods' edge exactly.
They went further along this side
adjoining Rauch's land, the squire reading
the measurements and angles

until, at a certain distance down,
he had a puzzled look. He walked
past the end of the dragging chain.
"Well, we will see." He continued
until he came to the main road.
He did not put a mark here,
but went back the length of Bauman's farm
along the main road. From the corner mark there
he measured with the chain back to Rauch's,
to a stone wall
that was a boundary between the farms.
Beyond this wall, a narrow lane
gave Rauch access to his fields
from the main public road.
"So," the squire said, holding the chain,
"it seems your land goes ten feet further
than your wall here shows.
It goes practically to Rauch's barn.
Sometime somebody, it seems,
made a mistake, didn't follow
the original measurements right.
Hard to understand,
but such things do sometimes happen. Of course
if that's how it's been all these years,
best to let it stay that way."
Ten feet would close Rauch's lane, and Rauch
could not easily get around his barn
on the other side. His house was there
and the slope was bad.
It would be a hard thing
to open a new lane to his fields. Thinking of this,
Bauman remembered the slight of three years back,
he remembered the sign: KEEP OUT.
It would be pleasant now
to show so that he could close Rauch's lane.
But if he spoke, he knew Rauch.
Yes, he knew him well. Rauch then
would refuse at any cost
to use the lane, use
something that did not belong to him.
Squire Benfield was right.
"Let it go," Bauman said.

WINDOW EAST, 1967

The photographer takes a quick long shot
down Crow Hill toward Bally and beyond
where the valley
holds winter air
as if in a flat white plate.

He passes a barn
and some sheep
and clicks a plain Palatinate
house front where a boy
takes him in to his mother,

Mary Gehman. She looks young,
wearing her Mennonite cap like a girl.
She smiles. Why
should there be a reporter-photographer
because "Linny" is in Vietnam?

It's typical of Linny to be there.
The medical profession was in his makeup
since the day he was born. Abe,
her husband, who has just come in, agrees.
"Abe had wanted to be a doctor," so that thought

hung over Linford's birth:
"He was a three-pound two-ounce baby
and no incubator in those days."
Still he lived and grew,
and he was "a fine boy, not too big." Played

in the ball park of the fields.
Easy-going seemingly—calm.
A strange thing: "From early childhood," Abe says,
"he liked
to use the knife." If

during butchering he saw anything
"a little different from the ordinary,
he wanted to cut it open
and see what the texture of it was."
So his hands learned.

Called by the draft but like his church
holding against killing,
he became a C.O.,
a hospital orderly.
From that

he had that longing
to become a doctor.
Nearly a decade later
when the Mennonite
Vietnam Christian Service

needed volunteers,
Paul Longacre asked Linny, now an M.D.,
and Linny said yes. "They're both there now,
and Paul's wife too."
Of the seventy

Mennonites now in Vietnam,
three are from Bally. Mary:
"They get fifteen dollars a month.
Linny's in the evangelical clinic
at Nha-Trang.

"The natives come,
the sick—women, children, older people.
No wounded, but some of our girls
do care for the wounded
further north.

"Linny's been there
two years.
This winter it isn't as rushed.
He's trying to learn Vietnamese.
He believes

'when the patient tells you
through an interpreter,
you lose a few details.'
He wants to learn direct,
at firsthand.

"They care for as many
as two hundred thirty a day.
Lots of eye cases." Linford writes,
"We'll be operating every forenoon.
Of course our regular clinic

will hum as usual. And the hospital
continues to carry a pretty high census
of acute illnesses:
plague, pneumonia, typhoid."
February 18—

"We did a procedure this morning
for a secondary cataract
that was completely new to me.
I'd never seen the instrument
that we used before."

Abe:
"Linny's aggressive.
He believes people die
because nobody does anything about it,
and he's doing something. There he can act."

So he's there, but
he wears a tennis cap and enjoys it
when the plane
taking him to Dalat
circles a waterfall. He writes:

"We should be finished with surgery
by noon, at which time all of us
will attend a pre-Tet dinner." Tet,
the Vietnamese New Year.
He plays tennis, afterward, on courts

one hundred degrees
in the shade.
He sends a snapshot of himself,
racquet lifted
in the Nha-Trang sun.

THE FRAGMENT

As spring lengthened under the Chaine Annamitique, Dr. Dana
    O. Troyer taught Linny the latest techniques of eye
    surgery. Him and Harold Kraybill.
"We're taking turns operating along with Dr. Troyer. I did
    a discission of a cataract on a seven-year-old Tribes boy.
Another case today was that of a thirteen-year-old boy with a
    piece of shrapnel inside the right eye. We localized the
    fragment by X rays and examination with an ophthalmoscope."
Mirror and pinpoint light, light without sensation.
"We put him to sleep with ether and made an opening in the
    lower part of the eye. Harold devised a magnetic tool,
    wrapping coils of electric wire around a bolt and hooking
    it up to the VW battery."
The fragment was unfortunately lead, so the magnet didn't work,
    but they got it out anyway.
Intense fighting to the north, "coming closer" along the China
    Sea. Increasing demands on the clinic by eye patients—
    cataracts and in some cases, wounds. "We're weary."

Linny went to the Hon Chong rock, a high point over the beach
    tinged with pink at sunset, weedy at low tide, and he and
    Harold, accompanying themselves with their two guitars,
    sang "*Christ Is Risen,*" or, as he wrote, they sang in the
    hospital or the TB house,
and the Vietnamese outside listened on grass mats,
    with round hats and white gowns.
Mary wrote back: "How we do pray and wish for peace!"

DISCONNECTED
(Winter, 1968)

On Crow Hill at dawn, Marvin Hofmeier
looks at the new snow blown
thick with March moisture
across the night,
weighing everything down.
A pine branch
on the west side of the hill
is pressed to the earth's surface
like a hand put out
to save the tree from falling
and he thinks,
The strong fingers
are fastened,
and he does not like
that unnatural snow weld
of bough to ground.
He thinks of Linny Gehman
now in Vietnam.
Recent attacks,
have they overrun his hospital?
His folks worry.
These doctors, these do-gooders,
going off to a foreign country
when there's so much
to be done at home.
To his surprise
the branch he saw bound down
shakes itself free
and moves evenly
in the morning air.

A MEMORY OF WORMDITT

Arnold Haase-Dubosc was visiting Fred Braun
and, the talk turning to the Anabaptists, he said:
"I grew up in Wormditt, a small town
in what was then East Prussia. It is now Poland
and the town name is now Orneta. When I was a boy,
I remember there was this certain house
lived in by Anabaptists. I even think
it was used by the few Anabaptists
as their church. At any rate we children always
went around the house, we didn't go near it.
We were warned
not to touch these people.
Anabaptists were '*tauflos,*'
'without baptism,' they were the 'old outcasts'
as the Jews were the 'new outcasts.' I don't remember
that I ever even saw any of them."

THE COW:
THE LIFE OF WALTER SHUHLER

Large wet nurse of human babies,
just freshened, left out alone
in Walter Shuhler's meadow during her calf's weaning,
she bawls restlessly. Shuhler this year
has almost eighty cows:
forty-six milkers, thirty heifers.
The years have waved the stiff-tailed houris
into his barn, a procession
as long as his patience. They are in the barn now,
in their stalls. Only in the meadow
a fallen willow holds one cow
fenced. It is night. The wind on the hills
blows softly as a killdeer
darts over the stops of the stars.

"I was one of nine boys, no girls—"
Born almost sixty years ago
along with the new century,
in Lycoming County, near Bastress.
There he stayed only a year.
Joseph, his father, then
hauled the whole family out to Kansas
to the sailing plains
where they could have "three hundred acres"—
where it was flat and easy.
Easy, yes, but, with Osage orange hedge
and only slight undulations of the plain,
it was unfamiliar
and there was no certainty:
Some years the drought killed everything.
They remembered home then
when in the worst year "you made something."
In snow
they hauled all back again—
stock, horses, chickens—
and took a few-acres farm
at Kraussdale. After Kansas,
that Kraussdale smallness felt good.

Nine boys, nine boys,
a baseball nine,
the ball cracked over
the field-end pine.
The pine grew.
The boys gave up
diamond
and baseball caps.

On Route One Hundred, not far from Bally,
next to Owen Gerhard's place,
Irwin Henry had opened a small quarry.
He had a daughter, Florence, born country girl,
good-natured and able to do.
His farm, neglected
because of the quarry, needed working.
When, at picnics of the Catholic Church,
young Walter Shuhler met Florence

406

and liked her, that was it.
They'd work the farm,
so she would live as a wife
where she had lived as a child.

"It's hard at the start," he says.
"At first we raised chickens in summer
and steers in winter. I went out to Lancaster
and bought the steers when they were thin,
put them in the barn here and fed them.
Fifteen head each September,
some from the Dakotas, one year Texas,"
hungry leatherbacks.
"At least they gave fertilizer,
and in April, May, or June,
I sold them as the market was,"
then from the incubator's door,
two thousand baby chicks, so
steers and chicks, chicks and steers,
a seesaw of the seasons until:
Joseph, named for Shuhler's father,
Herman, Ralph (named for Shuhler's brother),
and Mathew ("Matty"),
four new "hands," all willing.
When Joseph was old enough to help,
all the feeding steers were moved out
to make way for a planned transformation.

"To start, we bought about twenty
Holstein purebred two-weeks-old calves."
Two and a half years for these
to freshen and come to milk,
two and a half years of waiting
and all the feed going out
and little income coming in,
trucks piling up the silage
and wet tongues drawing it down.
"I had good luck. All raised all right."
Before he started to ship milk,
he had four Guernseys. These he kept—
golden pitchers for the butterfat—
"but I bred to the Holsteins."

Yes, this matter of breeding.
"A cow now gets in heat
and stud is needed. Not many anymore
use the bull as in the old days. One calls
for the 'insemination man.'
Another name is 'the technician.' He comes
with a syringe and chilled semen.
Well, you know how it is.
It's almost like a doctor.
He injects it so."
Shuhler says "one has to do it."
The semen is from the purest-bred bulls,
ten thousand dollars a head
such as no single farmer can afford.
Nine or ten inseminator men
are always cruising with their bottles
in two-way-radio cars.
Yes, it's modern science:
"I haven't lost a cow in ten years.
The herd is strong. No Bang's Disease
to be spread by the bull.
The calves are better all the time."
Looking toward a neighboring farm,
he says, "Heffner
is the only one keeps his own bull
or keeps to the old ways.
I don't agree with him, but—"
This age that comes on now—
the sky marked at night with strange streaks,
satellites—this scientifically efficient age
has the hurt of its benefits.
"You feed the cows 'top production,'
only the best, and it burns them.
In the old days you gave them their hay,
corn chop, linseed oil meal,
and you turned them out in summer.
Now they stay in the barn all year round,
balanced feed, measured protein—
it's a kind of stress.
It worries me.
Something they need is missing."

But he goes with the times,
and every improvement he can make
he makes. Look now at a modern barn.
He works with his four boys,
and every motion is precise.
It is a *ballet mécanique.*
One boy brings circular bales
and unrolls hay in front of the stanchions.
Shuhler fixes over a cow's back
a strap to hold the milker.
The cows get the habit of it
and are ready for its electric hands.
In five minutes the milking is done,
the four udders pulled and drained,
and the machine moved to the next strap.
The son whose job it is takes the milk
and runs with it (runs!) to the cooler.
A few cats watch from a distance,
left over from the old days
when a farmer might lift an udder
and shoot milk into their mouths.
The machine has no deviation
into humor—works one way.
In an hour and a half
thirty cows are milked, then the machines
are unbound and put away,
removed from their electric saucers.
The automatic manure-cleaner
revolves in its trough and stops.
All is quiet. In the hush,
the barn becomes an old barn again
(even with the *forschuss* gone),
and the cows stir and low.
Shuhler pats one on the flank. He says,
"*Dubble*—that in the dialect
means 'spotted'—she's a pet.
All are pets. Minnie, Donna, Lynne.
Cassie, Susie, Lucky, Linda, Bootie—
Boots. Yes, each one is different.
One won't kick, another will.
Some are nervous, others not.
Some are shy, others will come to you.

There are some, in the temperament,
just like their mothers. Others
have their own ways." Rough tongues
rasp in the easy silence.
"My brother Ralph, who is the priest,
says perhaps the beasts have souls,
something anyway. Yes, he comes
sometimes and helps, but I do not pay him.
He has taken the vow of poverty."

In the first night-dark
Shuhler crosses the wide lane end
to a shed near the house.
Here he picks up a long stick
and, going to two trees behind the house,
hits the limbs. Roosting chickens,
who have learned his will, jump down.
They shall not be in the trees at night.
No, they shall go into the shed.
The fox still makes his rounds in the dark. Florence,
standing in the kitchen door
near the stars,
hears from the meadow a renewed bawling—
Mmmmmmbaaaaaaaah.
It's that just-freshened cow.
It seems to her nice,
somewhat like it used to be.

ODE TO A NEW DISCOMFORT
(Walter Shuler)

What is this discomfort I feel
about machinery, the need to turn my back
to the silage-blower
and look down to the dying willow?
Kneeling in church, I hear
the Latin words, wanting
not only their pauses between the bells
that ring my childhood back,

410

but a past beyond that.
Now all just goes ahead.
Machinery. I know
it took ten men on three wagons
to get the silage in by hand.
With no time to wait,
they cut grass in the morning
when it was wet and heavy.
Corn fodder was hard to haul too.
Now two men do it all quickly,
grass running in the blower
up to the silo's top—
a kind of grassy sump pump.
The tractor too does everything fast,
rolls fast on the ground—six furrows
and only a smell of gasoline
behind the rubber haunches. Sometimes
I miss the smell of horse urine.
The harness still hangs in the barn there,
but the whinny's gone.

THE ANVIL

In the door of the barn, Shuhler sits on a stool,
in front of him the traditional tool,
der dengel-shtock—
dengel-shtock on which to beat a scythe,
to straighten its blade, to sharpen its wide
crook—
dengel-shtock, that friend of the past,
one of the friends the fields outlast.

Automatic milkers don't help him now;
no help the gadgets that perplex the cow,
that natural thing.
He wants to think and he needs the tap
of a hammer on the blade of a scythe, the rap
and rhythmic lulling
that, years before the "insemination man,"
helped him summon up his fields and plan.

411

MISPLACED KANSAS

In nineteen forty-nine,
when the Walter Shuhler farm
was about fixed up as a dairy,
a cyclone came up Butter Valley.
Sunday evening, "a little before nine—
twenty minutes to nine," the sky darkened.
"We were in the barn. Didn't hurry.
We had this and that to do,
but as we came to the house,
we saw it was very black,
and I noticed a flickering. I said to Florence,
'It's a cyclone over the hill there.'
I recognized it from Kansas,
we ran then. I wanted to pull the electric switch
in the cellar. I told the family,
'Keep away from the windows.'
Lucky they were all inside.
When I pulled the switch, it was pitch dark.
I could see flashes. I could see rafters fly over.
I didn't know they were from my own house.
There was a kind of deep roaring hum
that the wind and pressure make.
Everything was rocking and shaking,
whatever could shake. It was over
in about fifteen seconds.
We were the worst hit in the valley.
The house roof was off altogether,
and the chimneys. Most of the window frames
were pushed right in. Outside,
everything was mashed up. The silos down.
All the big trees were over, flattened.
You can still see the stumps.
It came from the south
and was only a few hundred feet wide.
We were hit right in the middle.
If it wasn't for the house that split it,
it would have taken the barn. As it was,
when the house split it,

412

one part went down this way
and took the roof off a small pig stable.
The other part went that way
and took a chicken house, everything—
took it all away. The chickens
were scattered on the hill and next day
came walking back. I heard a few
were down in Clayton close to that
manufacturing place down there.
The barn wasn't hit,
but on the barn's side near the house
about fifteen feet of boards
broke where the house roof blew against it
and pushed the frame about two inches.
But just so the barn stayed. Lucky
the cattle were in the barn, it didn't hurt them.
I had started to make a hen house
out of a temporary corncrib.
I had two two-by-fours
nailed with eightpenny nails,
and the wind tore one of them to pieces
and didn't touch the other.
Still it wasn't as bad as a fire.
But it was bad enough.
The trees that were over broke fences.
We were most of the night clearing the lane.
The next day,
shingles, tin, and nails lying all over
in the meadow and the fields.
If the cows eat wire or nails,
it will kill them, so we carefully
cleaned off the meadow first—that was still
where we mainly fed the cows—
and let the cows out. We put
a canvas over the house roof
and four days later, by Thursday,
we had the roof back on.
It was a cyclone, all right. Strange,
there never was one before
and never has been one since.
I've seen it in Kansas, a cloud
let down a wind funnel that would shoot along

faster than you could run
and everything it touched was gone.
But who'd think
that Kansas would chase you here?"

MARY GEHMAN TALKS
ABOUT HER FATHER

Mary Gehman sits in the living room,
a low-ceilinged room that looks out
on a field on Crow Hill's east slope.
On the wall across from her, a motto:
"In quietness and confidence
shall be your strength." The kitchen stove,
visible through an open arch,
has many drafts and checks carefully balanced
to offset the early April cold.
"My father"—Elias Kulp—
"was a strong man,
very energetic, hardworking.
He was impatient, never claimed to have much patience,
but he was loving.
I was still a little girl
when we came to Bally
and rented first a hundred-acre farm
down the hill from here. Father favored it
because it had a cellar spring.
The land was in bad shape. We called
one field 'the peach-orchard field'
because it had stumps of a peach orchard
that we had to take out—typical.
Many don't appreciate hill land."
But her father was willing to work it,
patient with land.
She helped him and scooted after him.
She went to the creamery with him.
"He enjoyed singing.

He sang 'In the Sweet By and By'
in German as he drove along."

At the table they prayed. His voice
had a fervor of thought.
It was a kind of predestination.
He had an aptitude for talk,
and "when he was in his forties,
he was nominated to be minister
of the Bally Old Mennonite Church.
Four drew lots and he was chosen.
He began his ministry at once."
None had special training then.
He stood up and spoke from the pulpit,
a prophet from the fields, a flail of God, his forehead
blunt with God's will, inflexible
for the Bible and its truths
as generations of his faith
had brought it on and understood it.
He tried in that understanding
to be without worldly accommodation,
to live by faith: Menno's love,
proofs of that love as God's love
for all men, rejection then
of any kind of violence.
Enough the single command, to love.

The church wanted its leaders
to be like others—to work.
Elias bought a fourteen-acre farm
further up Crow Hill and worked it.
He also drove a mail route. But, working,
he found the demands of the church
increasingly took his time.
The church sought him out for evangelism,
for it was noticed
he could pour the light of God's lamp
into the listener's soul. It was as if
he spoke directly to each one
who listened to him. These services

for conversion and revival
"might keep him away
for ten days or two weeks.
He had to hire a substitute driver
for the mail route,
and farm work suffered. But he did it."

Mary had been in school in Bally
with a farmer's son, Abraham Gehman.
When she was nineteen,
she and Abe got engaged. A year later,
in nineteen thirty-one,
"we got married. It might not seem
a great time to get married,
at the beginning of the Depression,
but the Depression didn't mean much.
We never had much money,
and Abe just kept on farming.
We bought here on Crow Hill,
two farms up the hill from Father's,
and here we were to be from then on.
We truck-farmed. And we kept sheep
to supplement the farm income."
They now have a large flock.
Out behind the barn the old ones
stand trembling in the still-chill weather
in spite of their heavy fleece,
or lie like barrels
that winter has left on the damp ground.
"We have thirty old ones
and get maybe thirty-five young ones
every year. Abe
shears them at the end of April
when the cold rains are over.
He ties the wool from each sheep
in a bundle and takes all the bundles
to Reading and sells them in the 'wool pool.'

"It was good, when the children were growing"—
she has had ten children—
"to be near Father. The children often
would slip off to his house,

and Linny especially
would sit on his inside steps
and listen when he talked.
I guess Father was more patient with them,
you get more patient as you grow older.
Anyway they all liked to go. You learn
from somebody like Father," somebody
who had a light on his tongue.

BIAFRAN MONODY, 1970

A road with some red dust, rust of the harmattan haze
blowing down from the Sahara in veils,
in fogs and penetrations,
        a cover,
a coating of faint blood on the cassava fields
        near the Cross River, laterite blood
blushing and paling up from rock.
On the road, a naked girl
unsexed by starvation
walks ahead of others, protein-hungry.
The Niger, great Niger,
        glistening elbow above the delta, drooping
        in its green slot.
What has pulled Linford Gehman here
                from the hill
                where a gawk of guinea hens
is the only revelation of the air,
                and peach-tree stumps
are lost in merely the mist of morning?
Not russet and yellow clothes,
the blue-clothed West, the white-clothed North,
        Balewa's robes with cloth ribs
flowing like bronze sadness
across his breast, Balewa
dead now.
Not mud houses, thatched cones toward Umuahia,
                not terraces
opening rain-forest dikes

417

against the coastal swamps—a people:
"Be not afraid, Renascent African . . . wake up
        and claim your heritage
        or be forever destined to draw water"
                Zik.
No, only children,
the children's line of oval eyes,
hunger.

"I came in by night on the Loftleider,
a plane from Amsterdam
down to Sao Tome, then by a Joint Church Aid DC 6
to Uli airstrip.
That's on the road from Onitsha to Owerri."
Linny's voice tends to be monotone,
nothing exaggerated.
"A young Canadian took us
to Ubulu to the relief warehouse,
and we slept there on air mattresses
on the floor; with me, Wally and Evelyn Shellenberger
who had been three years
at Abiriba Hospital,
also Atlee Beechy,
Dean of Students at Goshen College
who had just been on the Federal side.
He had had to fly to Amsterdam and back
to reach the east. I knew him from Vietnam.
The next morning
the Canadian drove us to Umuahia, the capital,
and from there we drove to Abiriba Hospital."

Nigeria, fifty-six million blacks,
where no whites own land. Africa
facing whites equably;
black doctors, black nurses,
most speaking some English
or good English. Ibo children reaching
with grace for all that books
could give them. "At the hospital
at first I took care of the clinics,
saw outpatients from eight in the morning
to two o'clock in the afternoon.

418

But after the bombing we were reluctant
to work after eleven in the morning.
We began at seven
and tried to have most of the patients
returned to their homes by eleven.
I would alternate with the Biafran doctor
in taking the emergency calls that came in."
He did surgery, worked
"in much the same way I had done
in Vietnam. Casualties were sparse
until February twenty-sixth
when we got those two hundred
in one day, from Ozu Abam.
The hospital was moved later, and two Biafran doctors,
Dr. Odim and Dr. Udoji,
were put in charge.
The difficulty was to get medicine.
Biafra had wonderful doctors,
but what can a doctor do
if he doesn't have medicine?
And if a patient doesn't have food,
the medicine isn't even good." Children
were fed "pap" from corn, yams, or cassava (garri),
they lacked protein, so
they thinned dangerously.
Now even pap was scarce.
"You could go in any village,
could walk through the streets and find
signs of malnutrition.
Some of the reporters would create the picture
that all of Biafra was this way.
Actually the studies that were done
showed fifteen to twenty-five percent
dangerously malnourished.
Of the remainder maybe half
were hungry. Still it seems likely
that at least a million died.
You could see the starved all over. Only
about two hundred tons of food a night
came in on the airlift,
and maybe four hundred were needed.
It was protein that was needed

to stay alive. For the children especially.
Dried codfish was flown in
from Scandinavia. CSM,
dried milk, from the United States.
Caritas International unloaded the planes one night
and the next night the World Council of Churches,
and we received our supplies
from the WCC warehouse.
But never enough.
Quite often, during this time,
there would be three or four children in a clinic
who would be severely malnourished,
so bad that at first, I remember one Tuesday
two or three died
right in the Okporo Enyi clinic.
We used to take intravenous fluids with us
for severely dehydrated children
and we would put them on the table
and give them the fluid at once,
and then the last two months
a sick bay was set up
at Ibere about ten miles away
and we would take two or three of the worst cases
from the clinic to the sick bay.
At first we noticed
the ones we took to the sick bay died
shortly after we took them there
because we were taking only
the most malnourished children,
the ones who were almost dead already,
and we realized then
that they had reached a point
that their condition was irreversible,
given the conditions
under which we worked, so
though it's a difficult choice to make,
we knew we didn't have enough food for everybody
and we had to give it to those
we had found through experience
could be saved.
Those who could be saved
we gave three meals of protein a week,

420

then they lived." The waiting line
of children in the street
approached doctor and nurse, backs bony, hair
graying and uncurling from starvation.
"A QUAC stick,
a Quaker Arm Circumference stick,
took their measurements,
the height by the stick,
their upper-arm circumference by a band,
and from the correlation
selected the ones to be fed."
Sometimes some fled
not away from but to the doctor's arms
and clung as to a mother.

East of the Niger,
slender white faces of spirits,
female death masks with narrow eyes,
    bared teeth,
    and rows of tribal cicatrices
across the foreheads. To be propitiated.
    Maji knife-masks
    and sickles curved upward, the yam-cutters.
Spirits of the yam shrine.
In houses, behind the mud-arched doors under sun rivers
    of grass,
ikenga, idols of good fortune,
horned forms
    with "attributes held in the hand."
Everywhere along riverbanks—
    combs, crests, helmets
and other erections and defenses
against hunger.
Ibo children
go hungry to school past sounding
water rites, rituals, and morning rains.

ABIRIBA AFTER

After the war, the Quaker Service,
invited by the Ministry of Health
and the state government, with three doctors started
reactivating Abiriba Hospital.
The hospital had lost
all its medical equipment, and a Friend
reported it had missing
"2/3 of its roof." Still
ninety percent of the staff
was back. The townspeople cleaned out the wards,
burned all the brush off the ground, and took
roofs from nonessential buildings
to reroof the hospital. Every person
gave three sticks of bamboo
to make beds. The one building now
with its small staff
on its cleaned grounds,
served the Chafia Division,
which had a population
of over two hundred thousand.

BO-CAU

May 6, 1972:
clouds blow over Crow Hill
and over delicate lilac tufts
just opening by the downhill windows
of the Gehman's house.
In the kitchen
Bo-Cau is walking barefoot.
"Nothing on your feet!" Johanna cries,
and sweeps Bo-Cau up laughing into her arms,
but the laugh controlled.
This is a child whose body memory
carries Vietnam's grief:

"People who have gone through so much suffering
are resigned to almost anything,"
Abe says. Hurt, but against the hurt, love
in Bo-Cau's large eyes, in her upper lip that lifts to love
in a seeking, sensitive arch.

When Linford recruited Johanna for Vietnam, his sister
was a Goshen College graduate
and had taught school: she was strong and small, slim,
with straight black hair trimmed thin down her neck
and with large dark eyes
so that later on,
wearing a conical straw hat tied by its under-chin ribbon,
she could pass unnoticed for a Vietnamese.
She joined the International Voluntary Service
to teach. To get ready to teach,
she went where Linny was, to Nha-Trang,
to study Vietnamese. "There
I didn't learn much more
than about the tonal language."
When she was assigned to the city of Sa-Dec,
south of Saigon where the Mekong River branches
to empty into the sea,
"Neighbors' children helped me learn to talk."
She lived in a white boxlike house,
and an older girl she shared the house with, Xuan,
helped her even more.
"I was teaching high school English.
I found this orphanage nearby
and started to work there.
Americans are supposed to help, aren't they?"
Then Minh Hang, "That was her name, the name
the nuns at the orphanage gave her
on her birth certificate, but when she cried,
she sounded like a mourning dove,
so I asked if they had doves in Vietnam
and they did. The name for a dove
is Bo-Cau, so I called her that."
Bo-Cau was born December eighteenth,
nineteen sixty-nine,
in a Sa-Dec hospital and was abandoned by her mother
who went back to Saigon to continue

whatever the war had made her into.
The baby was sent to the orphanage.
"She was so perfect
I fell in love with her.
I watched over her carefully,
but in spite of that, there in the orphanage,
in the contagion there
(the orphanage was really filthy),
boils appeared on her head, staph.
What I did for her then during the day
wasn't enough. The orphanage lack of care during the night
undid what I had done,"
so she asked permission to take Bo-Cau home,
and they let her. After that, Bo-Cau
became hers, her child,
the small head gradually smoothing over,
the dehydration, from which so many died,
stopping.
She slept on a mat on the floor,
penned in by bolsters, or on a bench.
Lying on her stomach, she lifted her head up,
staring out at the strange clean room.

To keep her safe,
Johanna carried her by day
in her arms or on a bike or sampan.
As Bo-Cau grew, they traveled on "the Honda—
I put a diaper over the handlebars
to protect her,"
and they rode through streets where,
in a town physically the size of Bally,
thirty-five thousand people lived.
"Everybody knew her
because I carried her, because she was mine
and I cared for her. They asked what I had done
for the staph. I told them, hot compresses,
I told them what to do. No, they wouldn't. Everybody,
even the nuns in the orphanage,
scraped the baby's back with a spoon
'to get the bad air out,' the 'poisonous air.'
They scraped till the back was raw."

424

Bo-Cau's back was smooth.
She grew. She got strong.
She watched lizards run on the walls.
She watched rows of boats moored together
on the river. "She imitated.
Little children in Sa-Dec walked around
carrying things on their heads to sell—
sweet potatoes, peanuts, corn, manioc,
all kinds of rice cakes.
Bo-Cau put things on her head."
When she was twenty months old,
in August, nineteen seventy-one,
with South Vietnam elections scheduled,
"We in the IVS
did not have our contracts renewed.
Perhaps Thieu
didn't want Americans there in the countryside then
who could speak Vietnamese.
Pressure was put on volunteers
to go home."
Johanna stayed on, determined
to adopt Bo-Cau. It was a risk, it was slow working
through the American Embassy in Saigon,
but by October she had permission
to take Bo-Cau with her,
her legally adopted daughter though
still a "nonpreference immigrant."
They left with only Bo-Cau's orphanage clothes.
In Hawaii some "lady" gave her clothes.
Mary says:
"We met them at the airport. Bo-Cau
was clutching a little pink suitcase.
Johanna had a suitcase,
and Bo-Cau would watch her
and when Johanna put her suitcase down,
Bo-Cau would put hers down."

"It was hard for her," Johanna says.
"She had no experience of cold.
She slept with me, she always does now,
but she couldn't understand

being under covers.
She kept her hands out and they'd freeze.
I put mittens on them."

Now she is here
in the Crow Hill spring.

Johanna puts on her shoes
and Bo-Cau pats their soles, helping her.
She runs across the floor.
She sings without words
"*Jesus Loves Me.*" "*Gioi lam,*" Johanna says,
pronouncing it "yoy lum": "That means 'very good.' "
She talks with Bo-Cau still in Vietnamese.
"Sometime we'll go back and visit
and I want her to be able to talk. '*Di dau roi?*' "
she says as the dog goes out.
" 'Dee dow roy?' means 'Where has it gone already?'
and '*an com*' means 'eat rice,'
which means 'let's eat.' Abe
is '*Ong-Ngoai,*' Grandfather,
and Mary, '*Ba-Ngoai,*' Grandmother."
Johanna holds up
Bo-Cau's green plastic lizard.
Bo-Cau folds her arms and bows
and says, "*Xin phep*" (seen fep),
asking politely for it.

"But Bo-Cau is learning English too.
She can count—
'One two three four.' "
"One two three four," Bo-Cau says
and counts to ten, pleased.
"*An com,*" Johanna says, announcing lunch.
"*An com,* Dwight," Bo-Cau says to her uncle.
And after lunch
she sleeps.
Johanna puts her on the living room couch,
and with house sounds around her

426

she sleeps in a guarded trance.
Always that need of a presence, sleeping.

When Bo-Cau wakes
into the living room,
she is delighted, Ba-Ngoai near her
and "Boppy."
"She can't say the *m* in Mommy.
Don't call me Boppy."
"Boppy."
"Mommy."
"Boppy."
"Mommy."
"Mommy."
"*Gioi lam.*"

Now in a clear voice she is singing
"Baa baa, black sheep"
and playing a favorite game, the cones.
The cones are rough-textured cardboard spools that stick together,
that Johanna's sister Rhoda
brings from the Bally knitting mill:
"All Wool, Charcoal Brown," "Natural,"
"Dark Oxford," "Special Blend."
The spools with their labels now
stacked one inside the other go upward
into a tower. Bo-Cau
hands the snug tower to *Ong-Ngoai*
to pull apart for her
so that she can line up rows
of cones like faceless soldiers on the plain of the floor,
kneeling intent,
her black hair falling around her neck
in its straight fringe.
As she reorders the cones
back into a tower,
beyond the living room window the east field
"sweetened with rain," as Abe puts it,
flashes with an oriole.

The day goes. At night when evening deepens,
when reading is done,
one by one all go to bed, going up
the stairs beside the kitchen stove.
All except Johanna. Bo-Cau understands,
accustomed to their staying up
for the "eleven o'clock news," that TV
flickering bridge to Vietnam telling
how it is there now in the crisis
of the Vietcong attack on Hue. But Bo-Cau is tired.
Lying on the floor, she does not see
the spreading band of light. She puts her small legs
up against Johanna and sighs.
The screen shows a road outside Hue
with civilians fleeing, women
carrying babies in panniers hung on shoulder yokes,
a long line of women moving like desperate dancers,
and in Hue itself
"a line of emergency civilian militia,"
some being little more than boys.

Bo-Cau yawns and waits.

THE HOSIERY MILL

Rhoda Gehman works in the hosiery mill
in Bally. "I'm a knitter.
I run eleven machines.
A knitter can run from ten to twenty,
depending on how many are push-button—
automatic. They're getting automatic down there.
Each machine makes one sock
except the toe is open. The 'looper'
has to close that on a looping machine.
That used to be a certain way by hand,
but that's going automatic too."
As in the shoe factory in Boyertown,
jobs are specialized: examiners,
pairers ("they pair the socks by hand"),

428

boarders ("they put the socks
on a hot metal board
to give them the crease"), finishers
("they put on the labels").
A hot press "puts on the stamp."
Then there is a designer,
a man who makes designs for the socks
"right there. One day
a girl had on a skirt
and the designer liked the design,
so he made a sock design to match it. The machines
used to make all plain socks,
but they're working a lot now
on these pattern machines."

Rhoda, who is unmarried,
has been there thirteen years.
They had forty-six machines when she came.
Now they have three times that many.
"They built a new part
into the woods." And as the mill grew,
it became more automated.
"They have a can or basket
the finished socks fall into.
Some fall in attached
and you have to cut them apart,
but now they're getting these hot pinchers
that come together and separate them."
So productivity is increasing.
"I make now
twenty dozen more socks a shift
than when I came. Then I made forty-five,
now I make sixty-five."
She works five days and Saturday morning. They get
a half hour for lunch ("the machines shut down")
and the mill stays open around the clock
in three eight-hour shifts.
"The married girls work best in the night shift.
One who does is Pat,
Honey Miller's daughter—
she has three or four children.
She works from ten thirty at night

till six thirty in the morning.
Such mothers, with children—
I don't know how they do it.
They sleep during the day
a half hour here, an hour there."
The mill has time clocks and penalties,
and no union. "They have
more bosses than regular workers"
as the automation is extended.
"They say the yarn is so expensive.
They don't want any bad socks. Sometimes
on a machine making a sock
one needle goes wrong and the rest go on. Then
all the socks will be bad. To catch that
and call the mechanic, you watch."
Rhoda and the other knitters
watch as thread
emerges from the point of each spool cone
as if from a spider's spinneret.
The spools are behind the machines.
"You step between the machines
to replace the spools, and you must
be careful. It's easy to get caught.
When the spool is empty,
you must replace it quickly
and knot the thread in a small knot
or you wreck the sock.
With some machines now, the end of the spool,
when it runs out,
makes a drop in the tension, then it stops
so you can put on a new spool."
So almost all is automatic now.
Boxes of spools
with all the different shades of color
wait, piled up, to feed the hunger
of a mill that is a single machine.

ADAM AND EVE

George Hunsicker says,
"My great-great-great-grandfather was
one of twins. His name was Adam
and his twin sister's name was Eve.
The family tells it
that he left Germany
to avoid fighting in war and came alone
to this country.
The thing is, today
with me liable to be called for this Vietnam thing,
I might leave this country
for the same reason he came to it."

EVASION ?

A non-Mennonite says to a Mennonite: "I know
you're against war, but you pay taxes."
The Mennonite says: "If the whole church
agreed to a common stand,
I'd join, I'd tax-resist,
but I don't want to go it alone.
I go as far as the church goes.
And say this for the church:
If I did decide
not to pay taxes,
the church would defend me legally."

SIGHT

Josephus Gerhard
is more than half blind. Time weighs and is slow.
The alarm clock of birds at dawn
wakes him. Awake, he knows
he sees best with his ears, but "ennihau"
one day it's over.

TODAY'S MOTHER

A woman says to a friend:
"My children are getting up in years
and I think of their children,
when they'll have them. I have pity
for the children born from now on.
Of course grandchildren are a blessing,
but even so. If I got pregnant—
I still could, you know"—
she hesitates, but only a moment—
"I'd do away with it."

STREAKING

"At the Gilbertsville auction last week
three young men stripped and streaked.
The police kept them moving, wouldn't let them stop. Well,
everybody thinks that's so new,
but there was this young woman, years ago,
took off all her clothes and ran through the orchard.
Yes, that was just around here."

432

WILDI ROS
(Wild Rose)

"Yes, there is this Herta," he says.
"Often I think of her. Old now like me.
One would know much about people
if one could know about her.
Her ancestors on one side were English—
Turner their name. She lived as a girl
over by Unami Creek—Swamp Creek—
and that was a wild piece of country
at that time. Copperheads
lying among all those ledges
even the Indians feared.
Yes, the last mountain lion around here
was shot there. There she lived
always secluded, always a shy one,
with her two brothers and a sister.
One day Harmon Creger came by.
He got a glimpse of her,
and at that glimpse he made up his mind
this was the girl he would marry.
He was a determined man.
He had been orphaned in his childhood
and adopted. He had fought up,
working in the fields, carrying meat
in baskets as big as he was
to sell along the roads. Then he went to school,
studied books by main strength
until he knew what others had neglected:
the nature of soil.
So he prepared himself to farm
before he bought his farm.
He was twenty-five
when he had the first glimpse of Herta
and began driving there. Often far off
she heard him and hid in the woods.
Of course he couldn't hope to get there
without being heard. Rocky country
and the steel rims of his buggy wheels

grated on the stones. He told me—
I knew him well later—
that he talked often with her father only
and hitched up the buggy and drove home
without having seen her at all.

"Then something happened, I don't know what,
but he went into the woods.
I think she had climbed a tree—
no, I don't know what happened,
but I suppose there was force used.
Some end to that untoward courting.
Whatever it was that ended it
a marriage was soon begun.
But, was it good?
That woman was still wild as a pheasant,
and note now her five grown children.
Not one is married. And she—
flies to some inner room
if you should even come to the door.
Makes Harmon send people away.
He mastered the soil, his farm always
such as demands respect.
He can get the best out of a field,
can make it do double for him.
But his wife, *net*—that's different.

"I met a man grew up with Harmon.
I mentioned Harmon to him.
'You know him?' His look
said something more than the words,
so I pressed him. He said,
'We used to go swimming,
a bunch of us boys and Harmon,
and always when we got undressed,
we felt ashamed. It shamed us
that we didn't have what he had.'
That made me think—that.
It could be some are too powerful.
A woman is not like a field—

434

more like something in a flower bed
that should be handled so. Herta
maybe not even that, a *wildi ros*
not meant for the hand at all."

HUNTING SONG
(Harmon Creger)

Ai, but he hunted ill.
Ai, but he hunted ill.
The shrew in the grass
had watched him pass,
crouched beside her sill.

Ai, he forgot the sun.
Ai, he forgot the sun.
The fox in the meadow
had barked at his shadow
and so he had come and gone.

Ai, he forgot the wind.
Ai, he forgot the wind.
The doe in the wood
had lightly fled
as she caught his smell upwind.

If only he had been still.
If only he had been still,
but the greennecked mallard
alarmed in the shallows
had veered behind the hill.

Ai, hunter, ai, hunter, ai, hunter
with his gun down at his side.
The rabbit's lair
was always near,
and there the quarry hid.

CREEK SONG
(Herta)

As she walked by Unami
that told her where it went
by the pounding blood of its autumn mud,
her eyes of sixteen
looked, against her eyelids,
at dark blood of her own
that frightened her and lightened her
and made her want to sing.

As she walked by Unami
in the mid-August heat,
she held her hands like hard breastbands
over her restless breath.
The pike that swam the ripples
slowed its pulsing fin,
and its mottled spear rushed at her
and so her hands dropped down.

As she walked by Unami
on the first of May, she saw
darkness pour from a sycamore
as if from a wound.
It might have been a shadow
or wind in opening buds,
but she had to close her staring eyes
to stop the rising mist.

As she walked by Unami
on a crust of fallen snow,
she touched the splice of forming ice
over the current's flow.
Her arms within her coat sleeves,
her blood within her arms,
cooled like the creek, had learned to keep
beyond the reach of storms.

436

THE PLAYER

The ground snow reflects light on the sycamore,
flickering over green, purple, and gold bark,
then rising toward another white,
the bark of the upper limbs.
A boy
touches the base's mottled idiom,
pushing and again pushing.
Seventy feet above his head,
small brown buttonballs begin to swing
in unison, the trunk motionless,
but they, a crown of hanging ornaments,
running in a great alarm of nowhere,
clappers of a thousand bells
all silent and all
strung to the bell cord of his hand
that gives to their tossing its far noise
on the glockenspiel of the clouds.

THE ART OF FRAKTUR

On the mailbox, in illuminated
Gothic letters, CLARENCE G. REITNAUER.
It is a small white house
on the road to Huff's Church
not far from Seisholzville, and this Sunday, a day
of pouring floribunda and mock orange,
the house has visitors. Two,
a man and his wife,
want Reitnauer to inscribe for them
a birth certificate
in the almost-forgotten art of *fraktur,*
fill in name and date
and add as decoration a rough
spray of leaves, whatever he wants, something
to make the writing memorable.

He sits now at his wide desk.
He pulls out drawers of ink bottles,
rows of pools
glittering red, green, black.
Fraktur.
Palatinate scribes
originated a handwriting drawn
from a sixteenth-century German type face
called *"fraktur,"* itself a copy
of medieval manuscript.
Each letter was separate from the others, so
the writing seemed a writing of breaks—
Fraktur-schriften. In that art were written
Haus-segen, house blessings; *Taufscheine,*
birth and baptismal certificates;
wedding certificates; inscriptions
in family Bibles. The *fraktur* artists
gave these strokes of beauty to sheets
that were for many families
the sole record of their having lived.

Reitnauer now
dips his pen's nib into the black pool
and copies the name and date given him,
then on the white space he puts color—
leaves, a trace of tulip,
and a *distelfink,* a goldfinch
flying bright-winged toward the future.
His visitors like his work
and ask him about himself.
He is glad to talk.
He was born in nineteen hundred "on a farm
down the road from Seisholtzville—
a store and hotel, also years ago
they had a wheelwright shop there
and a dozen houses, that was the whole thing. You know,
the Walker Granite Works were only started
around nineteen seven."
His great-great-grandfather was a Seisholtz
His grandparents lived with his parents
and he was the only child and "spoiled some.
I didn't much like farm work.

438

I loved a blacksmith shop.
I liked to work with wood. Even
I'd buy nails
with money I was given for candy.
When I grew older and wanted
to go to college, my folks said no,
but let me go to a business college.
I got my certificate—" It hangs now
over his desk: "28 February 1922."
After graduation
he was working in the office
of a planing mill. As he walked
from the office to the working area,
his old interest in wood came back·
"Those shavings drove me wild,
I had to be in the shop."
He worked in the shop twenty-eight years,
then worked as a cabinetmaker.

In nineteen forty-four he received a letter
from the famous "frakturer" and illuminator
Irwin P. Mensch, a neighbor down the road
near Mensch's Mill. The letter
was addressed and written in a script
of perfect curves, like tendrils curling,
exactly graduated, a mastery
such as he had never seen.
He was attracted. He talked with Mensch.
Mensch like himself
had gone to a business college.
"He told me, 'I had trouble with writing.
I had stubby fingers. I managed
to get a certificate,
but the head of the college said to me,
"You have the worst penmanship
I ever graduated." I was ashamed.' "
He studied calligraphy then on his own
and trained himself to a feather sureness.
Going further, he taught himself
the art of *fraktur.* There were examples.
A handbook of *fraktur* art
was compiled at Ephrata, at the *Kloster,*

"The Christian ABC Book,"
with alphabets in various sizes
designed by Sister Anna Thomme
to serve as models. Mensch
became a master of it. Reitnauer:
"I had no hope to be as good as him,
but I liked it and wanted to learn.
I did learn." Now
he is one of the few
left to carry on the art.

The visitors notice in the room
many objects of interest. Reitnauer
has long liked to have these things around him,
artifacts, memories:
a left-handed grain sickle, the curve in it
predating the "cradle," a hook
for a harness trace, tools—other things kept
that meant something in his life. In a cupboard
is a pretty ruby-colored glass.
"It was a glass of my grandmother's sister
and as a boy
I always liked ruby and gold.
Funny how as a kid
you take a strange liking to something.
One day came my great-aunt
with the ruby glass wrapped up for me.
And there it is. I have also
this lard lamp my grandmother had
when she was single. Which I dug out of the ground one time
and kept." It has the shape
of a small rusty boat smelling of earth
and with a chain-attached pin "to lift the wick."
"Here too is something, this *Shdivvel Knecht,*
this bootjack. I had as a longtime friend
the Reverend William Rupp of Souderton
who wrote a weekly column in *Deitsch*
under the name '*Der Busch Knibbel*' (the clodhopper)
for the Pennsburg *Town and Country.*
Bill got sick. He asked me
to take the column over for a few weeks.
Then he died. Well,

440

I'd become used to the column,
so I continued. But I had to have
a pen name for myself.
I thought of this *Shdivvel Knecht* here,
the least important *Knecht*. Let me explain:
Do you know about *Der Gross Knecht?*
I see you don't. On a farm there used to be
an old hired man called *Der Gross Knecht*.
He could plow, do any kind of work.
Almost every farm had one.
He was the regular man.
Then there would be *Der Glea Knecht*,
a boy who could hunt eggs,
throw down the hay, do such things.
Such boys were out of big families
where they had to hire them out.
But a *Shdivvel Knecht*,
that would be the least of the hirelings,
one who could do very little.
When boots were too small, outgrown,
or one's feet swelled and the boots stuck,
a *Shdivvel Knecht* would pull them off.
Here it is, here's the little V,
raised by a little prop,
that caught the boot heel. Bootjacks
are rare now
except among those that ride horses
or among sportsmen. So I took that name
and I write under it still."

But *fraktur:* "After I started,
I learned enough that I could make
envelopes for sick people.
Those in hospitals.
During the war, World War Two,
I sent illuminated addressed letters
to servicemen: it was something
they liked, and I sat often
until late into the night
addressing and writing such letters.
I sent over a thousand
and I've saved nine hundred and fourteen pieces

of mail that I received back." Now
he is asked to do many inscriptions,
Bibles, birth certificates,
and for *Huffa Karrick,* Huff's Church,
where he teaches Sunday school,
he each year designs a cover
for a special program, an annual
"Pennsylfawnisch Deitsch Sunndawg Shule," the cover
pleasant with color. He shows his visitors
the *fraktur* lettering and illustrations
he did for a booklet,
Penna-Dutch Almanac Beliefs.
"If you change your underwear
between Christmas and New Year,
you will get boils."
"You should urinate on the ground
where you plant parsley
and you will get a lot."
"Soap should be boiled in the increase of the moon."
"If you want to have a nice white roof on your barn,
just wait till it snows."
The booklet cover has a red barn
and large red flowers. He calls his wife, Bertha,
who comes in and is introduced.
"I want you to know," he says,
"my wife helps me. All alone she hand-colored
a thousand of these covers."
The visitors admire them. She says,
"I'm like Clarence,
one of those can't sit around
and do nothing." He says,
"Next year is our golden wedding.
We were married
April fifteenth, nineteen twenty-two.
I made this book:
'This book is made for
and dedicated to my wife
Bertha S. Reitnauer.' " It has in it
stories and poem written in *fraktur*
Gothic in the thick
in-shadowed up-and-down lettering.
A poem:

442

Take time to be holy;
The world rushes on;
Spend much time in secret
With Jesus alone.
By looking to Jesus
Like Him thou shalt be;
Thy friends in thy conduct
His likeness shall see.
                W. D. Longstaff
The lettering is a wall of flourishes
thrown against the verse.
All, this sheaf of verse and stories,
the *Almanac Beliefs,* the *Sunndawg Shule* program,
the birth certificate he has just done
and many others earlier, year by year,
stand here
illuminated like a house blessing, a *Haus-segen,*
to say the events of life, though local,
are important and should last.

THE TWO LANGUAGES

Clarence Reitnauer says,
"It happens, you know,
sometimes I'll forget a word in English.
It just won't come to me.
I wanted the word for *doppick*
and it was gone. I had to wait and think
and then it came—*clumsy.*
Well, you know it is not really *clumsy*—
it's *doppick.*"

DICTIONARY WANDERING

Certain persons can almost
take a day off
in the dictionary.
In the *Pennsylvania-German Dictionary* published
by the Pennsylvania-German Society
October 8, 1919:
"*Dunkelfarwich,* dark colored."
"*Dunschdich,*" a word that means and sounds like "vapory,
    moist."
"*Rangsdewasch,*'herdsman's cow melody."
"*Kauderwelsch,* jargon."
"*Bucker*" means a "castrated dog, rascal, hardened mucus removed
    from the nose. In part of the Palatinate this is a term
    of abuse. Possibly from the F *bougre* (heretic or worse)."
Many dialect words are Germanized English: "*abtscheckte*" is
    "object."
In C. Richard Beam's
Abridged Pennsylvania German Dictionary
published in 1970:
"*Buschwaecker*—1. one who lurks in the bushes or on the edge
    of woodlands and shoots down pigeons that escape in
    shooting matches. 2. one who lurks in the bushes and
    shoots off the game which others are chasing."
"*Dank (saage)*—to refuse an offer of candy, etc. *Ich saag
    Dank, ich hab Schnitz im Sack.*"
Words can be a ravishing giveaway.
Delia Longacre calls the dialect
"an insidious music."

IN THE MUSEUM

In the Perkiomen Seminary Museum
of Pennsylvania German arts and crafts
are some tapestries woven by historic girls:
"This work in hand my friend shal have

444

When I am dead and in my greave
    "Lydia Yeakle Her w 1799"
In the center a castle holding a man
nearly as large as the castle;
two turrets with bird weathervanes, the birds
in a strange wind
pointing opposite ways.
Another tapestry:
"To you a present
This shall be
And may you long
Remember me 1858"
and
"I love you" "Papa"
on the small cloth squares.

A showpiece of the museum
is the Irwin P. Mensch corner
where that master's calligraphy and *fraktur*
cover two walls. His weightless drawing
puts birds of an extraordinary lightness and grace
on branches,
under blossoms, or winging
up in blue air.
His famous desk in the corner
is completely inscribed with the Twenty-third Psalm,
the Gettysburg Address,
and other texts,
but his best work is on the walls, *fraktur*
written with the typical "breaks" of the pen, ink
applied rapidly and drying
into winged signed
messages to friends,
lines of letters like the skills of women
leaning over their worked words:
"This work in hand my friend shal have"
loops and curves little more
than the wind's work in a white sky.

SELFISH GATHERING

Delia Longacre relaxed her body
in shadow, only her long hair reaching out to moonlight
on her pillow. She went to sleep
with no sense of surrender, suddenly
not there. She breathed
a long time without images,
the languor of her body
unimpelled and swelling pleasantly
to the mons veneris in the arch
of unconsciousness.
She turned, her head
completely open to the moon.
Three men and a woman were walking
along some dusty rows of potatoes—no, it was corn—
and stopped at a row end. It seemed
as if they were talking
about something that had to do with hunting,
with keeping hunters off their land.
Dust
swirled around their heads
and she, or some part of her,
was at a table
where appropriations—long printed estimates—
were being raised and lowered
like blinds at windows
and there was a sound of anger. Windows
full of fire opened and closed,
and she was at a different gathering.
Heads of state,
presidents, prime ministers, chairmen, leaders, a few remaining
     kings, shahs, and supreme highnesses,
were saying,
"Why don't we get together to stop war,
settle everything peacefully. All of us
would have twice as much as we have now."
All voted
to try to find a way
to do it.

446

BEING CHRISTLIKE
(Daniel D. Wert, Sr., Lancaster, 1968)

"We still have some who, like the Amish,
are afraid of involvement,
but those in the Mennonite Volunteer Service
feel you're not being Christlike
if you're not becoming involved
with people as they are.
So they're trying to do this."
He meant the church's program of VSers,
those kids from the fields, students,
doctors, and teachers
serving for fifteen dollars a month.
He said, "Ethnic background
doesn't determine your human worth.
This has always been basic
in the Mennonite belief.
Mennonites are affected
by this middle-class whites' civilization
or culture that we have in America,
but basically their background
has not been one of prejudice.
Mennonite faith was born
in a time of suffering.
It was a movement
by a small group originally.
They followed this idea then
of believer's baptism,
separation of church and state,
and this meant suffering.
This of course meant they emphasized
brotherhood and equality
and spoke against the hierarchies.
Mennonites
up until now have never been
political activists,
they believe you should work
with the individual primarily,
but there are times when being quiet,

447

being silent, is wrong,
can put you on the side of the wrong."
Speaking about his son Robert
working in a unit house
in the Washington ghetto,
he said, "He has no feeling
that he's reaching down
and pulling somebody up. He almost
thinks like the black, I believe.
It's rather interesting—
Robert and my other older son both
are dark, so if Robert lets his hair
get a little bushy, long,
and lets his sideburns grow,
he fits in pretty well.
I don't know whether they have
some Indian blood or not,
but every once in a while
there are dark Germans.
We don't proselytize. We are just there,
our young people and our ministers,
to be with people as they are."

CHICAGO

Donald Kraybill says:
"The Mennonites are changing
from nonresistance to nonviolent resistance,
and it's difficult. It needs care.
The moral issue gets harder to think through."
Safe—in a sense, safer, less troubling—
is the one-to-one concept: deal directly
with another single human being.
Fred Braun is thinking about that
as he drives with Don,
a Pennsylvania VSer (VS, Voluntary Service),
in a blue Volkswagen bus from the Chicago Loop
to a Southside Mennonite house
at 6750 South Green Street,

448

his visit a liaison
between Washington Township and Chicago,
Butter Dahl and another kind of valley.
Don is from the West Eighteenth Street unit,
but decides to take Braun to the South Side house:
"Not that you'll see very much tonight,
but you'll see more there."
From the Lakeshore Drive
and the Martin Luther King Drive
Don turns
into an avenue of small stores,
not smart, definitely non-Loop. Traffic lights
blink. Night
is a smell of stockyards, a puddle
of animal heat wetting these dark precincts
where blacks are housed
in transit, Don says,
either to full poverty
or hopefully to something better.
As the bus goes deeper in, Braun reads
on a building side
in large white flowing script,
"Del-maniac Gangsters."
"That's a local gang," says Don,
"ten-to-twelve-year-olds.
The Pimpstones are still younger,
the Supremes are fifteen to eighteen.
Two blocks away, the Disciples.
The police have a ten thirty curfew.
Every kid must be home by then.
Not that they all are,
but it helps cool it." Off the avenue
on a heavily shadowed side street
between dim streetlights,
Don parks and, getting out,
asks a boy, "You know where Paul is?"
The boy flees. The building they come to,
a facade of unlit windows,
is locked in front. The back-porch door
also locked and unanswering, but they hear a flurry
of basement voices below. Don knocks
on the basement door.

449

"Who's there?"
"Don. Is Paul there?"
A whisper of conferring and the door is
cautiously opened by a kid
used to suspicion. Paul Smith,
a pleasant thick-haired young man, a VSer,
comes to greet them, and the kids drift
away and resume playing, hard but not loud,
like a radio turned low.
"Do these kids belong to the gangs?" asks Braun.
"Oh yes," Paul says. "All of them.
As soon as they find there's things to do here,
they come. And we take them. Nothing said
about gang affiiliation. The way it is,
the streets fight one another.
I keep track of the streets.
You can tell usually if they're out or not.
The five- or six-year-olds will come and alert you
or you hear shots.
The older teen-agers have guns
and there's often shooting in summer.
We've had stray shots go through the house windows.
The only deliberate shooting we've had here
was one kid shot a thirty-eight
at the door of the unit vehicle.
I don't go out at night if I don't have to."
Paul leads the way upstairs,
lighting up a room
with sofa and chairs, the comfortable
echo of Crow Hill. Paul: "Here the kids
belong to clubs—a certain time each week
for each one. Six with the boys,
two with the girls: there's gymnastics,
tumbling, wrestling, boxing.
We rent a gym and have basketball
and try to have all age groups play—
it takes some careful scheduling.
Weekends we have trips
around the city—museums, bowling."
"And of course there are many kids we work with
alone," Don says. "Many kids don't have fathers,
and their mothers have long-hours jobs,

450

so they don't get much love, much attention.
You try to substitute. Like one kid
had no bath at home. I had him take showers
and washed his clothes in the washing machine
and dried them in the drier
and at least he was clean.
A couple of days ago was report-card day.
I went over the report cards.
Some had poor conduct checked,
and I went into that with them
to see if there was something they could do."
Now a man in casual clothes, young,
relaxed, with a look of authority, comes in.
He's introduced to Braun as Maynard Brubacher, pastor
in one of the two Chicago Mennonite churches.
The tie between church and unit house
is close and it is natural
for Maynard to come by.
Don is saying:
"One kid we'd worked a year and a half with
was picked up for burglary
and I went to court with him.
When he was out on parole,
he broke into our apartment
and had to go back to jail—
automatically, for breaking parole
so that's how it will be with one kid,
and then another
you'll work with just two weeks
and you'll get a response."
"We take them all," Paul says. "We keep
on with everybody." Maynard nods.
An older kid, tall and thin, comes
three-stepping up the stairs and drifts over to Don.
Tapping him on the head, he says, "How'd your
basketball team make out?"
"We didn't," Don says. "We lost."
"If I'd been playing, they'd have won."
"You're the best, of course."
"Yeah."
"Talk the best game, anyhow," says Don.
Pretending indignation, the kid says,

"Take that blue bus and go,"
and laughs and three-steps back down the stairs.
"That's one we count on," Paul says.
"We give him special attention.
A kid like him may go to college.
His father lives at home and his mother is strict.
Goshen, Bluffton, he could make it."
Braun asks Maynard
about his church. Is it "black"?
"You mean integrated? Yes.
The membership of my own church
is about sixty-five percent black
and about thirty-five percent white.
Two of our team ministry
are black, but we have
no Negro VSers. We need them,
but we can't find them. We don't yet have
many such young people to draw on.
In time it will change.
We'll have here what we need, the young
black and white working together.
Not just the 'farm boys' we have now,
good as they are, but blacks too.
Christ put it well—
'Henceforth I call you not servants;
for the servant knoweth not what his lord doeth:
but I have called you friends.' "

CONGO FROM THE PILGRAM ROOM

Suzanne Hilty, an Ohio
Bluffton girl going to Bluffton College,
carries her books and a small
interior parcel of amusement and caution
up to the Pilgram Room,
a student meeting room on whose walls
are hung flags, symbols, and the reproduction
of three pages
of "the first printed book by Pilgram Marbeck,

452

Strasbourg, 1531."
"The Necessity of Outward Ceremonies."
On a card adjacent to it:
"1528 Marbeck became an Anabaptist . . .
and moved to Strasbourg . . . the only city tolerating
Anabaptists and other dissenters.
Consequently many quite different spirits
found refuge in Strasbourg." Among them,
"Sebastian Franck,
Jacob Kautz, Johannes Bunderlin,
and Caspar Schwenckfeld. They held
that all outward ceremonies
were irrelevant and should be abolished.
The true church, they said, is invisible
because it is a purely spiritual
church." Marbeck's booklet
attacked them, the title running:
"Clear answer to some articles,
which are being spread by erroneous spirits
by letter and orally . . ."

Sue
from the summer of '68
to the summer of '70
carried her "erroneous spirit," heir
of the dissidents,
a dark, true, and pleased self
but with misgivings,
to Africa. She says:
"PAX, a program for fellows
wanting to do alternate service
and study with it to get college credits,
had decided to let girls in." A freshman,
she volunteered for two years in the Congo.
She learned French in Canada,
and at Kinshasa in the Congo—
that once two-part Bantu and Belgian city
now one—she took courses
in African economic development, African religion,
African culture, and African history under
professors from Bluffton and Bethel
"and one Congolese professor,"

Ohio's flat open spaces preparing
to walk in the rain forests. After Kinshasa
she was assigned to teach
at a Methodist mission in the interior
near Lodja, a few miles—"fifteen kilometers"—from it
in a small village.
"The students, young people,
came from all over, from the Central Region mainly.
I had six classes of thirty-five to fifty-five,
both sexes," this slight, light Bluffton girl.
"I taught anything.
Religion, technology, physical education.
I taught in the French I had learned,
which was everybody's second language."
Having French,
these young people right from the brush
wanted to learn English. They were verbal internationalists
eager for languages—"Americans don't like languages,"
they said,
and imitated her English skillfully.
Every word pleased them:
"But being from different tribes,
there was tension—you know, like we might be with relatives.
If they were mad with one another, they'd say,
'You were slaves.'
Some were older than I, and I had a problem:
Keeping them in order
was like trying to keep fifty million grasshoppers
in a basket with your hands."

At first she lived in a Mission house
with three to five other single women. Then wanting
to know more about how Africans lived,
she changed to an African home—
Mama Ahata with a niece and three granddaughters
"and a steady flow of visitors"
on that edge of plain, surrounded by forest.
Thick undergrowth, rifts of flowers
in the green, "It was constantly flowering."
She was in Lumumba territory.
"All the village had known him. His brothers

were still around. There were bullet holes in the ceiling,
and most of the people here had spent time
hiding in the forest." Not far
from Wembo Nyama.

She began studying
the Batetela tribal language, Otetela,
helped by several students—
Wetshi André, Utshinga Woto Cathérine.
She began to get
the unique sound and feel of the language
that combined into an expressive entity,
a stirring of spells by which, cautiously,
she might herself, experiencing differences, change
as the words changed, taking in
the watched ovals of faces,
lips and tongues with their slight movements.
Otetela
had three tones, "and various sliding combinations of sounds"
more "subtle and delicate than English."
Its words and phrases
were often patterned like music, with musical pitch:
"Konde konde konde" a sentence with three homonyms,
"The alligator did not eat the beans,"
the meaning
depending on three tonal differences.
She found her interest, before long,
was in images. Images leaped everywhere
like a cloth unrolling, full of color.
She decided to do a paper
on "Otetela Word Pictures."
"Utundja utema l'andja,"
"Put heart on the outside."
The name of an acidy fruit, "al-amonamona,"
"eat and smile."
"Lulimi shosola katchikela unyo ukandukandu."
"The tongue throws a word, leaves the mouth embarrassed."
(Think before you speak.)
"Djingadinga y'untu."
"Person of just a little smoke." (Not worth much.)
A man coming home from a distance:

"Mbudja l'anya wa wad'endi,"
"Put him in the arms of his wife."
"Nkokokoko," "Coming loose,"
"Tshukudo," the noise of lifting a basket from the water,
onomatopoeia like
a girl holding her arms wide, imitating
a heron with wings spread, courting.
"Tuki dia lune, kikitsha ekulu olo ta."
"Like a palm tree planted, put your feet down firmly, fight."
"Just like a tree that's planted by the water,
I shall not be moved."

When she had finished her paper, she said
to those who helped her with it:
"Lusaka uku apopo wa mvula."
"Thanks like raindrops."
And this sound of thanks, in syllables of three tones
and no distance,
continues yet
in this windowless Ohio
room of Pilgram Marbeck.

THE FIRST PROTEST AGAINST SLAVERY

Five years after Francis Daniel Pastorius
came to Germantown,
he and three other Quakers—
"gerret hendericks
derick op de graeff . . ." and
"Abraham op Den graef"—
at a meeting held "ye 30—2 mo—: 1688"
drafted a protest against slavery,
the first on the American continent.
The document was done in English
written out by Pastorius
and it still exists in his clear, fine hand
with many sweeping curves:
      "These are the reasons why we are against
the traffick of men Body, as followeth: Js there

any that would be done or handled at this manner?
viz., to be sold or made a slave
for all the time of his life?
How fearful & fainthearted are many on sea
when they see a strange vassel,
being afraid it should be a Turck,
and they should be tacken
and sold for slaves into Turckey."
Pastorius had had this experience of fear
on his way to America.
"Now what is this better done as Turcks do?
yea rather is it worse for them, wch say they are Christians;
for we hear that ye most part of such Negers
are brought heither against their will & consent;
and that many of them are stollen.
Now, tho' they are black, we cannot conceive
there is more liberty to have them slaves,
as it is to have other white ones.
There is a saying, that we shall doe to all men,
licke as we will be done our selves;
making no difference of what generation,
descent or Colour they are.
And those who steal or robb men,
and those who buy or purchase them,
are they not all alike? . . .
In Europe there are many oppressed for Conscience sacke;
and here there are those oppressed wch are of the black Colour.
And we, who know that men must not comitt adultery,
some doe comitt adultery in others,
separating wifes from their housbands
and giving them to others;
and some sell the children of those poor Creatures
to other men. Oh! doe consider well this things,
you who doe it;
if you would be done at this manner?
and if it is done according to Christianity?
You surpass Holland and Germany in this thing.
This mackes an ill report in all those Countries
where they hear off, that ye Quackers doe here
handel men licke they handel their ye Cattel.
And for that reason some have no mind
or inclination to come hither,

457

and who shall maintaine this your cause
or plaid for it? . . .
we contradict & are against this traffick of menbody.
And we who profess that it is not lawfull to steal,
must lickewise avoid to purchase such things as are stollen,
but rather help to stop this robbing and stealing
and such men ought to be delivered out of ye hands
of ye Robbers & sett free as well as in Europe.
Then in Pennsilvania to have a good report,
instead it hath now a bad one
for this sacke in other Countries.
Especially whereas ye Europeans are desirous to know
in what manner ye Quackers doe rule in their Province;
& most of them doe loock upon us with an envious eye.
But if this is done well,
what shall we say is done evill?
        "If once these slaves,
(:wch they say are so wicked and stubbern men:)
should joint themselves,
fight for their freedom
and handel their masters and mastrisses
as they did handel them before;
will these Masters and Mastrisses tacke the sword at hand
& warr against these poor slaves,
licke we are able to believe, some will not refuse to do?
Or have these Negers not as much right
to fight for their freedom,
as you have to keep them slaves?
        "Now consider well this thing,
if it is good or bad?
and in case you find it to be good
to handel these blacks at that manner,
we desire & require you hereby lovingly,
that you may informe us here in,
which at this time never was done, viz.,
that Christians have such a liberty to do so,
to the end we shall be satisfied in this point,
& satisfie lickewise our good friends & acquaintances
in our natif Country,
to whose it is a terrour or fairfull thing
that men should be handeld so in Pennsilvania."

458

What then happened to this Protest
signed by the four Friends?
The monthly meeting of Quakers
found it too "weighty" to "meddle with"
and referred it to the Philadelphia
"Quarterly meeting."
The Quarterly meeting said it was
"a thing of too great a weight
for this meeting to determine,"
and referred it to the "Yearly Meetting."
The Yearly Meeting tabled it.

THE LIFE OF AN OBSTINATE AND LITTLE-KNOWN FORERUNNER SAINT, BENJAMIN LAY
(For Jim Peck)

Benjamin Lay was born
at Colchester, County of Essex, England,
in sixteen seventy-seven.
His parents were Friends and taught him
Quaker principles, but his learning
other than that was small.
After he was early apprenticed to a glovemaker,
he farmed for his brother,
and from this innocence
went to sea. He was a sailor
for about fourteen years, once
leaving his ship and going inland
to drink a draft of water at Jacob's well
in "Syria," where "the Savior of the World"
had talked with the woman of Samaria.
In appearance he was noticeably
misshapen, about four and a half feet
in height, hunchbacked, with a contracted body
and with extraordinarily thin legs
that hardly seemed strong enough to hold him.

In seventeen ten
he found himself a small hunchbacked woman, Sarah,
and married her and left the sea.
Nothing much is known of his next few years
except that he had audience
with King George the Second, to urge him
to drive "hirelings" out of the church,
quoting Milton to him to that effect.
The Quakers asked him to "disunite" from them,
perhaps finding him too political,
but he still admired their principles.
In seventeen eighteen, he and his wife
went to the Island of Barbadoes
and lived there some years,
seeing the African slave trade carried on
and becoming "singularly enlightened"
by the treatment of slaves
on the West Indian island plantations.
He let it be known as his opinion
that slavery threatened "awful retribution
from the Omnipotent and regardful Parent
of the whole human family."
Blacks, aware of his concern for them,
gathered around his house
in hundreds until they were prevented.
He himself was so harassed by slave owners
he decided
to "seek asylum in another country."
His wife too wanted to go,
worried that in Barbadoes
she might be "leavened into the nature
of the inhabitants,
which was pride and oppression."
In seventeen thirty-one, this man and wife
came to Philadelphia,
hopeful of a new life.
They were soon much disheartened.
Even here in "the city of brotherly love"
and in Penn's province founded by Quakers
was slavery. The worst was
that Quakers themselves were the slave owners. True,
their slaves were better treated,

460

but that meant nothing to Lay. The "system"
was "altogether unrighteous,"
and he spoke out strongly against it.
To give himself a better base
for his opposition to slavery,
he moved to the country,
buying a few acres of land
between Germantown and the old York road.
He now had a plan:
he built a house like a cave,
planted a small orchard and several walnut trees,
and became a vegetarian,
unwilling to eat what had been killed,
and he and his wife spun cloth
for their own clothes, of tow—
that is, not of animal hair.
So they kept their needs utterly simple,
so they provided themselves the groundwork they needed
for opposing slavery, especially
among the Quakers, since Lay
"could not endure the idea
that, professing as they did,"
any of them should hold slaves.
Having this thought,
he conceived a way to dramatize it.
The Friends were holding an annual meeting
at Burlington, New Jersey. Beforehand,
he prepared enough pokeberry juice
to fill a bladder. He fitted the filled bladder
into a large Bible-like volume
with the inside pages cut out. His appearance
now was "grave and benignant"
and he had grown a long white beard.
He put on a military coat and sword
and over these buttoned a greatcoat.
So he went to the meeting
and placed himself in a "conspicuous" spot,
and in the midst of the proceedings:
"Oh, all you Negro masters,"
he cried, "who are contentedly
holding your fellow creatures
in a state of slavery during life . . .

you must know they are not made slaves
by any direct law, but are held
by an arbitrary and self-interested
custom, in which you participate. . . .
You might as well throw off the plain coat
as I do"—he threw off his coat,
revealing his uniform—and said
that they might as well consider it "justifiable
in the sight of the Almighty,
who beholds and respects all nations
and colors of men with an equal regard,
if you should thrust a sword through their hearts
as I do through this book."
He thrust his sword through the bladder
and streams of pokeberry juice like blood
flew out over those sitting near him.
He had the satisfaction
that he had at least produced discomfort.
At another meeting he devised
another way to try to reach their hearts.
There was a deep snow on the ground,
and he stood outside the gate
with his right leg and foot
entirely bare. As Friends went in,
unhappy at the sight, they tried to reason with him
about his exposing himself—
"Ah," he said, "you pretend compassion for me,
but you do not feel for the poor slaves
in your fields, who go all winter half clad."
Another instance of his methods:
A neighbor of his had bought a Negro girl,
"tearing her away by avarice"
from her parents. This man
had an "interesting child,"
a boy of six years old.
Lay beguiled the child into his house
and kept him amused all day.
At night the father and mother came
running toward Lay's place
obviously in the greatest distress.
Lay went out to meet them.
Sympathetically he said,

"What is the matter?" The parents cried,
"Oh, Benjamin, Benjamin, our child is gone,
he has been missing all day."
Lay said, "Your child is safe in my house,
but what about the sorrow,
which you don't seem to think of,
of the parents of your Negro girl?"
And he gave them back their child.
He wrote a book against slavery
with "powerful appeals to the judgment
and feelings," and distributed it free,
especially to young people.
On the last page of the book
was this engaging statement:
"Thou art lovingly entreated to excuse,
amend, or censure as it thee please:
but remember that it was written
by one that was a poor common sailor,
and an illiterate man.—B.L."
Governor Richard Penn,
Benjamin Franklin, and others
visited Lay in his "cave."
His influence was widely felt.
Not long before he died,
in his eighty-second year,
in seventeen fifty-eight,
he was visited by a friend
who told him the Society of Friends
had just come to the determination
to disown such of their members
as could not be persuaded
to desist from the practice of holding slaves.
Lay rose from his chair and said,
"Thanksgiving and praise
be rendered unto the Lord God.
I can now die in peace."

THE TABLE

In nineteen sixty when the census was taken,
a wire service picked up a picture
of sixteen children, news
in a time of less large families.
A woman in Kentucky wrote:
"Dear Mr. and Mrs. William Miller
Just reading my paper when I saw your picture
of yourself and large family,
I am 70 years old
and the mother of 16 so you see
why I was reminded of past days. . . .
'Blessings on those little ones
Whose work is yet undone
Blessings on those little feet
Whose race is yet unrun.'
Mrs. C. W. Clifton."

William Miller, always known as Honey,
was born August fifth, nineteen twenty,
the first son of Frank and Mary Miller.
He had eight younger brothers and sisters—
many sisters, he got well used to girls.
"I went to school with Marie Kline.
She was born the same year as me,"
daughter of Raym Kline, the loom tender.
"She lived five years on Crow Hill
near where Nevin and Ivy Yost are now,"
and Raym moved then down into town.
Honey tells how that went:
"He bought a house on Main Street,
and they rolled it right straight down
through Fox one block
to near the Bally Block and then sawed it
right in half and made two houses of it.
Old George Melcher did that."
Here Marie grew up and Honey
still kept an eye on her.

When they were twenty,
they married one November day
in the Catholic Church,
the Church of the Blessed Sacrament.

Now they themselves needed a home.
Not much below Isaac Stahl in Bally
was a two-story frame building
Amos Whitman had used
as an undertaking parlor.
It had this gloomy reputation,
but after Whitman died,
Tom Shute bought the place
and made himself a home of it
Now Raym Kline bought it
with Marie and Honey in mind.
"He did a lot of work on it,
made what had been the funeral parlor
downstairs into two rooms
and put in a bathroom upstairs.
At first we rented it from him
for twelve dollars a month, but then
he said we'd better buy it
and sold it to us for what he'd paid,
not charging for the work he'd done.
That was his wedding present." Soon
children began to appear on the porch.
The Millers had six girls in a row:
Patty whose full name was Patricia,
Constance, Janet, Christina (Tina),
Susan, and Margie. Only then, a boy.
The first boy, William Junior,
was born on the first girl's birthday,
something later he objected to.
"He wanted a birthday all by himself."
Now came Nettie (Antoinette)
and the twins, Kathleen and Eileen,
nine girls to the one boy. And now
the house had to be expanded.
They made two new rooms in back,
and cutting through for a door,

465

they found coffin handles in the wall.
The kids threw the handles back and forth.
Still more babies.
Two more boys at last
but along with them four more girls.
In all, sixteen children.
Their clothes were durable.
The cellar, small, was large enough
to keep many sacks of potatoes.
Luxuries faded off
with fifty-four meals a day.

At first they had a normal-sized
dining room table,
but the family outgrew it
and it was unhandy not to have
one table where they all could eat together.
But such a table must be long and strong.
It was an engineering problem
that Honey gave much thought to. One day
he happened to look up at a picture
hanging on the wall:
The Last Supper, Christ and his Disciples
at a long table. It was supported
by sets of crossed legs that took the weight.
"I got lumber and copied it.
Made it myself.
It was just what we needed.
You can see, it worked out just fine."

THE GLAD TIDINGS MENNONITE CHURCH

Today being Sunday, the sandwich shop closed,
in the housefront church at 344 Brook Avenue, South Bronx,
in a room behind the altar
Pastor Eugene Shelly sits at a table end with six men and women
    down one side and six down the other side
for Bible study.

Some are from the Service Unit on East Nineteenth Street.
    VSers. Two are Puerto Rican.
On the women's heads, the Mennonite cap.
Nehemiah 8:
"(Ezra) before the water gate . . . read in the book in the law
    of God distinctly, and gave the sense, and caused them
    to understand the reading."
The people wept, but Ezra told them, 'The joy of the Lord is
    your strength,' and told them not to weep."
Pastor Shelly says, "The Jews perhaps mourned for having broken
    the law, but Ezra wanted them to rejoice that they had
    the law. He wanted gladness, happiness."
"So they keep the law?" one asks.
"Yes. To be happy. Could the gods of the peoples around
    Jerusalem—Baal and those others—could they give
    happiness?"
"No." No.
" 'Give me understanding, and I shall keep thy law; yea, I
    shall observe it with my whole heart.' "
Salmo (psalm) 119.

At eleven thirty, church service begins.
Some members are "in retreat."
"We aren't many," Pastor Shelly says. "It's like the Coffee
    Hour, which we aren't having tonight. Let's come up around
    the organ and sing."
They gather at the organ, Puerto Ricans, blacks, VSers, four kids
    caressed by the grownups.
"Jesus, I my cross have taken,
All to leave and follow Thee:
Naked, poor, despised, forsaken,
Thou, from hence, my all shalt be—"
"Tranquil river, let me ever
Sit and sing by thee.
Tranquil river, let me ever
Sit and sing by thee."

After the singing, after the service and benediction, many go
    from church upstairs to see the pastor's wife, Martine,
    and the Shellys' newborn baby, Michael.
The baby sleeps on Martine's arm.
"Who does he look like?"

"Well, he has my forehead," Gene says, smiling and indicating
    his own receding hair.
One asks about "the robbery."
Gene says, "The church window's broken, we haven't had it fixed
    yet, and they stepped in that and got to the fire-escape
    ladder, and the window was open for air. So they came in
    while we slept."
"Lástima,"
thieves in the pastor's apartment.
The run-on and murmur of voices slackens until only an out-of-
    town visitor is left. Gene says,
"You think it's bad we had the TV stolen.
One night somebody called me at two o'clock in the morning.
    It was to tell me my car, that I keep parked outside,
    had one of the wheels gone.
I went down and found the car jacked up and no right rear wheel.
You can expect it in this street."

Gene was born in Lancaster, but was brought up in the "Deep
    South," absorbing there "the attitudes of my peers."
He went to the Eastern Mennonite College
in Harrisonburg, Virginia,
attended seminary there and from there, still from the South
    and inexperienced, not fully taught,
took over this church.
"You saw this street. It's unbelievable. At first I thought
    nothing could be done.
I still wonder.
I get help from the VSers here in this house
and from the brothers and sisters from the Unit House on
    Nineteenth Street,
but even so. Still
you have to do something.
I try not to let what I do and plan get too far ahead of the
    congregation,
but the need for local leadership is desperate. Two things:
Housing. Some tenants are organizing against the landlord,
    and need help. We're thinking, the church I mean, about
    'adopting' one building, helping them get together.
Medical care. A woman, and maybe with kids, has to spend
    six hours now waiting in a clinic. What I'd like is a
    doctor to volunteer to work here.

468

But that isn't easy. They go abroad. And we so much need a
     doctor here.
Mennonites in the rural areas
don't know that work in the cities helps *them,* is important to
     them. Like,
there's a drug problem now in Lancaster County,
kids taking drugs. But it spreads from the city. Here in
     this block
nearly all the older teen-agers take drugs. They come in and
     talk with me, tell me how they steal, how the pushers push
     it, where they cut it.
They show me their arms.
We do what we can, work through certain ones to rehabilitate,
but the problem, like many others, is part political, isn't it?
     We Mennonites
haven't tended to join community groups.
It's considered dangerous and secular, and it is dangerous.
     But we, being under the lordship of Christ, must do it,
     must join with others,
if we're to accomplish something."

A LITANY OF HOUSING

In early nineteen seventy,
thirty South Bronx clergy, seeing
not steeples, not churches
beside churchyard trees and protected bushes,
but never-ending blocks of poverty—these clergymen
prepared a statement on housing
in the form of a litany. On a certain day
all thirty went down to City Hall
to a City Council meeting—
such meetings are open to the public—
and took their places in the gallery.
"Then," Pastor Shelly says,
"something rather good happened,
an accident. The clergyman the Council was expecting
to open the meeting with prayer
didn't come. We suggested that one of us

469

give the prayer instead.
We were a cross section of the clergy—
Protestant, Catholic, Jewish—on the whole
conservative, and the Council President
Sanford D. Garelik and another councilman
stood reverently to hear us.
We gave our litany:
'O God the Father of all men,
>> HAVE MERCY UPON US
O God the Son, who suffered at the hand of governors and
>> chief priests,
>> HAVE MERCY UPON US
O God the Holy Ghost who enlightens every man that comes
>> into the world,
>> HAVE MERCY UPON US
Hear our prayer, O Lord, as we cry out for the homes in which
>> Thy people dwell. In your compassion help those forced to
>> live amid inhuman conditions, especially in the South Bronx.
>> LORD, HEAR OUR PRAYER
From ice on top of water in the kitchen; from the collapse of
>> bathroom ceilings; from water running down the bedroom
>> walls,
>> GOOD LORD, DELIVER US
From bits of paint and plaster in the babies' beds,
>> GOOD LORD, DELIVER US
From garbage in the hall and on the stairs; from garbage in
>> the streets and in the cellar; from garbage on the sidewalk
>> and the cars; from garbage in the courtyard and the alley,
>> and in every other place,
>> GOOD LORD, DELIVER US
From the sicknesses of little children: from rat bite and lead
>> poisoning; from colds, bronchitis, and pneumonia; from
>> malnutrition and from starvation,
>> GOOD LORD, DELIVER US
From the abysmal hopelessness of families; from the rage of
>> fathers; from the despair of mothers; from drunkenness
>> and addiction, and from apathy,
>> GOOD LORD, DELIVER US
From a bureaucracy that cannot see; and seeing cannot act,
>> GOOD LORD, DELIVER US
From hearings that cannot comprehend,
>> GOOD LORD, DELIVER US

From all excuses, postponements, and delays; from redundant
   investigations, inquiries, studies, and reports; from
   referral and reconsideration, and from all subcommittees,
        GOOD LORD, DELIVER US
From all emergency telephone numbers and emergency repairs
   that bring frustration faster,
        GOOD LORD, DELIVER US
From promises that are made but never kept; from housing
   meetings that are dreamed up but never held,
        GOOD LORD DELIVER US
From the excuse that the City Council has no power, but only
   the Mayor; that the Mayor has no power, but only the State
   Legislature; that the Legislature has no power, but only
   the Governor; that the Governor has no power, but only
   the Congress; that the Congress has no power, but only
   the President; and from all buck passing,
        GOOD LORD, DELIVER US
From attempts to belittle human dignity by labeling those
   who cry out for justice as anarchists, communists, troublemakers,
   and corrupters of youth,
        GOOD LORD, DELIVER US
O God of Abraham, Isaac, and Jacob, protect this generation
   of Thy People.
        LORD, HEAR OUR PRAYER
O God of Moses, deliver the oppressed from bondage.
        LORD, HEAR OUR PRAYER
O God of the Prophets, confront the conscience and stir up
   the will of all in power and authority.
        LORD, HEAR OUR PRAYER
Hear our prayer for the relief of human need.
        LORD, HEAR OUR PRAYER
Remember the soul of the child living on East 138th Street
   who died because of no heat in the building.
        LORD, HAVE MERCY
Christ, have mercy.
        LORD, HAVE MERCY
O Lord, hear our prayer,
        AND LET OUR CRY COME UNTO THEE.

                                            AMEN.' "

MAY 15, 1970

Two black students killed by police in Jackson, Mississippi.

The Mennonite Glad Tidings Church Sandwich Shop is filled
    with kids, all aware of these killings but casual,
combing Afro hair with metal combs,
mock-boxing in the window, entrances and exits
    a constant human ricochet. Five little girls
run under the counter gate to the rear room.
Ray Siegrist says, "We get to know them across the counter.
    We're doing all right, nonmillennially speaking."
Richard Frey rushes sandwiches: "Yes? Yes?"
Pastor Shelly opens a dripping can of ham.
Miriam Shank is passing out penny candy and "strings,"
    Swedish longtubes of Red Strawberry.
"What's the news from Mississippi?"
"You mean Mississappi."

THE FATHER
July 12, 1970

Pastor Gene Shelly
is the son of a pastor, Paul Z. Shelly,
who is now visiting him from Alabama. Pastor Paul:
"The Mennonites back in the nineteen forties
had an 'itinerant evangelism'—
that's what they called it when they started
sending workers down to the South.
Also the 'Apostle Paul Way.'
Now they have
twelve preaching points there."
His own "preaching point"
is the Bethel Community Mennonite Church.
Here he preaches "alike
to Baptist, Free Holiness, Methodist,
any who want"—his is the only church there.

472

"I have an associate, a pastor,
has a Negro church not too far off
at Freemanville: Oak Drive Mennonite Church.
It's been trouble,
but not that bad
When there were threats earlier, and the sheriff
warned the pastor he couldn't 'stand behind him,'
the pastor was amused. He said,
'Well, if they burn my house down,
I guess I'll have to build another.'

"Things in the South are changing
To those that need, I quote the Bible:
the thirteenth chapter of Acts,
three men put their hands on Apostle Paul's head
to send him forth on his ministry. I say,
'Of those six hands, four were black,
including "Simeon that was called Niger." '
When one says 'nigger' in my presence,
I challenge it. I heard this:
In a group of men the old question came up,
'Would you want your daughter to marry a Negro?'
One said,
'I have a relative married a Negro
and she's getting along, but I have another
married a Pennsylvania Dutchman
and she hasn't had a happy day since.'
When I told him I was Dutch, he was embarrassed.
But I laughed. You hear the truth sometimes
by accident. *Net?*"

READING VERDUIN

Fred Braun, a descendant of those Latinists
who wrote poems at the furrow's end,
milks a goat
and goes to his study to read. As he reads, he feels
momentarily alone, then
in silence a strong

inner mobility, a motion
through the page—first to the immediate scene
(or idea), then to his own thoughts.
He is reading a book by a Calvinist,
Leonard Verduin, *The Reformers
and Their Stepchildren,* recommended to him
by Daniel Wert. It has as theme
the definitions of heresy, organized
chapter by chapter around the epithets
used against the sectarian radicals
in the sixteenth century:
*"Donatisten! Stabler!
Catharer! Sacramentschwärmer!
Winkler! Widertäufer! Kommunisten!"*
Men and women wearing these angry labels
refused to lose themselves in the larger Church,
Catholic or Lutheran,
and were killed for it (*The Martyrs Mirror*). Braun
is thinking about this and about
the theory of the "just war"
still quoted, still used by the Church
or by good men. Solutions
turning always to the sword, to slaughter.
Luther and Muenzer—about them:
Luther in so many ways admirable,
full of peasant practicality, a good father
and good adoptive father. He was cautious,
but in his one great moment
he was firm: "My conscience
is captive to the Word of God.
I cannot and I will not recant. . . ."
But this same Luther,
when the Peasants' Revolt got going,
could say, "They should be knocked to pieces,
strangled and stabbed, secretly and openly,
by everybody who can do it,
just as one must kill a mad dog."
And Thomas Muenzer, the peasant leader
whom Frederick Engels called a "democrat"—
this Muenzer who quoted the Bible
but believed in reason and the future—
this Muenzer could write:

474

"Is it not Christ who said:
'I have come to bring, not peace, but the sword'?
What can you do with that sword?
You can do only one thing:
If you wish to be the servants of God,
you must drive out and destroy the evil ones
who stand in the way of the Gospel.
Christ ordered very earnestly
(Luke 19:27),
'but these mine enemies, that would not
that I should reign over them,
bring hither, and slay them before me.' "
It's a horror, Braun thinks,
to quote that verse so unlike Christ.
How do we know, how did Muenzer know—
Luke being copied and recopied—
that some biased copyist did not
slip that verse in for his own needs?
At any rate, the peasants did slay.
They killed nobles and priests
and burned many castles and monasteries until
soldiers were brought in,
and blood flowed in Menno's "torrents,"
and the peasants, who even Luther had said
had been "tried too far,"
were slaughtered by the tens of thousands,
as usual more they than their oppressors.
Through all this, Anabaptists
held to their belief in nonviolence
though one thing Braun knows of: One day
a group of Anabaptists carried swords,
thinking that a show of being armed
might save them from attack. It did not,
and when they were attacked, impulsively
their swords flew out and killed.
So near is the danger, anger. The command,
"Love your enemies,"
is almost beyond men's strength, yet—
there it is in Verduin's book—
a remnant of the faithful
repeated the command. Flemish Lollards
(*lollen,* "to sing softly and soothingly")

"sang their 'heresy' into men's hearts":
They lived then
with that reasonable sweetness
that looks today from plain-secters' eyes.
Braun is reminded of Elias Kulp
who through a long night—
he once told Braun about it—
read Christ's injunction of loving-kindness
and acknowledged it. And thought.
Thought is hope,
and Mennonites believe that love
is not only Christ's great command
but that it defends and overcomes
"with less death." But, for that, clearly
men must be trained in sanity, seriously.
It must be the politics of their soul.
Provocations must be prepared for,
men must be ready when provoked.
The willingness to die rather than kill,
the will not to kill
must, like an absolute, spread to all.
Braun thinks, Is it possible?
One must believe it possible
if anything at all is to be done.

PLOWING ACCIDENT

Pat Giagnocavo was plowing
when his plow handle hit him in the chest.
The plow had caught on a stone, and his two big horses
levered the handle up against him.

`Now, as he lies in bed,
the hills get dark and draw his dog's whine
into the marked birches. He hears the truck,
filled with birch cuttings,
following the spring's still-icy ruts
down to the valley.

476

He lies on his back. His ribs
breath by breath lift a heated brick,
and Monday becomes Tuesday
against the fading slits of his stove.

He sleeps and his hands grasp again
the continuing plow of his mind.

LIFE

Wesley Kaesemeyer walks across his neat-raked barnyard
and stops where a rail
balks the cattle. The cattle low.
The air is cool.
"Yes, so it is. Got to get in the fodder.
Got to get in fodder and feed.
Got to get all in now, enough
to last through."

THOMAS FORSYTHE'S RED

Down the black cinder path
behind the Barto railroad station,
in a many-roomed square frame building
like an enlargement of his pigeon loft,
Thomas Forsythe houses
all seven of his children and their children.
An engineer, he works
in the nearby pumping station
for the oil line that runs its cleared track
"straight as a string" over hill and valley
"except where they miss a right of way."
For many years he was outside
"walking the line," knowing
something like bird flight across ground.

At rivers he did not hesitate,
but swung out on the cable crossing
where the iron cord hung in the air
and so followed the straight line through.

In nineteen thirty-four,
Harlan Edge, a local pigeon fancier,
gave him two pairs of birds to start, first
of those appealing heads, round-eyed
and specked with a wedge of white over the beak,
those pets he soon handled knowingly,
spreading the wings, counting the "flights,"
fanning the tail, and with a stroke down the back,
dropping them into the basket, "ready."
Two years later, his passion fixed,
he was the secretary
of the Lenape Pigeon Club,
and not only he but his wife and a son
lived for the pigeon loft—their loft
was a convenient outbuilding
thirty yards behind the house.

In all their years of flying
the Forsythes' favorite bird was "Red."
"Wayne Rigner, in nineteen thirty-six,
brought me a pair of Wegges," Forsythe says.
"The hen put some sticks together
and between them laid two eggs.
She sat from four in the afternoon
till ten in the morning, then the cock
took the short shift till four.
You can say this for the cock,
he lets the lady sleep at night."
After the regulation eighteen days,
one of the pair of eggs hatched out
a spiny baby pure red all over.
While cock and hen had sat on the nest,
both—such is the instinctual design—
had prepared for a special function:
at the baby's first fluttering,
papa or mama opened beak
and the little one plunged into the craw

478

and found there "milk," a secretion
in return for which, as he ate,
all his body shook with ecstasy.
By some chronometer of need,
as he grew, the secretions changed,
gradually coarsening
until he was ready for whole grain.

One morning in mid-April,
soon after the new bird's birth,
Forsythe came into the coop
with a small aluminum band.
On this band was printed
AU 36-303,
which would be the identifying number
for this pigeon's entire racing life.
He fastened the band on the small leg.
The Forsythes called most of their birds by number,
but as this "squeaker" grew
in his pure rosy flush,
they began to call him Red.

At a month he was a full-grown squab.
At six weeks Forsythe picked him up
and took him to the young birds' pen
where he continued squeaking
until he was two months old—
then his voice changed to bass
and he squeaked no more.

He was let out now to fly,
exercising around the loft,
testing the sight of either eye. A pigeon
has two distinct fields of vision,
either one of which
can be suppressed at will,
but more, each eye has at its center
a heavy layer of dark pigment—pecten—
and so can face the sun unhurt,
staring at it straight on,
and by that same dark veil, it is said,
can see the stars by daylight.

(Are the stars a possible compass?)
As the weather warmed in late spring,
Forsythe got out his training basket
and took Red and the other "young birds"
up the Congo road to a hill
from which, straight across the valley
greening in its soft panels,
they could see the loft. He released them.
They rose and made
two circles and a half and headed out
and were home when he got there.
Then he took them to Guldin's Hill,
three miles on toward Boyertown,
and let them learn to fly home from there.
The training always continued southward,
following closely the same line
the birds would follow in their races.
After Guldin's Hill, the hosiery mill
at Boyertown, then "I swung them
back and forth across Route One Hundred,
always south,
then to Yellowhouse, Baumstown,
Elverson, Churchtown, and Gap—
from Gap I took them to Cochranville,
from Cochranville to Conowingo Dam.
Then they were ready to race."

The first Sunday in September
was the first race for the young birds.
This year, nineteen thirty-six,
somewhat after six o'clock
the Thursday before the race, Forsythe
and his son Robert took a basket
and went out to the young birds' pen.
With Robert checking and Forsythe scooping,
they began to fill the basket:
Red was one of the first chosen.
As Forsythe's hand pursued him,
he stepped aside and from the bellows
of his breast roocoocooed, glancing up
clean, stonelike in his red contours
that narrowed smoothly to the beads of eyes.

480

"Come here, son." The hand
enfolded him and dropped him,
still protesting, into the basket.
When the full team had been chosen,
Forsythe went outside and got feed,
his part to be put in the shipping crate,
and so he walked down the cinder track
to the station. At the station platform
five men had already gathered,
and the claw of the countermarker
was fastened to the platform's edge,
opening its four nails toward the birds,
nails that would release a rubber band
over each bird's inserted leg,
the bird's identification for the race.
Forsythe's near neighbor, Howard Fluck,
recorded the countermarks. Rigner
with a wink asked Fluck to tell the number
of one of his pigeons. "Fifty-nine."
"Wrong! Sixty-seven! By God,
he can't tell his own birds."
"Tom here, he's got a redbird. He can tell him."
Forsythe slipped the countermark on Red
and took him to the shipping crate.
"Three o three." "Right, three o three."
Below the voice, Red settled into the dark,
roocoocooing once,
as the hinged door snapped shut.
With the countermarking done,
the loaded crate was ready
to be shipped to Perryville, Maryland,
the first "station" flown by the young birds.

Sunday, Forsythe as club secretary
got a wire from the "liberation point"
giving the time the birds were let go,
and could see in his mind the multicolored cloud
that over the distant city would form
as the birds climbed, spreading in line
and circling, "getting their bearings,"
seeming to go only to return,
but at last "really going."

Soon, for the birds are fast,
the race committee gathered at the clock
in Forsythe's kitchen, waiting for the "timers."
A timer is a small clocking device
that brings in a bird's countermark from the loft
to prove the exact flight time.
"Hardly worth a timer for you, Tom.
We could watch you from the loft here."
"Seconds count," Fluck said.
"Maybe the bird don't come to hand
even when it's in the loft."
"That's so now," another said.
"A woman's needed for pigeons.
Let the wife take the timer
and, by God, they'll jump to her hand."
"Perfume—it's the perfume does it."
All at Forsythe's could see the open sky
waiting. The air began to get that strange
pressure as if light thickened
and the blue of the sky deepened,
or as if up from the horizon
a tegument stretched. Forsythe waited,
and now the sky was empty
and now specks were visible, coming,
that flurry of flight
so instantaneously there. The pigeons broke,
each going to his or her owner's loft. Soon
Forsythe's wife brought the timers,
and Forsythe looked for the countermarks—
"best two birds" for his loft—
but of the two, neither was Red's.
Red was on his mind,
a bird so "like," so clean,
and he asked, "Did Red come in?"
"Yes, he's in now," his wife said.
"About fifth, yes, he was fifth."
As Forsythe helped Fluck
do calculations of the speeds—
they worked them all out then by hand—
he was glad that Red had come back.

Red in the following five years
won only one "first in race."
He was never a very fast bird,
but he was dependable.
"The tougher the day, the better he done."
He was the first of Forsythe's birds
to fly five hundred miles in a day
and so was his first "day bird."
Whenever the club had a pool
of "nominated birds for one race,"
Forsythe always nominated Red,
and Red won many such pools
when faster birds failed to come in.
Always as the timers reached the kitchen,
the family asked, "Is Red back?"
for sometimes some were lost—
sometimes more than half.
Red passed every danger and returned,
tired, slipping quickly into the gate
that closed him into the chirring loft.

Red mated early, choosing the hen he wanted,
to whom from then on he was faithful.
Oddly enough, he chose three o one,
next in the loft's numbers to himself.
His wife, like him,
was not particularly fast,
yet together they bred winning birds.
Also
every flock has a natural leader. Red
made himself leader of the flock.
The flock did well under him
and he flew all the "five hundreds."
He also flew an occasional six hundred.
Forsythe remembers one six hundred.

"The birds were let go in Carolina.
at five o'clock a Friday morning."
It was Armistice Day. It rained.
It was a bad day for flying.
The first bird to come in

belonged to Herbert Fronheiser
who did not "do it justice,"
for he and his family had gone
to the Armistice Day parade
and the bird "popped in" untimed.
Fornheiser for years afterward
blamed himself for that negligence.
Even so the bird won the race,
the only bird to arrive the first day.
Forsythe stayed in his loft
watching till after dark.
Rarely a racer comes in after dark,
but a good one sometimes will.
He watched up till nine o'clock.
Then he went back to the house.
He went into the front room
and caught one of his granddaughters
and petted her, little thing
soft and peaceable. Next day
early he was watching.
He wondered where Red had spent the night.
It might have been on a roof somewhere
that he had rested, on some outbuilding—
perhaps a coal shed.
They come down so sometimes
on a familiar shape,
on a likeness of the loft.
Then when they are rested,
they leap into the air and fly on.
He walked back and forth in the yard,
looking repeatedly toward the sky.
The day was clearing. It was good
to see the pit holes of the sky
filled with sun channeling its light
out and down. At noon Pappy Edge came
and walked the path with him.
Pappy knew how much Red meant to him.
"You go eat," he said,
"and I will watch. No more are in.
Maybe Red will be second."
So Forsythe nervously ate,
and came back with his wife to Pappy.

Now all three paced the yard path
so near the polished railroad tracks
and the gawky apparatus
of the oil pumping station.
The sky that had been cloudy
now had winked clear, its blue
throbbing and becoming heated and giving
a sense of intent space
over the edges of the trees.
At four o'clock Forsythe happened to be watching
the exact center of sky to the south
when nothing became a point
and the point began to vibrate,
enlarging into the scissors of wings
recognizable in their color,
and he called out, "Red."
Strange that so small a thing
as that advancing, plummeting body
could twist him so—be such a relief.
Nothing seemed nicer than Red's landing,
the spread and blocking of his wings.
A quick leap and he was in. All know
a good flyer does not eat or drink
but flies without feed or water
straight through the daylight hours,
even the second day flies straight through
and at the loft,
though the feed trough is full,
goes first to water. So Red,
his countermark in the timer, drank,
was safely home and "second."

In Red's sixth year, Forsythe
no longer put him to race.
The time had come to "retire him."
Retired, he continued to breed racers
who wore his courage with a faster wing.

Early in the spring of forty-two,
on a cold day
when the wind came down from the hills
with an odor of melting snow,

for the first time that year Forsythe
let Red out, to exercise him. "He was sluggish.
He had only
gone up a short distance
when a hawk struck him.
He wasn't dead when I picked him up,
but the claws had gone right through him
and he died in my hands."

THE WALL

Joe Heimbacher likes it, the barnyard wall,
though the red stone begins to crumble
and the coping breaks.
It is a solidity
once in the mind,
now in the rain,
unweathered in the affection of his eye.

A SONG OF THE SEASONS

Spring comes on fast, throwing violets up Crow Hill.
Elda Maria Schwenk puts a single *veiolich* in her dark hair.
The sun warms and thaws.
Small surface stones rustle against Heimbacher's plow.
    Sweat wets him. It rains a stint of starting and stopping,
      g'yupping and whoaing across his hilltop field.
Daniel Dengler cuts his day's boards in the coffin factory,
    "that hotbox."
Mary Hertzog scrubs a stain of sparrow-wing maple seeds from
    her front-yard well cover.
In the Uhrs' fields, noon leaks a green dampness.
Dengler reaches for a board that was ripsawed from the center
    of a tree, not noticing it holds a steel-jacketed bullet
    fired in the Civil War. So death flaws one coffin.

486

Heimbacher's harrow pulls up a flint arrowhead,
      nudging another death.
Mary Miller walks under the maple trees at Fred Braun's and
      smiles because Braun says he lives undersea. The sea—
      those trees she planted when she was just a little twig
      herself, twenty-five long years ago.
Still, the manacles of work are fastened on the wrists of
      summer.
Still, shadows re-form over Crow Hill as clouds, and differences
      and delights race on the meadow.
In Amos Schultz's Ovid: "Apollo leaned down to the hyacinth
      and inscribed it with his own grieving words, 'Ai ai.' "
"Ai ai," Heimbacher himself says, but not in sorrow.
Hyacinths are the color of the back of Schwenk's porch, a blue
      robe hung on the wall.
In the Hertzogs' front yard, nasturtiums flick their small
      spurs, petunias haul trumpets of disorder into the fence
      pickets, and sedum throws its mustard luster along the
      ground.
John Birmelin packs loose mud at the roots of his ballads.
      He laughs at meter and makes new sounds.
About a person he doesn't like he writes, "A dumb wondernose."
Heimbacher's pigs have snouts like snuffling coins, hunting
      in ooze. Purslane is named for them: "seibaertzel."
      They roll and frolic in it. It is pig romp.
Phlox align their diamond hedges. Wheat chases the hay.
Elda Maria sees husks of shagbark hickory nuts flying open
      on the branches like the dried blossoms of tulip trees.
      Storms swing scythes.
As the wood thrush shivers, the fields call, pitiless overseers:
pumpkins sound their drums, and corn bends to the pheasants,
      marauders with loud tails whistling toward winter.
The rewards of heaven drop into sacks. The year is safe,
      the barns full.
Above Uhrs' hill, oaks wrap themselves in the few leaves
      that are left.
Water rakes the pastures like hens' claws. Cold curtains of
      rain thrash on the Kemps' washpole birches.
Ivy Yost heats up the skyward cannons of her chimneys.
Along a side road toward Josephus Gerhard's, a *staagefens* of
      seven thin-split rails sifts the first snow.

A fox breaks the new ice. In Braun's hillside waste,
    jewelweed crumbles with the yarrow, and darkness binds
    the sumac's eyes.
The stars go cold. The nights go indoors.

THE REVEREND JOHNSON IN HEREFORD

The Reverend Johnson, when young,
before he was a reverend
or went to Germany, thought,
Hereford, that's a beautiful name
and a beautiful community.
I wish I might live there someday.
Not least in the wish
may have been Hereford's being
close to his beloved uncle,
Josephus Gerhard, who lived
just down the road. Hereford
was a simple crossroads,
but it was more than that.
The general store—then Fred Huber's,
now Jim Althouse's—and post office
had always on its front
a martin house flying a summer draft
of purple martins. Next to it, a lawn
behind a low gray stone fence
defined a perpetual coolness.
A few more lawns, a few houses.
Hereford. Young Elmer Johnson,
as he came through it, felt
a return of his mother's quiet there,
Susanna of the green calm.
On the eastward hill toward Chapel,
Joseph Griesemer's place, the house
a rise of sharp colors,
the pillars of the two-story porch
bright yellow, the gutters
strips of blazing blue set over stone:
it was a brilliant perch hung

488

over the floor of the valley.
Johnson thought it much the best house
in the neighborhood, so it stayed
in his mind in the seminary
and in nineteen four as he sailed
for Europe. Ten years later
he had come back from his work there
and was looking for a place to live.
Driving with Allan Stauffer
from Pennsburg to Hereford,
he passed the Griesemer place,
Surprised, he found it boarded up.
Unpainted and in neglect,
it still spoke to his heart
with that hover against the valley.
Stauffer told him, "Butcher Kriebel
bought it a year ago.
He needed the land for his cattle
and used the barn. The house, no."
Johnson said, "Be kind enough
to drive me to Butcher Kriebel."
Kriebel said,
"Well, if you think to rent it,
you must see it. Come."
So they drove back again.
A thread of sun touched the kitchen stove
under the high ceiling and high walls
that had the same simple splendor
of the outside. The house responded
to the new tread going through.
"I want it. Yes, I want it."
Kriebel put his hand on a door.
"I will paint and paper," he said.
Always that kindness. So it was done.

Here for seven years
Elmer Johnson and his wife, Agnes,
a niece of Josephus Gerhard,
lived as tenants and friends
of Andrew Kriebel, the butcher.
From their porch,
Hereford, a green annunciation

from spring through fall,
and in winter, a resting pause. Here the Reverend Johnson
took his lifelong stewardship
of the Reformed Mennonite Church in Bally.
Here he started his collection
of the Bibles of the valley,
the record of birth days and death days,
a reliquary registry.
And here his only son, Rolland, was born.
After seven years,
in confirmation of this being home
and to fully settle down,
he bought a nearby farm
across the Hereford-Bally road
and there built himself a stone house.
It was not easy,
when the time came to move to it,
to leave the Griesemer place,
that bright gaud of the fields,
that enameled tabernacle,
or to leave Andrew Kriebel
as their landlord of the hill—
no, no move is easy.

In his new Hereford house
the Reverend Johnson
stayed to his pastorate's end, then
when his wife died and his son's wife died,
in an access of dejection,
he thought of "leaving it all,"
of going to Hartford, the retreat
where he had once studied, where he had taught,
yes, a flight from here
back to the world he had once lived in
and that he would return to again.
He sold his home and told a few friends,
but came Andrew Kriebel and said,
speaking perhaps for all,
"I have heard what you think to do.
You shall not go. No.
You shall still stay with us here."
Kriebel bought a house

490

up the Chapel road
two hills past the Griesemer place,
and with a kindly authority
there told the Reverend Johnson to stay.
There he has stayed to this day.

At eighty-five—he is now that age—
he is still active
though it may be "doing nothing."
He takes buses "around.
I loaf, and when I loaf,
I like to do just what I want
from minute to minute." He has come
to that holy idleness
he has earned. As he wants,
he stops in the Althouse store
and talks for an hour or two
by the unblackened stove
in the vibration of its winter heat,
or he watches through summer's open door
the blue of the purple martins.
He lives yet in Hereford Township.
He rents a box in the Hereford Post Office
for eighty cents a year
"to be part of the place."
In the store, his voice, unpulpited
but as deep and wide-reaching as ever,
ranges back across his life,
summoning up its years of wandering,
and at times becomes still
while over store and field and hill
spreads the appeal he first felt
like Susanna's calm, and wanted,
and has since had, his home.

ROSE GERHARD

Rose, Owen Gerhard's widow,
lives alone in the old house
that now includes the tenant house,
the two houses now brought together—
a large place for her aging self.
What memories in it, that here Owen's
father and mother—Josephus and Elizabeth—
began their married life, and here
she and Owen too began. "Owen
married me in nineteen ten. Then
his parents moved down the hill
to let us have this larger place. Yes,
some days Josephus helped,
but it was up to Owen." She remembers of Josephus
how much he liked people. "That was his nature.
Even in church when there were strangers,
he went right up and talked to them." He was deacon
in three Schwenkfelder churches,
at Hosensack, at Washington, at Kraussdale.
"We went one Sunday to one, one to the next,
and then to the third.
We always knew the Gerhards. When I was little,
they used to come to our house to dinner
and we went to their house. I remember
how Josephus liked horses!
He used to get horses from Jake Wallach
and fatten and train them
and then Wallach sold them. And of course
he had his own. Twenty—more!"
So many memories of this house.
Children: Frances, Paul, Richard, Robert,
"and with Owen and me and the hired help
at harvest—sometimes it was nine to feed.
Now and then
the Reverend Johnson ate with us. Once
he ate two sausages, then he said,
'Now don't look,' and he took a third one.
Another time

492

he wanted to rest. I said,
'Take off your shoes,' and he did
and took a nap."
The gentle laugh of Elizabeth's daughter-in-law
who is herself a Schultz (her maiden name), maybe
"a twenty-second cousin" to both Elizabeth
and Elizabeth's nephew, Elmer Johnson.
She wanders the kitchen floor now,
getting a small vase
filled with wild hyacinths—"They call them bluebottles"—
that her granddaughters brought her
She puts them in the light of a window
and stops to look out.

THE PENNSYLVANIA
GERMAN SOCIETY MEETING, 1972

After the morning session
Dr. David Hottenstein lets his poodle,
Pierre François, trot his black fat
unclipped self down the Pennsburg lawns,
lawns that were once
colonial fields and woods.
"Pierre François,
come back here now. I don't clip him
over the winter, but my daughter Mary Harriet
will clip him for the summer. He's bright.
He'll get up in my lap
when I'm in my old clothes,
but not when I'm dressed up. . . .
My son David?
He never became a doctor.
He's the first nondoctor Hottenstein
in four generations. But he has this connection
with medicine, he helps with work
on atomic research in cancer."
Hundreds now
have left the Society's morning session.
The Reverend Jack R. Rothenberger

spoke on the ecumenical ideal
of Caspar Schwenckfeld, "the irenic nobleman
of Silesia," who stayed a layman
and in his simplicity wanted
a "universal, peace-loving, serving, and saving church,"
and believed such a church
already mystically
existed in God's love.
"A good meeting," David says.
"Mary worked hard for it. You should see
how she's reorganized it there
at the society headquarters. Letters
coming from all over the world that she answers—
plain, nothing put on,
just her own way of writing."
He and she live now
in the old Hottenstein plantation house
near Kutztown. "We're restoring it.
Not renovating, restoring."
John Heyl at the morning session
showed slides of it, including the ballroom
that the Henry Dupont Museum at Winterthur
brought and reassembled there. "So now
if I want to see my old ballroom,
I have to go to Winterthur."
Pierre François, agreeable Huguenot, trots on
with the levitation poodles have. "Well,
I see Mary up there. She must be tired.
I must get her now and take her home."
Home to the old family house
in the vale of Maxatawny.

ED KULP AND CAMERA

It's an ordinary day, the sun just rolling up, as Ed takes
    his camera and goes out.
He is glad for a day to be rid of the Bally Block's heat,
    dust, and snoring August blowers. The work slows.
    No night shift now.

The years are getting on. Mamie's getting older. I'm
    getting older.
And it seems so long since son Willis went west that time with
    Mamie's folks, with Harvey, and got that love for it.
    Nothing I could do. Got that love for stone, chalcedony,
    streaks of whiteness, what's in and under stone.
Studied there, got his degrees there. Stayed there.
He was prospecting for water when the drill tore his arm off.
"Shit, I don't need the arm," and he's still there,
    wandering those Colorado rocks.
Buddy's married and settled in Roanoke.
Miriam's married. She comes and visits.
Mamie and I manage.
I have my camera.

The lens's window may be dark for days, but then the shade snaps
    up on a fringed gentian that sways and steadies in its
    trembling dew, or a phlox, or a snapdragon opening its
    yellow mouth, or one bright harebell.
Even grass is beautiful, the light on it the way light falls
    sometimes on a child's knee, or on a factory belt. I
    flash it up on the wall and Mamie laughs.
But the single flower, the "I" of the flower trying to get
    through from stillness.

He walks down to the *shwamm*. The swamp is where the cardinal
    flowers are, but today there are only two and the petals
    are imperfect. The eyes are blurred in both.
He wanders over to a nearby pool where there may be some fern.
    At the pool edge, small frogs jump, each sounding its
    cro-ak of alarm.
Small ripples of mist float over the water, constantly renewed
    out of the edges, the water motionless. Cro-ak. Cro-ak.
No fern. There are silken cinders of white sanicle, thoroughwort
    growing through the shoulders of its stemless leaves,
    jewelweed batting its yellow eyes.
But he wants none of these.
He notices a gleam of nettle. When he used to run barefoot
    as a boy, he'd scream in the nettles, the *brenas'l*.

With his camera bumping on his chest he steps into the woods,
    and at his feet a jack-in-the-pulpit shakes its furious
    red scalp lock of seeds. It has an onion root the Indians
    ate. He ate it once. It was bitter.
Toward Barto, Saylor's mill turns saffron in the low yell
    of the millrace.
The day gets darker with the woods.
Kempie, Koiner, Katie, Kurt, Kelly, Karla, the grandchildren—
    he misses them. Ahead,
shadowed,
a dead chestnut rears up its trunk, opening eyes where limbs
    have fallen, other limbs still there
as the tree strains up.
He stops,
he begins to get the pale form's shape:
arms chilled by wind and rain, the chance permanence of the
    rain's breastbands, the silver drapery of the snail around
    the stiffened knees, the knees scarred.
A scarf down the long bole, a streak of veil, of
    shroud.
He lifts his camera. He puts his eyes to the vertical viewer
    and adjusts for light, for distance. His finger presses
and he has it,
the live American ghost.

WILBUR SCHULTZ'S BOYS AND GIRLS

"We grew beards for the centennial at Macungie.
Yes we did." The gallery of his children
laugh as Wilber Schultz touches his beard:
"I'm growing one for the Emmaus Centennial,
but I may shave it off a few times first."
The six children lounge lopsidedly,
some dressed, some about to get dressed.
"How do you like these six musicians,
who'll play tonight at the Miller family reunion?"
"I'll play tuba, stuck with it," Robert says.
Louise likes the accordion, Herbert
the trombone, and Martha the clarinet.

496

Doris makes the saxophone "moan."
Johnny can ream out the trumpet
with a mean cadenza.
Papa Wilbur makes eyes with his fingers
on the potato of the ocarena.
Louise and Doris beat tunes on the glockenspiel
like their great-uncle Isaac Stahl.
"Isaac's brother Thomas
was a foresinger." "Mmmmmmmmmm."
"He was a fine potter, too."
"He sang once—"
"We'll play some solos, duets, and trios—" "Yeah,
but we should have practiced more."
"Martha played with the fire-company band,
but she resigned." Shouts:
"Quit." "Petered out." Martha
is indignant. "I did not!"
The bearded Wilbur says,
"Tonight they'll play their first concert. You know,
The Success March, The Courage March.
It goes from lessons and solo work
into the organization."
At least two hundred seated Millers—
men, women, and children—will listen
as the moon cuts over the roof
of the large pavilion in the woods,
and the Schultz kids,
clattering their notes in the night,
will help make the reunion bright. "Yes,
as I said, the Stahls. Their father Charles
had a pottery on Indian Creek
and made more practical things—water jugs,
apple butter crocks. Well, kids,
are you ready to go?"

FROM A LETTER FROM RALPH BERKY
in answer to an inquiry about John Simmons

"The late John Simmons
sang second tenor in the quartet, a troupe
that warbled together for a period
of about twenty years
from 1927 on. In the early part
we did concert work, a capella,
and memorized. When John and the other two boys
married and had families,
we did less—and less—singing,
and only on special and rare occasions.
The other two were Russell Bechtel,
baritone, and Ed Kulp, 2nd bass.
Yours truly was first tenor.
Three standby numbers were 'Old Friends,'
'Kentucky Babe,' and 'Fairest Lord Jesus.'
I wrote for the quartet many years ago:
'Hear the bells, Bally bells, ring along ding-dong
How they ring, how they sing night and day ding-dong
Bells of home, bells of love, ring along ding-dong
How they sing, how they cling evermore ding-dong.' "

INTERIOR

Russell Bechtel is in the store alone.
A man comes in
in blue dungarees, carrying
a rat hound with ears like lilac leaves.
He says, "I carry the dog
so he don't do no damage."
"He's a nice dog," Russell says,
tickling the ears.

498

There is one side to groceries.
Across from them, the other goods:
shelves of seeds in bottles, picnic plates,
and back of pie tins, cautious cosmetics.
Joe Heimbacher comes in
to buy a summer hat. Ed Kulp's
eleven year-old Miriam
walks in with Russell's Janet
not to buy, to "visit."
The big front door again flashes open:
John Simmons, in to barter potatoes.
"Will we sing tonight?" he says.
"If we can catch Ralph," Russell says. Stanley appears
and puts on his apron and stands
ready to serve the trade.

BAUMANN'S GARDENS OF BABYLON

In the red of Rome Beauties
and other speckled crimsons
rattling on the endless lift,
the apples rise—

waves of seconds
carried up
to the knives beating evenly
as a heart, and loud.

From large
apple butter barrels a cloud
of steam out of copper coils
eddies toward the cider trough,

then winds the top of the press
where the circling knives cut
the apples into layers of pulp.
Around the pulp

a boy and a man silently
fold the wrapping cloths,
and square by square pile up the slats
until

they move aside as the tower slides
into the press's jaws,
and the turn of its great screw
begins. Then

down the sides streams of juice
fall like pillars, sweet and columnar,
level by level, a city of hanging gardens,
a Babylon,

formed momentarily between the apple-butter barrels
and the pile of refuse,
rusted remains of fruit waiting
to be shoveled away.

DECISION

Edwin Fox goes behind his house
to the greening slope where his beehives
turn their backs on departing winter,
bright troop
he must soon give up.

Some Italians buzz by, saying,
Stay a little off. Lively now
in the April sun, they make ellipses
above the stands. They need stands.
If the box is too near the ground,

the winter skunk, prowling and hungry,
knocks at it and having stirred
the guards whose instinct drives them down,
he lays his tail out
and the bees crawl on and so he eats them.

500

Bees need man's care. If he gives his hives up,
none of his boys will start again.
It's getting like the ministry, he thinks. None
want any more to go in.
Yes, his generation

may be the last
to have the beekeeper's interest.
Bees are work and many are saying,
They're no longer worth the trouble.
Well,

danger to that double sweetness,
the apple and honey, if the wing
depart with the sting, and the disdained,
so small,
prove to be the indispensable.

AT WAYNE KEMP'S PLACE

The roof that has been silent under snow
changes to a sound that comes and goes
in the incessant touching of a drum,
quickening to a roll, now wavering.

Trees that have had lines of white and steel
accept an interregnum of gray buds
that fall and grow and fall and grow again,
the rapid seasons of a single rain

A REQUIEM FOR JOSEPHUS GERHARD

Down, all the way down, doubly down
in the skin of earth
smoothed so well by his own hand,
ai, there he is,

501

king of stumps, dispensing blessings
over the gullies of clover,
ten decades shy from Millside,
ai, there he is.

Given at last to the roses,
sunk into the gold eye of the wild rose,
palms wet with psalms,
ai, there he is.

The locust free at last, tired
and resting in the glaze of birth,
wings closed over his vanished stick,
ai, there he is

where the risked windrows cry
under the triumphant reaper,
where the last windows look,
ai, there he is.

His, the weight of cows
under the horns of their bawling,
gathered at the twilight's fence,
ai, there he is.

His, the rush of horses
at sundown in the forebay's shadow;
master of the grass ramps,
ai, there he is.

Let one horse rear for him
in the powerful harness of that time
with crackling bridging and bridle—
ai, there he is.

Let the saddle, dark, be his,
burnished with snows and sleepings.
Hooves of beatitude,
ai, there he is.

502

Let him drive the summer roads,
he who built the toll roads,
pennies to town and safe grain,
ai, there he is.

Strawberries, such an episode
of one woman absorbed,
oh, fully absorbed into himself,
ai, there he is.

Like berry leaves that darken,
and runners run out fresh,
the green is there again,
ai, there he is,

Union and communion,
but locks of solitude
with keys of only barley seed,
ai, there he is.

Mourning dove in whistling palace,
calling with three falling notes
outside and in the ear,
ai, there he is.

Affirmative speaker, H. A. Schuler,
negative, A. S. Berky.
To the debating friends,
ai, there he is.

Affirmative, the cornfields
with bayonets of August
from sight to flame—
ai, there he is.

Negative, the original acres,
all the Octobers of his crops
bare with the penury of June,
ai, there he is.

Blood of his heart inside out,
blood of his unrelenting will
shaken over the horses' rumps,
ai, there he is.

There is his blood, there is his body,
there is the statement of belief:
"We do love one another."
Ai, there he is.

There he is in his body
and his body in the ground,
in the gully that at last
only his own length could fill.
Ai, there he is.

THE ENDING DEITSCH
(Linford Gehman)

"I don't speak *Deitsch,* never did.
The people of my generation
speak English. We can listen to the *Deitsch,*
but can't speak it.
In my father's childhood it was different.
His parents talked the dialect to him.
In our house, no. My parents
might talk it to each other,
just very occasionally,
but they never talked it to us children.
And that's true generally.
It's something, some feeling against it,
maybe some shying away from German
during World War Two. Radio? TV?
I don't know what it is, but the *Deitsch* is ending,
it's just the accent now.
Up towards Alburtis and Macungie it's a very heavy
Pennsylvania German accent,
but what's remarkable
is they can't speak the *Deitsch,*
none of the people of my age."

THE QUARRY

Fred Braun walks ahead of Walter Shuhler.
Ralph Berky wears his boots
in the mid-August wet.
Saint-John's-wort shines its little reflector
up from the quarry floor
that once was bare,
that once advanced into the enlarging wound
of the hill. Shuhler says,
"They tell that nature cures all.
It seems so." The quarry
that exposed the hill
like a lantern throwing
light and dust from its chimney
has now turned out its wick.
Trees fill the quarry floor,
so that the curving cut can be reached
by only one remaining track. The cut
has a bright line of gravel and quartz
at its base and shows sand.
"It might have been a seashore once,"
Shuhler says, "so it looks."
On the ledges hang flowers
like nests of hungry young birds.
Ralph says, "Sometimes barn owls
nest in quarries,
but I see none here, none of their droppings."
Virginia creeper climbs a fissure,
and wild grape turns its hands out
over the red wash of the lower stone.
In the cut is a cave that, Ralph says,
he and a friend once explored,
having to crawl much of the way: "It goes in
a hundred ninety-nine feet to water.
At the end of it we dropped a pebble
and we could hear it splash.
It made us nervous
and we were glad to get out, I can tell you."
They backed out,
glad to be free of that mole hole.

A fence of sucker shoots now bars the cave,
and a white ash, rooted in gravel,
reaches up toward the quarry's rim. Walter's Florence
came here to call her father,
and here the roads of the township
slipped out and grew hard.
All green now is the stone crusher—years
of the shaggy ropes of poison ivy
hold its walls upright.
Of the self-healing quarry
only a curve of cup remains,
only an aperture of petals.

WILSON MOYER LEAVES
BEFORE THE RAIN

Trees, roiled with a wind
sweeping under thunderheads, thrash slowly
all along the ridge. The headstone
of Mountain Mary's grave
reflects the quick knife of lightning.

Nearby, Wilson Moyer cuts weeds. He is deaf.
Driving the mower,
only as a shuttling across his eyes
he hears the rattle of the blades
and only as trembling, the tread of his horses.
The two horses march aligned
with scimitars behind their fetlocks.
As lightning flashes,
he opens his hand, listening.

This is the continuous field, unworked now
except as he mows it
but which his father tilled. He mows it
with a last attachment. As he stops,

drops of elemental rain, heavy,
follow him as a deity of sorrow
turning with the horses. Going in,
he walks toward a falling veil.

THE CROWS OF KROPPA BERG

"The crows
come years ago like clouds,
come down black on a field
and eat the rows."

But now, wary, slow,
cawing,
caw caw caw,
they lift one by one and fade:

no longer raid hens' nests
or corn rows.
The saying,
"Poor enough to eat crow,"

is remembered yet against the old ones,
the hoarse ones
with eagle heads.
They go

over Kroppa Berg
as the heat grown. Their call,
the sawing voice
ever present

and forever going,
sounds yet in the air.
Winged,
challenging

through the taller trees
or the horizon's wall,
like summer itself
it sings as it recedes.

THE LAST STONE

Joe Heimbacher has a hilltop field,
which is flat and has an outlook.
It also has stones. Whoever opened it
removed most of them
but left four boulders, perhaps
believing them outcroppings of the hill.
Three he hauled off, his drag
leaving wakes on the field
as on a sea. Only one defied him,
a two-ton pivot.

This stone he long planned to bury,
but year by year went by.
This spring it must be done!
All these years of turning aside,
the furrows bending—and disking, seeding,
and harrowing, and reaping the same—
no, it has to stop.

One day shortly after dawn
he and two of his sons
start to dig down beside the boulder,
their short-handled shovels in the cool
of the early April morning clanking
with a serious sound.
The hole they make opens a mouth of shadow
and takes the shape of the boulder,
but, to bury a boulder,
the stone must be separate
from the rest of the hill's stone.

One son finds the bottom.
His shovel goes inward and it is not
an indentation but a true bottom.
They spit to show their satisfaction.

They continue digging. Toward noon
the sun pours almost straight into the hole,
shadowing the shovel markings
along the sides in the earth and clay,
steps going down, the carpentering
of a low bed
boxed out in a reminiscence
of the lonely grave of humans
who, for lack of something better,
sometimes are buried in a field.
The hole is deep now and ready.
Heimbacher has brought a strong beam from the barn,
and he and the boys dig prying space
behind the stone and, fitting the beam in,
pull on it as on a lever.

The boulder as it hangs, a cap of lichen—
balk through so many working seasons—
shivers, tips.
A thrust, a cloth-rip sound,
and it falls with a great thud
to the bottom of the hole. The ground
stills. Sweat
cools on Heimbacher's arms.
He tells his sons to get their shovels
and they shovel all back to the even level
of the whole field, a bevel
like the long surface of the sea.
The field now has no marring,
no undue swell, and he can say about it
in one way at least: It is done.

Appreciation
for Help Given

With this book, as always, my son Jonathan edited me devotedly and ruthlessly through draft after draft, watching every aspect of the book's development, demanding to see every revision of every poem. Even at the distance of Copenhagen and Stockholm, he kept this invaluable guidance and supervision going.

Edward Field read through a near-final draft of the book and made many useful, important suggestions.

Many friends went over individual poems with me: among them, Jay Bennett, Joan Colebrook, Alvaro de Silva, Ben Field, David Ignatow, June Jordan, Jere Knight, Alfred Kroymborg, Naomi Lazard, Walter Lowenfels, David McDowell, Charles Norman, Robert Payne, Isidor Schneider, Walter Weiss, and Agatha Young.

My younger son, Daniel, and my daughters Elinor and Carol took a helpful interest.

Jonathan's Monika aided me with the Swedish language and material, in the Uhr poems and elsewhere.

Daniel's Erika designed the jacket.

Various and numerous (and beloved) grandchildren kept my mind fresh about children.

Liane Carrera made it possible for me to work full-time during a year spent in the south of France (and where I also wrote *Dry Summer in Provence*).

Of those in the Crow Hill area, Ralph Berky was particularly close to *Local Lives* and now and then used to say, "You might call on Alvin Albitz," or whomever, and would take me to the subject of a poem.

Andrew S. Berky gave me access to the resources of the Schwenkfelder

Library in Pennsburg and checked the book for accuracy.

John Joseph Stoudt also checked the book for accuracy.

Thomas O'Conor Sloane III loaned me his grandfather's collection of early books on the Pennsylvania German dialect and people.

Ellen Jaffe gave me several important books. So did Lawrence Gellert.

Among many friends on Crow Hill and in the vicinity who helped me (in addition to being subjects of poems) were the Reverend Elmer E. S. Johnson, Squire Frank Benfield, Walter and Florence Shuhler, Isaac Stahl, members of the Abraham Gehman family, Russell and Marian Bechtel, Stanley and Dorothy Bechtel, the Nevin Yosts, the Uhrs, the Hertzogs, the Millers, David and Mary Hottenstein, Ed and Mamie Kulp, Patrick Giagnocavo, Clarence G. Reitnauer, and the Reverend William J. Rupp.

Also helpful were Lee and Mildred (Jordan) Bausher, Mary Baylson, Linda and Michael Frye, and many members of the Mennonite Voluntary Service.

My wife, Helen, with me in the area, sensitively shared many of the experiences of the book.

The following notes try to make a more detailed acknowledgement of help and sources:

The Reverend Elmer Johnson took me to see his "beloved uncle," Josephus Gerhard, and told me stories about him.

The Dialect draws somewhat on *The Pennsylvania Germans,* edited by Ralph Wood, Princeton University Press, 1942.

The Emigrants: I was reading Miller Williams's *Halfway from Hoxie* (Dutton, 1973) and came to *For Becky with Love the Eighth Year of the Slaughter* and decided to try a villanelle, working from a variant of his first line, "Whose tongues are twisted and whose hearts are shrunk."

B. Franklin's Change of Heart draws on *The Story of the Pennsylvania Germans* by William Beidelman, Express Book Print, 1898.

It was my father, actually, who tore out the house wall in *Censure.* He lived with me on and off and did remodeling, good workman that he was.

Mennonite Beginnings draws on several sources, including W. R. Estep, *The Anabaptist Story,* Broadman Press, 1963, and *Instead of Violence,* edited by Arthur and Lila Weinberg, Grossman Publishers, 1963, and of course *The Martyrs Mirror,* Herald Press.

"They Brake Bread" uses quotations given in *War, Peace and Nonresistance* by Guy F. Hershberger, Herald Press, 1944.

Behind Germantown draws on *The German and Swiss Settlements of Colonial Pennsylvania* by Oscar Kuhns, Henry Holt and Co., 1901.

Wilderness is based on material in the William Beidelman book mentioned above.

The Schwenkfelders is drawn from *Practitioner in Physick* by Andrew S. Berky, published by the Schwenkfelder Library in 1954.

The Voyage is based on the detailed account by David Shultze and also on a letter by Johannes Naas in the two-volume *Journals and Papers of David Shultze,* translated from the dialect and edited by Andrew S. Berky and published by the Schwenkfelder Library in 1952.

Clausa Germanis Gallia draws from extensive research, but particularly from Beidelman's *The Story of the Pennsylvania Germans,* mentioned above, and from *Louis XIV* by Louis Bertrand, Arthème Fayard, 1923.

The Baker comes from James E. Ernst's *Ephrata a History,* edited by John Joseph Stoudt and published by the Pennsylvania German Folklore Society, 1963.

Wilbur Schultz kindly loaned me *The Life and Times of Amos Schultz,* written and published privately by members of the Schultz family and the main source for *Amos Schultz's Life, The Moving,* and *The Reward.* Obviously, the Reverend Elmer Johnson was also helpful.

A Memory of Twenty-nine. W. H. Auden, in a critical article, put me onto the remarkable modernity of ottava rima. My own handling of it, of course, is free.

Conrad Weiser is mainly based on the definitive biography, *Conrad Weiser* by Paul A. W. Wallace, published originally by the University of Pennsylvania Press and reissued by Russell & Russell in 1971. It also draws on *King of the Delawares: Teedyuscung* by Anthony F. C. Wallace and published by the University of Pennsylvania Press, on Edmund Wilson's *Apologies to the Iroquois,* a Vintage book, and on the excellent account of Weiser's interval at the Ephrata Cloister by Daniel Miller (*Conrad Weiser as a Monk*) in *Transactions of the Historical Society of Berks County, Volume III.*

The Model is drawn from *Apologies to the Iroquois,* above.

War Resisters is drawn from Dr. Preston A. Barba's *They Came to Emmaus,* published by the Borough of Emmaus, 1959.

How to Be a Spy is based on an unpublished manuscript, in the Pennsburg Schwenkfelder Library, that Andrew S. Berky kindly made available to me.

The Convention Hessians is based on *The Hessian Camp in Reading* by Andrew Shaaber in *Transactions of the Historical Society of Berks County, Volume III.*

Emmaus's Beginning comes from material in Dr. Barba's *They Came to Emmaus,* mentioned above.

The Church and Constantine owes some particularly pertinent detail to Leonard Verduin's *The Reformers and Their Stepchildren,* William B. Eerdmans Publishing Company, 1964, but I myself am responsible for the main tendency of the poem, an attempt to evaluate the Constantine change. (See also *Reading Verduin.*)

Herbert as well as Ralph Berky helped me with the series on the Berky family beginning with *Father and Mother.* Ralph gave me, to help me with the series, his brother Darius's copy of *History of the Hereford Literary Society,* 1904, from which the poem on the society is partly drawn, as also *Examination of Applicants for Teaching.*

Steve, in *Toward a Philosophy of Horses,* is actually a horse my father had when he was farming and that he let me ride as he plowed and harrowed.

Emmaus and the Civil War is from data in *They Came to Emmaus,* mentioned above.

The Hand is a story told me by Robert J. Schwartz.

My Swedish daughter-in-law Monika helped me with *A Memory of Sweden* and *Mama's Sweden.* The Uhrs have thus become partly her, something Mama particularly would not have minded. Mama told me how, in her time, Sweden encouraged the translation of novels giving a dark view of American life, to discourage emigration. At the present time it's hard for me to conceive, having lived in Sweden, why any Swede would not wish to remain at home.

The Life of Dr. Benjamin Schultz was written from material in *An Account of Dr. Benjamin Schultz of Pennsylvania* by Andrew S. Berky, published by the Schwenkfelder Library in Pennsburg in 1952.

Without Soldiers is partly based on *William Penn* by Catherine Owens Peare, Philadelphia, Lippincott, 1957.

Des Iroquois aux Galères quotes a letter from *Des Iroquois aux Galères, Le Boréal Express* (Trois Rivières, Canada), December 1965, p. 5.

Behold Beloved is based on *Baptisms of Indians in Oley Prior to 1732* by the Reverend John Baer Stoudt in *Transactions of the Historical Society of Berks County, Volume III,* and on quotations from original sources in Roy Harvey Pearce's *Savagism and Civilization,* Johns Hopkins Press, 1967.

Chief Papanahoal is a part transcription of two unpublished manuscripts in the Schwenkfelder Library in Pennsburg, made available to me through the kindness of Andrew S. Berky.

In *Blue Memory* I assume the Delawares followed a general Indian practice of hanging up gourds for purple martins to nest in, as described in Bent's *Life Histories of North American Birds,* Harper and Brothers, 1960. The Indian comment on the Walking Purchase is in Samuel Eliot Morison's *The Oxford History of the American People.*

Devil and *Friendly Association* are drawn from *The Journals and Papers of David Schultze,* mentioned above.

514

Ernst Fuhrmann is based on a talk I had with Fuhrmann and on a talk with Lotte Jacobi about Fuhrmann.

Lawrence Gellert gave me the rare *Life of John Heckewelder* published by Townsend Ward in 1847. From this I was able to write *The Exterminators*, with added material from Yuri Suhl's book, *They Fought Back*, Crown Publishers 1967, and from C. A. Weslager's *The Delaware Indians, a History*. Weslager's account of the massacre substantiates all the main facts in the Heckewelder biography, but there is this substantive difference in the two accounts: in one (Weslager) the converted Indians were asked by their unconverted brothers to move west, but refused. In the Heckewelder source, as given in the poem, they were forcibly removed by their western brothers. The main bearing of the poem is unaffected either way.

A few touches in *The Mines* are from *The Pennsylvania Germans*, mentioned above. I also drew on Berks County histories.

The Borough Best. Actually Isaac Stahl, the potter, was also Luther Koch, the bandmaster-composer, but I divided Stahl into two persons, one partly fictional. My family told me my great-grandfather, Emmanuel Welty Myers, composed band music, and it was a sister of my grandfather who sat under the table in *All Them Notes*. I have an inkwell given me by my mother that, she said, my great-grandfather used "with a quill pen" to write with, and, I assume, to compose music with.

Laurence Stotz, a forester, gave me the New Mexican material for *Local Light.*

Der Graabschteehacker. I wasn't privileged to know John Birmelin, but I had a useful talk with his widow, Elizabeth, and with his daughter of the same name. His son Martin became a friend and went with me through many of Birmelin's poems and through his brief autobiographic writings, and we translated his epitaph together. Dr. Preston A. Barba helped with his recollections and went over the whole poem with me. I drew further on a piece in *Selections from Arthur D. Graeff's Scholla,* published by the Pennsylvania German Society, 1971; on a first edition of *Harbaugh's Harfe* given me by Lawrence Gellert; and on an essay, *Pennsylvania German Literature* by Harry Hess Reichard, in *The Pennsylvania Germans*, mentioned above. Reichard calls Birmelin "probably the most versatile writer that has ever assayed to use the dialect." He says further, "He is a master phrasemaker and also has a remarkable memory for phrases and expressions used by the grandfathers."

The Foreground, Singing is drawn from John Joseph Stoudt's *Pennsylvania German Poetry* published by The Pennsylvania German Folklore Society in 1956 and given me by Ellen Jaffe,

The Shoe Factory. My father took me through this factory. He had a lifelong interest in factories and worked in one for some years.

Biafran Monody. I was helped with background material by the Nigerian Consulate in New York. I also drew on Elsy Leuzinger's *The Art of Africa,* Crown Publishers (originally published 1960), and on Robert Collis's *African Encounter,* Scribner's, 1960.

Adam and Eve is based on a story told me by Gerald Hoffnagel.

Some detail in *The Art of Fraktur* is drawn from Frances Lichten's *Folk Art of Rural Pennsylvania,* Charles Scribner's Sons and Bonanza.

The litany in *A Litany of Housing* was written by the Reverends David B. Wayne and Robert Meyers.

The wording of the statement against slavery in *The Germantown Friends* is taken from the reproduction of the original document in *The Life of Francis Daniel Pastorius* by Marion Dexter Learned, Philadelphia, W. J. Campbell, 1908. I give the statement partly because, though famous, it is so hard to come by. And it throws a strong light on colonial history. A light, I might say, neglected by most historians. Morison's *Oxford History of the American People,* cited above, does not even mention Pastorius. The most revelatory parts of history—as of ordinary life—are usually its specific detail, so my friend June Jordan wrote me: "Somebody said that love is revealed by exact attention to actual detail/actual/composing substance of the thing/event/person."

Edward Kemp of the University of Oregon Library supplied me with the *Memories of Benjamin Lay,* Solomon W. Conrad's account of his life published in 1815. I was directed to this memoir by Janet Stevenson, who drew on it for her children's book, *Pioneers of Freedom.*

NOTE: There are many ways of spelling the dialect, and in quoting I've kept individual spelling and have not made it uniform. I checked dialect passages throughout with Ralph Berky, but he is not responsible if I am at fault. In some instances, the meaning of High German words changed in the dialect. The word "Fleddermaus" means butterfly in the dialect, where in German it means bat, and the word for bat in the dialect is "Schpeckmaus" (as in the John Birmelin poem). Family names also changed over the years: so with the Schultz family that started with other variants, including David Shultze.

516

Index of Titles